Gītagovinda and Odisha

Kṛṣṇa and Rādhā in amorous dalliance, painting on paper. Ashutosh Museum, Kolkata.

Gītagovinda and Odisha

Edited by
Dinanath Pathy
Bijaya Kumar Rath

NIYOGI BOOKS

Published by
NIYOGI BOOKS
D-78, Okhla Industrial Area, Phase-I
New Delhi-110 020, INDIA
Tel: 91-11-26816301, 49327000
Fax: 91-11-26810483, 26813830
Email: niyogibooks@gmail.com
Website: www.niyogibooks.com

Copy editor: Gita Rajan
Design: Nabanita Das/Niyogi Books

ISBN:978-93-81523-50-6
Year of Publication: 2012

Printed at: Niyogi Offset Pvt. Ltd., New Delhi, India

In memory of
Kedarnath Mahapatra (1911-81) who pioneered
research on Jayadeva and *Gītagovinda* in Odisha.

Folios from the Gitagovinda *palmleaf manuscript in the collection of Orissa State Museum.*

Contents

Preface

A few years ago, in the beginning of 1970s, Kapila Vatsyayan, the well-known scholar, was delivering the Artaballava Mohanty Memorial Lecture in Bhubaneswar under the aegis of Orissa Sahitya Academy. Although a question-answer session normally does not follow such memorial lectures, an enthusiastic young man in the audience, stood up and asked Dr Vatsyayan the obvious question. "Where was the poet Jayadeva born?" The learned speaker, widely acclaimed as an expert on the study of the *Gītagovinda*, promptly shot back, "Must be in a sleeper coach of a train in which his parents were travelling from Puri to Howrah." The entire audience burst into laughter and the interrogator felt humiliated. The then Chief Minister of Orissa, Janaki Ballav Patnaik was the chief guest and my role was to project slides through my carusal projector.

To me Dr Vatsyayan's answer, though a sarcastic response to a petulant question, revealed something the young man wanted to hear from her. Take the answer as a joke. The train which started from Puri and reached Howrah fell short of Kolkata; Burdwan lay still far away. She did not admit candidly that Jayadeva was born in Odisha but she almost said so.

The skirmishes that followed between the scholars of two neighbouring states on Jayadeva's birthplace revolved round a political issue concerning the building of modern Bengali and Odia identities. Gaganendra Nath Dash, in a well-researched article[1] advances three basic reasons and explains the controversies regarding Odisha's claims relating to Jayadeva and the *Gītagovinda* to Odisha. His main argument is that Jayadeva was a saint or a saint-

Facing page: *Erotic couples sculpted on the temple of Koṇārka.*

Page 9: *Jagannātha, palmleaf painting, Museum Rietberg Zurich.*

---

1 Gaganendra Nath Dash, "*Gītagovinda* Traditions: A Medieval Debate and Its Impact on Modern Oriya Identity', in *Text and Context in the History, Literature and Religion of Orissa*, Ed. Angelina Malinar, Johannes Beltz and Heiko Frese, pp.342-344.

poet who dedicated the *Gītagovinda* to Lord Jagannātha of Puri as his devotee. The second argument is based on traditional accounts which sought to establish that Lord Jagannātha was very fond of listening to the songs of the *Gītagovinda*. The third argument centres on the controversy over the singing of the *Gītagovinda/Abhinava-Gītagovinda* in the Jagannātha Temple which was undermined by the traditional accounts contained in *Bhaktamāḷā* written in Sanskrit, Bengali and Marathi and *Dārḍhyatā Bhakti* in Odia. At least, for the last four hundred years there were concentrated efforts from several quarters to claim, Jayadeva and the *Gītagovinda* for Puri, Jagannātha and finally for Odisha. Gaganendra Nath Dash, uses Benedict Anderson's famous expression, 'the imagined community' to explain the interaction of certain forces and counter forces. We would like to honour the imagined Odia community and its sustained effort to gather possible and probable evidences, for I would like to believe that, in advancing arguments and counter arguments, the person or the imagined community which satisfies present practices and traditions ultimately wins.

Below: *Brochure and First Day Cover issued on 27th July 2009. Earlier palmleaf drawings have been subverted by modern folk painting of Jayadeva.*

This compendium is all about the Odishan tradition concerning Jayadeva and the *Gītagovinda*. The wealth of material brought to light and included in this book would appear to leave no scope for misrepresenting the birthplace of Jayadeva. For the last two decades we do not hear the voices of dissent, but one cannot apparently treat the matter as closed, for the mindset is presumably not dead. It bared its ugly fangs when the Department of Posts, Government of India

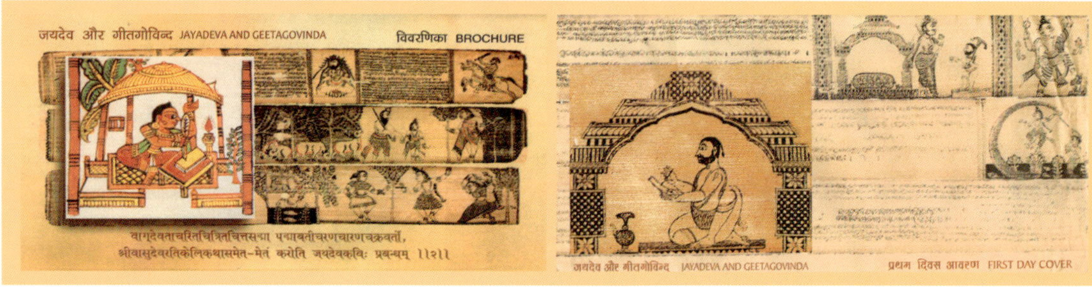

published the stamps and the first-day cover on the *Gītagovinda* in 2009. The citations as well as the visuals had no cultural focus. But this was probably due more to ignorance than intentional mischief. I wanted to bring in the issue, because it obscured a holistic view of the *Gītagovinda* and projected it in a poor light.

But I am confident that these issues will not deter the readers from appreciating the beauty of the *Gītagovinda*. My editorial colleague Bijaya Kumar Rath and I consider compiling and editing such a volume in collaboration with the renowned scholars as our prime duty. We would like various dimensions of the poem and the poet to receive the attention they deserve.

On an individual level, I am involved in reinventing the traditional art motifs of the *Gītagovinda*, specifically those depicted on the folios of illustrated palmleaf manuscripts in terms of their contemporary interpretation. I have held solo exhibitions of my *Gītagovinda* paintings in the British Council Gallery and India International Centre Gallery at New Delhi. These paintings inspired by the *Gītagovinda* have travelled outside India, to Paris, New York and Kuala Lumpur. I am not sure whether paintings in this generation still form part of Odishan pictorial tradition unless one speaks of the tradition of the modern. These reinvented images show that the visual imagery of the *Gītagovinda* have the potency even to stimulate modern minds engaged in a creative journey to realise the beauty of the poem. Examples of this are the paintings of the Lotus Pond depicted below. The lotus has a symbolic value here: the cosmic process and the natural process of bees gathering honey (with all its erotic associations) occur 'at one place'. In the lotus, the cosmic process is made natural and

Above: *Śrī Rādhā, ink on silk. Artist-Dinanath Pathy, 1988.*

Left: *Lotus Pond, Oil on Canvas, 168 cm x 153 cm. Artist, Dinanath Pathy, 1997.*

the natural process is given cosmic significance through the lotus as a symbol. [See also "The lotus" in *Sacred and Profane Dimensions of Love in Indian Traditions as Exemplified in the Gītagovinda of Jayadeva*, pp. 177-197.]

On an institutional level, I have tried to integrate the three basic facets of the poem i.e. the literary, the visual and the performing. When I was the President of the Orissa Lalit Kala Academy, I was able to involve the Sahitya and the Sangita Nataka Academy in my scheme. We held an art exhibition, a performance and a seminar and it was realised that the poem does not limit itself to poetic and intellectual stimulations but its value as a source of creative enjoyment was much greater. Unfortunately, my successors and colleagues in the academies gave up the integrated approach, thereby undermining its long-term efficacy.

Of the various *Gītagovinda* related cultural identities Odisha possesses, three facets stand out distinctly. These are: Jagannātha, Jayadeva and the temple of Koṇārka. These three are so well-integrated with the land and its psyche that together they promote a distinct cultural and devotional tradition of human values, aesthetics and erotic beauty. The greatness about Jagannātha tradition is its mystery and the power to assimilate and evolve. As a concept, it functions on a popular level defying iconisation and classification. The concept of Jagannātha allows people to project their own ideas (as Jayadeva did in his poem) which are finally subsumed and returned to society as a novel idea. The *Gītagovinda* or the song of Govinda, the cowherd god Kṛṣṇa, was initially sung for Lord Jagannātha in the temple at Puri by the poet and his spouse. The paraphernalia, that grew around its ritualistic application, remained wrapped in mystery. Jayadeva, as a name, is quite significant and he shares with Kṛṣṇa a similar

Above: *Jagannātha Pata painting in silk screen print, 20th century.*

Right: *Palmleaf* Gītagovinda, *Kṛṣṇa and Radhā in amorous dalliance.*

identity and in the process he develops his special relation to Kṛṣṇa. "The role of Kṛṣṇa's cowherdess consort Rādhā in the *Gītagovinda* derives its cosmic significance from the context of recurrent references to Śrī. Jayadeva's use of the epithet Jagadīśa, 'Lord of the world', for Kṛṣṇa in the first song is too similar to Jagannātha to be accidental—the *Gītagovinda* may well have taken shape in the richly syncretic environment in Puri in the 12th century" [K.C. Mishra, *The Cult of Jagannatha*[2] and Barbara Stoller Miller,[3]]. "Stoller Miller's observation that 'Rādha is neither the wife of Kṛṣṇa nor a worshipping rustic playmate. She is an intense, solitary, proud female who complements and reflects the mood of Kṛṣṇa's passion. She is Kṛṣṇa's partner in a secret and exclusive love, contrasted in the poem with circular *rāsa* dance' is more than justified."

The role of erotic energy in the *Gītagovinda*, its sexual passion (*ratibhāva*), antithetical modes of 'separation' (*vipralambha śṛṅgāra*) and 'consummation' (*saṁbhoga śṛṅgāra*) bring in an interplay of modes and result in aesthetic joy. This mysterious ramification in poetic sentiments brings the poetry to an intimate closeness of Jagannātha who is primordial and sensuous.

The temple of Koṇārka which symbolises the life energy of the individual and the world stands for passion which is made palpable

2 K.C. Mishra, *The Cult of Jagannatha*, p. 53.

3 Barbara Stoller Miller, pp.3-7. For a review of the accounts of Rāmānuja's life, see Dasgupta, *History of Indian Philosophy*, Vol. 3, pp.100-5.

Śankhanābhi Jātripaṭa.

Māhārī, *photo Sangeet Natak Akademi, New Delhi.*

through sensuous and graceful description of movements and physical forms. Both the *Gītagovinda* and the temple of Koṇārka as sensuous poems in words and stone at one level stimulate wanton desire and when the perceptual experience of sensuousness is restrained, it results in an aesthetic and devotional experience.

Jagannātha's dark, elemental and mysterious form arouses erotic devotion which when filtered through passionate emotion becomes poetry and when it flourishes exuberantly results in the beauty of the plastic form. There, these distinguished identities have the same verve, same vision and same mood as well as the same implications in life and culture which no one could deny with any amount of ambition and reasoning.

Out of the two different interpretations of the inscription on the wall of the Lingrāja Temple in Bhubaneswar issued during the reign of Gaṅga monarch Rāghava Deva (1156-70) and its earlier date notwithstanding, we are tempted to focus on two points; one the town of Kūrma Pāṭaka and the painting of Kānci Vijaya in the Śrīkūrmam Temple which is obviously beyond scope of the inscription. These two would be treated as arguments to link them to the cult of Jagannātha, the town of Kūrma Pāṭaka as supplier of dancing women (*Māhārī*) or singing women (*bhitara gāuṇī*, Telugu Sampradā) to the Puri temple and the Kānci Vijaya painting as the recognition of the link with Lord Jagannātha. These two seemingly far-fetched evidences become for us, points of references to uphold Lord Jagannātha with His linkages to the *Gītagovinda* (singing) in

our understanding of the working of the poem and rejecting its relations with the court of Lakṣmaṇa Sena of Bengal. Here, in this corollary, the songs, dance and the painting become the face of the *Gītagovinda* and an extension of the interpretation of the Lingarāja inscription. In the Indian cultural context, memory and myth are two significant rallying points to frame a new socio-cultural history. Therefore, the information contained in the Lingarāja inscription is vague and leaves room for various interpretations. This inscription raises several other questions which have remained unanswered. Who was Medamā Devī? Was she not a leader of *guḍisāni*, who wanted to please Kīrtivāsa before reaching her final destination Puri? Was she carrying the lamp or got one made locally? These questions and their answers are far more important to understand the vital link between Śrīkūrmam and Puri as well as the provable link of Medamā Devī to the poet or his poem. Most probably she sang the *Gītagovinda* and was aware of its being sung in the temple.

The editors are thankful that Srīvidyā Swamī His Holiness Mahāmedhānandanātha Saraswatī, our former colleague in the Department of Culture, Government of Odisha, then known as Dukhishyama Pattanayak, has so kindly written the introduction and also contributed the English translation of the *Gītagovinda*, both of which have enriched our publication immensely.

The editors express their gratitude to Bikash and Tultul De Niyogi, of Niyogi Books, who so kindly took up the responsibility for the publication of this book. We also thank Eberhard Fischer, Ramahari Jena, P. C. Dhir, Dillip Kumar Tripathy, Japani and O. P. Sud for supplying relevant photographs. Jatindra K. Nayak, Nityananda Misra and Soubhagya Pathy, who helped in compilation and editing, deserve warm appreciation.

Kancī Vijaya, mural painting, Śrīkūrmam Temple, Srikakulam, Andhra Pradesh.

Dinanath Pathy, Alice Boner Institute, Varanasi.

Introduction

Jayadeva, the celebrated poet of the *Gītagovinda*, though born and brought up in Odisha, is claimed to be their poet by Bengal and Mithila. Despite the close and intimate association of the poet Jayadeva with Lord Jagannātha and the widespread prevalence of the Rādhā-Mādhava cult in the Prācī valley, Odisha where Jayadeva's birthplace, Kenduli, is located, scholars of Bengal have all these years tried to claim Jayadeva as belonging to Bengal.

This introduction provides historical evidence as proof of the claims of Odishan Scholars that Jayadeva belongs to Odisha, not Bengal. Of the several facts in favour of Odisha, one significant point is the prevalence of 'Mādhava cult' in Prācī valley. It is this Mādhava that appears in Jayadeva's poems who sings:

"Rādhā-Mādhavayor jayanti yamunākūḷe rahaḥ keḷayaḥ"

i.e. Glory to the love-dalliances of Rādhā and Mādhava in solitude on the banks of river Yamunā.

Here the use of 'Mādhava' replacing 'Kṛṣṇa' is singularly significant since 'Mā-dhava' indicates the 'Husband of Lakṣmī, the goddess of wealth as well as the Universal Mother'. Jayadeva wanted Jagannātha to configurate in his poem and therefore brought in Mādhava (mā+dhava), husband of Lakṣmī. The eternal love play between Rādhā and Kṛṣṇa is regionalised in the images of Lakṣmī and Jagannātha.

The poet could have juxtaposed the word 'Rādhā' with any of the synonyms of 'Kṛṣṇa', for example, 'Rādhā-Keśavayor jayanti ' or some such expression. But the poet by associating the word 'Rādhā' with 'Mādhava' has elevated the position of 'Rādhā' from the mundane to a heavenly one. Of the vaiṣṇavite *ācārya*, Nimbārka proclaimed Rādhā (as the female energy) and Kṛṣṇa in divine sport. Mādhava images with four hands having conch and discus in upper two hands and a flute in lower two hands are found in

Facing page: *Kṛṣṇa, pata painting in silk serum print, 20th century.*

plenty in the Prācī-valley. This Kṛṣṇa-Viṣṇu form called Mādhava was the favourite God, who was worshipped by Jayadeva. An image of Kṛṣṇa-Viṣṇu Mādhava is on display in the Orissa State Museum. This reminds the viewer of the first verse of the *Gītagovinda*: '*Rādhā-Mādhavayor jayanti*'.

The following views of Odishan scholars in all fairness be taken into account by all contestants to arrive at a judicious view of Jayadeva's place of birth.

1.0. Jayadeva: not a court poet of Lakṣmaṇa Sena:

It is said that Śrīpāda Sanātana Goswāmī saw a stone inscription on the threshold of royal court in Navadvīpa containing the following *śloka*:

> "*Govardhanaśca Śaraṇo Jayadeva Umāpatiḥ / Kavirājaśca ratnāni pañcaite Lakṣmaṇasya ca//*"[1]// i.e. Govardhana, Śaraṇa, Jayadeva, Umāpati and Kavirāja were the five jewels in the court of Lakṣmaṇa Sena.[2]

It would certainly seem a concoction to frame a premise, basing on a nonexistent inscription of 12th century involving Sanātana Goswāmī of 16th century. Sanātana Goswāmī had never mentioned the existence of such an inscription, nor was it available at any point of time, as later claimed by scholars with a distinct bias. It would seem an extremely

1 Harekṛṣṇa Mukhopādhyāya, *Kavi Jayadeva O' Gītagovinda* (Bengali) 1983, p.3.

2 Suniti Kumar Chatterjee, *Jayadeva,* Sahitya Akademi, 1973, p.3.

erroneous and injudicious act, almost an offence on the part of a scholar to fabricate such historical untruth. The imaginary inscription mentioned above never seems to have existed primarily because the persons mentioned therein were not contemporaries and hence could not be mentioned in the same single inscription.

The above five personalities have been mentioned together in an *anuṣṭubh śloka* perhaps with the sole intent of trying to prove that they were in the court of Lakṣmaṇa Sena. But, in the following verse of Jayadeva, which lists these five persona, there is no mention of Lakṣmaṇa Sena:

> "*vācaḥ pallavayatyumāpatidharaḥ, sandarbhaśuddhiṃ girāṃ*
> *jānīte jayadeva eva śaraṇaḥ ślāghyo durūhadrute/*
> *śṛṇgārottara-sat-prameya-racanair-ācāryagovardhanaḥ,*
> *spardhī kopi na viśrutaḥ śrutidharo dhoyī kaviḥ kṣmāpatiḥ//*"
>
> (*Gītagovinda*-I.2)

Logically, if they were contemporaries and in the same king's court, the king's name should also have been listed by Jayadeva in the verse. Further, it should be borne in mind that the five poets mentioned in the above verse of the *Gītagovinda* by Jayadeva were not necessarily contemporaries. Jayadeva has tried to justify his poetic genius and in a comparative strategy simply mentioned the other four poets well known in their respective fields. Such an attempt has defined his own position in the annals of Sanskrit literature. Jayadeva was simply adhering to the tradition that had been followed by Govardhana and Bāṇa as well as others in mentioning predecessors who had excelled in their respective fields.

1.1. Govardhana, a court poet of Pravara Sena but not of Lakṣmaṇa Sena:

Govardhana mentioned by Jayadeva was Ācārya Govardhana, the celebrated author of the *Āryāsaptaśatī*. He nowhere mentioned his association with Lakṣmaṇa Sena. *Sena-kuḷa-tiḷaka* mentioned by him along with a list of other authors in one of the verses refers to 'Pravara Sena', the celebrated author of the *Setubandhakāvyam*. Udayana Ācārya, the younger brother of Ācārya Govardhana, son of Nilāmbara Ācārya, belonged to Odisha. Udayana Ācārya, the great logician and author of the *Nyāyakusumāñjali*, who went to the temple of Jagannātha only to find the doors of the Lord shut denying entry, perhaps due to his intense argumentative nature, was so enraged that he directed his banter and ire against the lord in the following verse:

Facing page:
Above: *Kṛṣṇa with Rādhā and* sakhī, *beneath the* kadamba *tree on the bank of river Yamunā, Orissa State Museum, 18th Century painted on woodenboard, Digapahandi workshop.*

Below: *Orissa State Museum Kṛṣṇa Viṣṇu Image.*

'Aiśvarya-madamatto'si māmavajñāya vartase, samāgateṣu bauddheṣu madadhīnā tava sthitih'[3] 'Intoxicated by Thy supreme glory Thou despisest me upon whom Thy very existence depended when Thou was attacked by the Buddhists' (translation mine). But this 'Naiyāyika Udayana'[4], who flourished in the last quarter of the 10th century belonged to Mithilā in the present State of Bihar, whereas the Poet Udayana Ācārya, the author of the two inscriptions in the Śobhaneśvara and Megheśvara Temples, was a native of Odisha and can definitely be assigned to the last quarter of the 12th century. None of the two had any connection with the Bhadury Brahmin family of Bengal.[5]

Udayana Ācārya, the author of the above two inscriptions is identical with Udayana, the brother of poet Govardhana, mentioned in his *Āryāsaptaśatī*. Both the brothers came to prominence with the help of great Viṣṇu Ācārya, who was at first a royal preceptor during the reign of Anaṅgabhīmadeva-II (1190-1198 AD), but gradually rose to the position of commander-cum-minister of Anaṅgabhīma III (1211-1238 AD). It seems very likely that Viṣṇu Ācārya belonged to the family of Udayana.[6] Udayana, unknown to Śrīdharadāsa, the compiler of *Saduktikarṇāmṛtam* had nothing to do with Lakṣmaṇa Sena of Bengal as he lived in Odisha in the courts of two local chieftains under the Gaṅgā-kings Rājarāja-II (1170-1190 AD) and Anaṅgabhīma-II (1190-1198 AD). Similarly Govardhana, not a single verse of whose *Āryāsaptaśatī* is found quoted in *Saduktikarṇāmṛtam* of Śrīdharadāsa, did not adorn the court of Lakṣmaṇa Sena and the term *sena-kuḷa-tiḷaka-bhūpati* of his work can more appropriately be applied to Pravara Sena, who is reputed as author of *Setubandhakāvyam* than to Lakṣmaṇa Sena.[7]

1.2. Śaraṇa's association with Lakṣmaṇa Sena - Not certain:

No work of Śaraṇa, mentioned by Jayadeva is available to us. In a verse "*vevah kupyatu...sevābhir yadi senavaṁśa-tiḷakādāsādanyāh śriyah*" (S.K. Sl. 1640)[8], Śaraṇa eulogises a Sena-king, whose name is not mentioned.

---

3 D.N. Shastri, *Critique of Indian Realism*, Agra, 1964, p.120.

4 ibid.

5 K.N. Mahapatra, "Govardhana Acharya and Udayana Acharya" *Orissa Historical Research Journal*, (*OHRJ*), Spl. Vol.82, p.169.

6 ibid, *OHRJ* Spl.Vol.82, p.170.

7 ibid.

8 Sridharadāsa, *Saduktikarṇāmṛtam*, Firma KLM, 1965, p.444.

In another verse '*bhrūkṣepād gauḍalakṣmīṁ jayati...*', Śaraṇa indicates a king who has excelled the splendour of the king of Gauḍa, which stands as a proof of his not being in the court of Lakṣmaṇa Sena.

1.3. Umāpatidhara and Dhoyī were in the court of Lakṣmaṇa Sena:

There is proof in the Deopara inscription of Vijaya Sena that Umāpatidhara was not only in his court but also in the court of his grandson Lakṣmaṇa Sena, since the interval period between the reign of Vijaya Sena and Lakṣmaṇa Sena was only 21 years (1158-1179 AD). As regards Dhoyī, there is definite evidence to prove that he was patronised by king Lakṣmaṇa Sena, in whose honour he wrote the *Pavanadūtam*.

1.4. Lakṣmaṇa Sena's capital in a state of flux:

There is no contemporary epigraphic or literary evidence to prove that Nadiyā was ever the capital of either Lakṣmaṇa Sena or his forefathers and successors. Two known grants of Vijaya Sena and Vallāla Sena and all the five grants of Lakṣmaṇa Sena dated within the first six years of his reign were issued from the royal camp of Vikramapura. Two later grants of Lakṣmaṇa Sena and those of his successors are found to have been issued not from Vikramapura but respectively from Dharyagrama and Phalgugrama, none of which can be identified.[9] *Tabaqat-i-Nasiri* written in 1260 after about 60 years of the death of Lakṣmaṇa Sena (p.555) and invasion of Nadiyā (p.557) records on hearsay grounds, "Rai Lakṣmaṇaiah whose seat of government was the seat of Nudiah and who was a very great Rai had been on the throne for a period of eighty years".[10] If we accept this account to be true, then we must accept the destruction of Nadiyā to be true, since it records, "After Mahammad-i-Bakhtyar possessed himself of that (Rai Lakṣmaṇaiah's) territory, he left the city in desolation."(p.559). In the footnote of the same page it is further written, "Mahammad-i-Bakhtyar destroyed Nudiah and leaving it in desolation passed onwards."

So it can be said without any fear of contradiction that no trace of the palace of Lakṣmaṇa Sena, destroyed by Muslim army could exist upto the time of Sanātana Goswāmī. Therefore, the theory of witnessing the so called controversial inscription on the gate of his palace is a fantasy and is not based on historical truth. The story of the discovery of the controversial inscription describing the connection of the five poets with

9 *History of Bengal* Dacca University, Vol.I, p.251.

10 Raverty, *Tabaqat-i-Nasiri* Translation, p.554.

Śrīdhām Navadvīpa, originated and was circulated in the post-Caitanya period, when Nadiyā came to prominence due to the birth of the great reformer Caitanya in that holy place.[11]

2.0. Jayadeva and Jagannātha:

Gītagovinda is sung in the temple of Jagannātha as a part of daily ritual. Jayadeva closely associated with Jagannātha the form of a 'gou' or bull symbolising Dharma. The bull followed the poet Jayadeva into a garden like '*Koili Vaikuntha*' of Jagannātha while he was plucking flowers and tuḷasī leaves singing the *Gītagovinda*. Jayadeva found the impressions of eight hoofs marked by the feet of the Dharma-'gou' and it moved him to such an extent that to immortalise the strange incident, he composed songs as *Aṣṭapadī* or eight quatrains. Jayadeva's association with Odisha is quite diverse and he occupies a unique position notwithstanding the role of other poets in their respective fields. Hence, Jayadeva's reference to four other poets of eminence belonging to different periods does not prove his association with the court of Lakṣmaṇa Sena.

11 Kedaranath Mahapatra, *Descriptive Catalogue of Sanskrit Manuscript of Orissa*, Introduction, pp.xxxxi-ii, Orissa Sahitya Academy, 1960

2.1. Jayadeva, a Pandit and Poet devoted to Jagannātha:

Jayadeva was a devotee dedicated to the temple of Jagannātha. He was delighting in singing the *Gītagovinda* in a spiritual fervour before his beloved God repeating '*Jaya Jagadīśa Hare*' 'Let there be victory to Hari, the Lord of the world, Jagannātha'. He found pleasure in introducing himself as a master conducting the (dancing) steps of Padmāvatī performing before Jagannātha. He has, therefore, called himself '*Padmāvatī-caraṇa-cāraṇa-cakravartī*' and taken pride in doing so for the pleasure of Jagannātha. He was never a court-poet. As a *vaiṣṇava*-devotee he dedicated himself to serve Jagannātha singing the glories of His divine-love.

How could a devotee dedicated to the cause of singing the glory of Rādhā Kṛṣṇa love, divert his attention to the royal court for petty benefits, monetary gains, or worldly fame?

Temple of Jagannātha, Puri.

Jayadeva despised serving in the royal court and considered himself superior to all who had earned reputation in scholarly debates. He therefore, had boldly, said:

> "*prākpratyak-pṛthivībhṛtah pariṣadi prakhyāta-saṁkhyāvatā-*
> *mahnāyādbhutatarkakarkaśatayā vicchidya vidyāmadam /*
> *ye ke'pyutkaḷabhūpate tava sabhāsambhāvitāh paṇḍitāh*
> *pattraṁ Śrī-Jayadeva-paṇḍita-kavistanmūrdhni vinyasyati //*"[12]

Jayadeva was bold enough to declare that he would place his sandals on the head of the scholars who through their loyalty and service are held in respect by the king of Utkaḷa, because he was a *Kavi-Paṇḍita*, a poet-scholar in the divine court of Jagannātha, the Lord of the Universe. Hence, Jayadeva who had introduced himself as a *Kavi-Paṇḍita* with an air of authority and had taken pride in calling himself a master of Padmāvatī, the danseuse, was a devotee par excellence and was never attached to any royal court.

3.0. Kendu-bilva on the river Prācī in Odisha:

Jayadeva in the *Gītagovinda* (*Aṣṭapadī*-3/8) proclaims: '*Kendubilva-samudrasambhava-rohiṇī-ramaṇa*'. He was the Moon born of an ocean or the great expanse of rivers Prācī and Kuśabhadrā that surround Kendubilva or Kenduli-*śāsana* in Puri district. In the past, Kendubilva was a large village but presently it is segmented into three settlements namely Kenduli-śāsana (settlement of *Brāhmaṇa*), Kenduli Deuḷī (seat of temples) and Kenduli Pāṭṇā (settlement of assorted caste people). See Revenue one inch map, Sheet No. 73 H. 16). The Kenduli area abounds in antiquities which can safely be assigned to the 8th century AD, if not earlier. Not far from this village is the famous *Triveṇī-saṁgama* (the confluence of the three rivers, viz. Prācī, Kuśabhadrā and Dhanuā), where a big festival is held every year on the new moon day or *amāvāsyā* of the lunar month of *Māgha*, which is called the *Triveṇī-Amāvāsyā*. According to a tradition Jayadeva used to take his bath here every morning and

12 Keśava Misra, *Alamkāraśekhara, Kāvyamālā* 1926, p.17. Readers may note the significance of the word *pad-tram* meaning sandals (*pad* the feet, *tram* to protect) that protect the feet.

worshipped Triveṇī-Mādhava. There is perhaps no other area in India, where so many finely chiselled Viṣṇu images of the pre-Gaṅga period (circa 900-1100 AD) can be noticed as one finds in the important villages of the Prācī valley.[13]

3.1. Kenduli in Bengal is a modern town:

The village called 'Jayadeva-Kenduli' on the bank of river Ajaya is modern and is so named intentionally to associate the village with the birthplace of poet Jayadeva. "The village Kenduli in the district of Birbhum completely lacks the archaeological significance and devotional environment which contributed in moulding the poetic career of Jayadeva. Significantly, the biographies of Caitanya do not mention Birbhum's Kenduli as the birthplace of Jayadeva. Had it been a sacred place, Caitanya, a great admirer of the *Gītagovinda*, must have paid a visit to this place at least once during his lifetime. But the contemporary *vaiṣṇava* literature is silent about any such visit."[14]

Vanamāḷīdāsa's *Jayadeva-carita* from single paper manuscript of sana 1208 or 1801 AD, edited by Atul Kṛṣṇa Goswāmi, was published by Bangiya Sahitya Parishad, Calcutta in Bengali sana 1312 or 1905 AD. "The work is of no historical value. Even the date of Jayadeva has been brought down by the poet from the 12th to his own time, when the feudal Raja of Burdwan would appear to have been the only big ruler known to Vanamāḷīdāsa."[15] Hence, it appears that in 17th century during the time of Vanamāḷīdāsa, perhaps there was another Jayadeva in the court of feudal Raja of Burdwan and he was born in Bengal. This Jayadeva of 17th century Bengal had been confused to be Jayadeva of 12th century Odisha and some scholars have mistakenly put Jayadeva (17th century) of Burdwan-Raja in the court of Raja Lakṣmaṇa Sena of 12th century.

3.2. Jayadeva's Kenduli in the hagiological writings:

Nābhaji, a Ramite of Rajasthan in his *Bhaktamālā* (written in Vikrama-Saṁvat 1642 or 1585 AD) in Hindi, Mahīpati of Mahārāṣṭra in his

13 K.N. Mahapatra, "New light on Poet Jayadeva", *OHRJ* Spl.Vol., pp.179-80.

14 ibid pp. 180-1.

15 Suniti Kumar Chatterjee, *Jayadeva*, Sahitya Akademi 1973, p.3.

Māhāri *performing dance in the temple of Jagannātha, painted on wooden board, manuscript cover, Orissa State Museum.*

Bhaktavijaya written in Saka 1684 or 1762 AD in Marathi, Kṛṣṇa Dāsa, a *Vaiṣṇava*-poet of Bengal in *Bhaktamāḷā* (18th century early part) in Bengali and Candradatta of Mithiḷā in his *Bhaktamāḷā* in Sanskrit have declared without ambiguity that Jayadeva was born in Kendubilva of Utkaḷa.[16] Modern Bengali scholars without bias have accepted Kenduli in Odisha as Jayadeva's birthplace.[17]

Another important work, the *Vaiṣṇava-Līḷāmṛta* (written in 48th regnal year of Pratāparudradeva i.e.1535 AD) in Odia by Kavi Mādhava Paṭṭanāyaka mentions that Jayadeva from Kenduli on the bank of river Prācī came to Puri after the death (i.e. in 1535 AD) of King Gaṅgesvara or Coḍagaṅgadeva, who took possession of Utkaḷa in 1112 AD and died in 1147 AD. It is also mentioned that Jayadeva left his mortal coil in Jagannātha-Purī before Gaṅga King Bhīmadeva or Anaṅgabhīmadeva-III (1211-1238 AD) ascended the throne. This king was a great devotee of Viṣṇu. It is further mentioned that this Anaṅgabhīmadeva built a dancing hall (*nāṭamandira*) in front of the sanctum-sanctorum of Jagannātha Temple and introduced the dance along with the singing of the *Gītagovinda*, perhaps to commemorate the association of Jayadeva and his immortal work the *Gītagovinda* with Jagannātha. It is said that

Priest worshipping Mādhava in Mādhavananda Temple.

16 Kedaranath Mahapatra, *Śrī Jayadeva O' Śrī Gītagovinda*, (Oriya), 1973, pp.52-68.

17 Brundavana Ch. Acharya, "*Kavi Jayadevanka Janmasthāna O' Samaya*", in *Oḍiśāra Kavi Jayadeva*, 1986, pp.29-36.

without listening to the *Gītagovinda*, his predecessor Kāmārṇava (1147-1157 AD), on religious grounds,[18] would not even sip water. It was again reintroduced by (Kavi) Narasiṁhadeva-II (1278-1307 AD) as a temple ritual.[19] In the 15th century Kavicandra Rāya Divākara Miśra composed the *Abhinava-Gītagovinda* in the name of Gajapati Puruṣottama Deva (1467-1497 AD), who eventually wanted to replace the one by Jayadeva in the temple ritual. But it is believed that Jagannātha preferred to listen to the *Gītagovinda* by Jayadeva alone. Again Gajapati Pratāparudradeva (1497-1534 AD) made the dancing in tune with the singing of the *Gītagovinda* by Jayadeva compulsory on the 8th July, 1500 AD.

4. Ancient Commentators on the *Gītagovinda* from Odisha:

A number of commentaries of the *Gītagovinda* was written by scholars belonging to different parts of India. It is quite significant that the first commentary *Bhāva-vibhāvinī* was written by Udayana Ācārya, the younger brother of Govardhana Ācārya of Odisha. Though Udayana was quoted in ancient works, we have not been able to get the work in print. The next authoritative commentary, the *Sarvāṅgasundarī* by Kavirāja Nārāyaṇadāsa, the great-grandfather of Viṣvanātha Kavirāja, the author of the *Sāhitya Darpaṇa* belonged to Odisha. It may be noted that Odishan commentaries being first in antiquity are the foremost and quite dependable in determining the text of the *Gītagovinda*.

5. Authentic Text of the *Gītagovinda*:

Many interpolations crept into the text of the *Gītagovinda* when handled by different scholars during the last eight hundred years. A definitive text of the *Gītagovinda* on the basis of ancient commentaries was a desideratum in the scholarly world, who often err in quoting an interpolation as the original text. Bajari Dāsa, an Odia translator of the *Gītagovinda* in his *Artha-Govinda* not only translated the text in the nine-lettered *Bhāgavata*-metre of Jagannātha Dāsa to make it popular, but also took commendable steps in the 17th century in determining the definite text of Jayadeva's *Gītagovinda*.[20] This manuscript was edited by me and was published as the first in the 'Odishan Oriental Text Series' by Government of Odisha in the Department of Culture in 1970 and it ran into 2nd edition in 1999.[21]

---

18 Jagabandhu Simha, *Prachina Utkala*, Orissa Sahitya Akademi, p.5.

19 Artaballabha Mohanty, *Mādalāpāñji* Ed. Utkala University, p.36.

20 ... - *Journal of Asiatic Society of Bengal*, Vol. LXII(1983),pp.96-97.

21 Dukhishyam Pattanayak, *Bajari Dāsa's Artha-Govinda* Ed. 1970.

6. Imitations over popularity of the *Gītagovinda*:

Jayadeva was the first and foremost to write a lyrico-dramatic *mahākāvya*. The music tradition of Utkaḷa worth its name took shape in literature and sculpture respectively as the *Gītagovinda* and Koṇārka in the 12th century Odisha. Both stand as testimony to earthly erotic love represented in divine garb. After three hundred years of Jayadeva's birth in this soil, Odisha, with the same spirit in its gene again, tried to produce the *Gītagovinda* anew called the *Abhinava-Gītagovinda* in its imitation in Sanskrit. Then the *Gītagovinda* found its expression in Odia language and literature in the 18th century. The *Kiśora-candrānanda-campū* and thousands of quatrains called *caupadī* by Baḷadeva Ratha and *padāvaḷī* (lyrical songs) of Gopāḷakṛṣṇa and other writers of *prema-līḷā* along with a huge number of metrical *kāvya* of Dinakṛṣṇa, Abhimanyu and others sang in divinity the human erotic passions as an art to educate the mass in the spirit of the *Gītagovinda* centering round Mādhava-Jagannātha as a conjointed form of Rādhā-Kṛṣṇa. An elaborate list of such imitations in literature is given by Kedaranath Mahapatra in Odia[22] and English[23].

Anthologies have incorporated in their body best specimens of literature that were available to them. *Saduktikarṇāmṛtam* of

22 Kedaranath Mahapatra, *Śrī Jayadeva O' Śrī Gītagovinda*, (Oriya), 1973.

23 "Influence of *Śrī Gītagovinda* on the Regional Literatures of India", *OHRJ* Spl. Vol., pp.419-444.

Entrance with painted stucco figures of Yashoda with Rama (Bala) and Kṛṣṇa to the 3rd chamber of Mādhavananda Temple.

Śrīdharadāsa is one such anthology. He has incorporated more than one of Jayadeva's *śloka* along with others. Twenty-six new verses of different styles available to us in the name of Jayadeva belong to poets bearing the same name. Even three of the five *śloka* said to be found in the *Gītagovinda* are interpolations. In the face of so many variations, it is certainly wrong to conclude by saying prima facie that Jayadeva was a poet of many styles.[24] Jayadeva lives in his immortal lyrics and the style he has perfected also speaks eloquently of his greatness. The adage 'Style is man' satisfies well in the case of Jayadeva and his work—the *Gītagovinda*. Even the *śloka*, "*mugdhe nātha....*". (SK-1/60/5) ascribed to Jayadeva is also current in the name of one *Śaṇkara*. Different styles show the existence of more than one poet by the name of Jayadeva in different times and as such no conclusion can be drawn from the quotations of *Saduktikarṇāmṛtam* that all the poets known as Jayadeva belonged to the court of Lakṣmaṇa Sena.

7. Jayadeva of Odisha, a universal poet:

All the hagiological works agree that (i) Jayadeva was born in Kendubilva, (ii) married Padmāvatī under the divine order, (iii) inspired Padmāvatī to dance by singing the *Gītagovinda* for the pleasure of Jagannātha at Puruṣottama-Purī, (iv) composed the *Gītagovinda* in Śrīkṣetra Purī also known as Puruṣottama-Purī, (v) the *Gītagovinda* was accepted in the

24 Suniti Kumar Chatterjee, *Jayadeva*, Sahitya Akademi (1973), p.19.

Koṇārka Temple - view from Nāṭa Maṇḍapa.

temple ritual and (vi) another *Gītagovinda* written anew by the Gajapati king could not get divine sanction to replace the *Gītagovinda* of poet Jayadeva. All these facts relate to Jagannātha Puri and Odisha alone. To bring in a king and his court is an exercise in futility because Jayadeva had only mentioned in the *Gītagovinda* about his most beloved lord Jagadīśa or Jagannātha, his birthplace Kendubilva and his beloved Padmāvatī whom he married under the divine approval of Jagannātha at Puri. It is again futile to search for the above for mere reasoning's sake anywhere else in India. Utkaḷa or Odisha Puri, the holy land of Jagannātha had reared the poet and had stood witness to the intensity of love and devotion the poet had for Jagannātha. The eternal song of love that Koṇārka sings in mute silence is nothing but the song of the *Gītagovinda* that had been later sung in this land by Upendra Bhanja. The *Gītagovinda* of Jayadeva still reverberates in the temple precincts of Jagannātha and within the hearts of Odias in the nooks and corners of Odisha as of all Indians and Indophiles elsewhere who love this immortal creation for its intense devotion and lyrical beauty.

Mahamedhanandanatha Saraswati.

HISTORY AND LEGENDS

Historical Perspective

Harish Chandra Das

The place where Jayadeva spent his eventful life and the prevailing religious tradition that shaped his career are of great historical significance. The village Kendubilva (presently Kenduli) in Pratāparudrapur gram-panchayat of Bāliantā police station in Puri district, located not far from the banks of the sacred river Prācī, witnessed the efflorescences of several religions such as Jainism, Buddhism, *Śaktism*, *Śaivism*, *Sūrya* cult and *Vaiṣṇavism*, the testimony to which are still extant in the form of temples, sculptures and monasteries. The religious, literary and artistic traditions of ancient Odisha infused in the poet the required sensitivity and inspired him to create, compose and sing the glories of Govinda, the cowherd god.

Kendubilva and many other villages on the Prācī valley[1] are littered with monuments dedicated to different cults. The Bhauma, Somavaṁśi and the Gaṅga rulers enhanced the religious significance of the sacred valley by erecting a number of temples for propitiation of different deities. Of the various monuments, mention may be made of the Svapneśvara Temple, Aḍaspur Jaina shrine, Rāmeśvara Temple at Rāmeśvara, the temples of Nīlakaṇṭa, Mukteśvara, Śaṅkareśvara, Angeśvara, Amareśvara, Grāmeśvara, as well as the numerous images of Mādhava, the sculptures of *daśāvatāra*, manifestations of Śakti; Buddha and Jaina images. These have a definitive focus on the grand religious synthesis and fusion that took place in the area. The circumstantial evidences, the ecstasy of religious efflorescence, the extensive archaeological remains of the Prācī valley, the intimate association of the *Gītagovinda* with Jagannātha cult and the spirit of popular legends and related practices drive us to the inevitable conclusion that Jayadeva was born in one of the *śāsana* villages known as Kendubilva.

1 *Prachi Valley Survey Report*, Ed. P.K. Ray, Orissa State Archaeology, Bhubaneswar 1975.

Facing page: *Gopīnātha, Orissa State Museum.*

Page 33: *Kṛṣṇa flanked by cows, palmleaf painting, Orissa State Museum.*

The *Brāhmaṇa śāsana* Kendubilva boasts of its enviable tradition as the birthplace of the poet Jayadeva. The village has rich relics in the shape of brick and stone temples and sculptures of *Śaiva, Vaiṣṇava* and *Śākta* cults belonging to the period between 9th and 13th century AD. The sculptures of Mādhava, Lakṣmī-Nṛsiṁha, Ambikā and Yogeśvarī are quite significant. Strangely enough a stone image bearing human physiognomy and having prominent matted locks, endowing it with a poetic aura, is worshipped by the local people as the sage Jayadeva. Ambikā and Yogeśvarī, two important goddesses, are worshipped by the local people with great reverence. The villagers remind that Ambikā was originally installed under a *vilva* tree, and Yogeśvarī under a *kendu* tree. The two trees *kendu* and *vilva* finally merge their identities in a settlement known as Kendubilva. Amibikā is now shifted to a brick temple. It is in this *Śākta* temple nearby that the *Gītgovinda* is recited in preference to *Śākta* prayers even on the occasion of *Daśaharā*. The recitation of the *Gītgovinda* in *Śākta* temples is a unique phenomenon symbolising the overpowering influence of *Vaiṣṇavism* over Śāktism and justifying people's love for the poet.

The local legend proclaims that Jayadeva performed a sacrifice in his native village. Two sacrificial posts, the remains of which are now seen in the precincts of Ambikā Temples, are stated to have been installed during the time of Jayadeva for annual sacrifice. As a reminiscence of the tradition, a sacrifice is also performed annually on the third day of full moon in the month of *Vaiśākha*. According to another tradition Jayadeva used to take bath at *Triveṇī ghāṭ* (confluence of Dhanuā, Prācī and Kuśabhadrā rivers) and propitiate Triveṇī Mādhava. To commemorate Jayadeva's daily bath in the river, people congregate at this sacred spot on the *Māgha Amāvāsyā*, the new moon day in the month of January/February. This event has also resulted in an annual fair. The two images of Mādhava now preserved in the Kenduli museum are stated to have been installed in the village during the Somavaṃśī period. It will therefore not be unreasonable to believe that Jayadeva was enamoured of Mādhava who became the protagonist of his poem, the *Gītagovinda*. To further enhance the importance of the village, Narasimhadeva IV installed the image of Nṛsiṁha and established the Vijaya Narasimhapura Śāsana in 1381 AD near the village Kenduli. The copper plate[2] grant of Narasimhadeva IV recovered from a tank near the Nṛsiṁha temple of the village, originally issued from Vārāṇasi Kaṭaka in 1383 AD, refers to the establishment of Narasimhapura Śāsana, donated to one Mahāpātra Naraharidāsa Praharāja. This *śāsana* is located very close

---

2 M.M. Chakaravarti, *J.A.S.B.* vol.LXIV, Part I, 1895, pp.128 ff.

to Kendubilva on the Prācī valley. The grant further elucidates the names of Olaṭapura and Aṭṭahāsapura Śāsana close to Kenduli established by Aṭṭahāsadeva, the youngest son of Coḍagaṅgadeva.[3] These facts indicate that the Kendubilva Śāsana might have been established by an illustrious monarch long before the rise of Jayadeva.

Prācī valley in which the village Kenduli is situated marks the fusion of Śiva and Viṣṇu. The fusion is mirrored in the archaeological remains of the village belonging to *Śaiva* and *Vaiṣṇava* pantheons.

The archaeological evidences of a synthetic cult prompt us to emphatically conclude that Jayadeva was born in Kenduli village and was attuned to the natural, social and religious environs.

Now the significant question remains regarding the historical perspective of such a great personality. In the annals of religious history all through the ages, the saints, preachers and protagonists of faiths played a pivotal role in channelising the trends of religions in accordance with the scheduled tenets. The religious history of India, so also its various regions abound with many such religious personalities who have been responsible in shaping the course of history. The religious history of Odisha is replete with achievements of such eminent persons who have left deep impressions on the cultural life of the people. Great exponents from Odisha and outside who visited this sacred land of Puri, eventually have made Jagannātha *Kṣetra*[4], (the abode of Jagannātha), their *līlā bhūmi* (place of consecrated activities) and Jagannātha as their ultimate goal in life. Jayadeva like others had spent a major part of his life in Puri. Therefore, historical conditions which favoured Jayadeva to flourish need a little more elucidation.

The political history of Odisha prior to Jayadeva and also during his time was at the peak of its glory. Coḍagaṅgadeva (1078-1147 AD)[5] founded the imperial Gaṅga dynasty, built the Kaliṅga empire

3 S. N. Rajaguru, *Inscriptions of Orissa,* Vol. III, Part II, 1975, Bhubaneswar, pp. 490 ff.

4 B. Mishra, *Purāṇu Maṭha Samskriti* (Oriya), 1988, Puri, pp.3-4.

5 K.C. Panigrahi, *History of Orissa (Hindu Period)*, Cuttack, 1981, pp. 154-158.

Viṣṇu Trivikrama, stone sculpture.

that extended from the river Ganges in the north to that of river Godāvarī in the south. This brought peace and prosperity to the region. Shifting of his capital from Kaliṅganagara in the south of Cuttack, at the centre of the empire, was not only a memorable historical event but was also expedient for consolidation and better administration of the empire. Soon after the capital was shifted, the monarch switched over to temple building activities. The temples of Mukhaliṅgam, Śrīkūrmam, Simhāchalam and Jagannātha at Puri, dedicated to Viṣṇu, amplify his religious, cultural and architectural achievements. The construction of the present Jagannātha Temple replacing the old and dilapidated one, rejuvenated his religious fervour and Puri sprang up as a *Vaiṣṇavite* centre of eminence. The visit of *Vaiṣṇava* saint Rāmānuja to Puri and introduction of *Pancarātra* system in the temple rituals greatly enhanced the religious importance of the *kṣetra*[6].

The religious history of Odisha prior to the advent of Jayadeva, reveals that the *Tantricism* of the time of Bhaumakara declined giving place to the rise of *Brāhmaṇical* order, particularly the *Śaivism* under the Somavaṁśis. The Gaṅgas who succeeded the Somavaṁśis now shifted their allegiance from *Śaivism* to *Vaiṣṇavism. Vaiṣṇavism* gained in eclecticism and esoterism found revelation in art, architecture, literature and in social life. The Gaṅga monarchs were wise enough to link the past religious tradition with their own ideals maintaining a sort of equipose, although they were evidently *Vaiṣṇavas* in faith with Jagannātha as their tutelary deity. The allegiance of Coḍagaṅgadeva, the great empire builder, to the great God Puruṣottama is evident from the construction of the Jagannātha Temple and his royal epithets like *paramavaiṣṇava,*

Kṛṣṇa-Viṣṇu from Dharmasālā, Orissa State Museum.

6 For a review of the accounts of Rāmānuja's life, see Dasgupta, *History of Indian Philosophy,* Vol. 3. pp. 100-5, Dasgupta notes: (p.100): "Most of the details of Rāmānuja's life are collected from the account given in the *Prapannāmṛta* by Anantācārya, a junior contemporary of Ramanuja in Barbara Stoller Miller, 1977. p.41.

paramabhaṭṭāraka, paramabrahmanya, Śrigaṅgacūḍāmaṇi etc. His change of religion is perhaps due to the influence of Rāmānuja who stayed at Puri in the early part of the 12th century between 1122-1139 AD. His visit to Puri and Śrikūrmam is clearly recorded in *Prapannāmṛta*[7] which mentions that the ruler of the region had been converted by Rāmānuja. In this connection it is expedient to impress, whatever might be the reason for mentioning Coḍagaṅga as a *Paramavaiṣṇava,* he did never neglect his ancestral faith, rather all along exhibited eclectic attitude towards all prevailing religions. The Korni copper plate[8] indicates, that Coḍagaṅga donated a village to Kīrtivāsa at Bhubneswar for maintenance of a perpetual lamp and another record shows that the ruler with all his queens visited Bhīmeśvara Śiva at Drākṣārāma and installed a perpetual lamp.[9] Several other epigraphs of the Gaṅga monarchs and their official records reveal their devotion to *Śaiva* and *Śakta* deities apart from their affiliation to the deity of their faith.

During the glorious rule of the Gaṅgas the religious savants, prophets and preachers thronged *Śrīkṣetra* to preach the gospels of their faith. Besides, Rāmānuja, the preachers like Narasimha Muni, Narahari Tīrtha, Jagannātha Tīrtha, Narasimha Yati, Vāsudeva Yati mark the efflorescence of *Vaiṣṇavism* and spread of their ideologies.

The *Mādalāpāñji*[10], the Jagannātha temple chronicles, relate that Ekajaṭā Kāmadeva, a great lover of the *Gītagovinda* never touched his food without listening to a few verses from the *Gītagovinda.* Ekajaṭā Kāmadeva is identified with Kāmārṇava Deva (1146-56 AD) in Madhukeśvara Temple inscription[11]. The *Mādalāpāñji,* though not a historical record, nevertheless relates to a chronology with historical inputs. Both Coḍagaṅga and his son Kāmārṇava were the disciples of Rāmānuja and devotees of Jagannātha and his consort Lakṣmī. Jayadeva seems to have been influenced by Rāmānuja's ideology of Jagannātha and Lakṣmī. According to a verse[12] of the *Gītagovinda,* Kṛṣṇa tells Rādhā that formerly she as Lakṣmī chose him as her consort on the seashore. As a result of this incident Śiva swallowed poison out of despair.

---

7 *Prapannāmṛta,* ed. P. Mukherjee, *History of Medieval Vaisnavism in Calcutta,* Orissa, 1940, p.28.

8 S.N. Rajaguru, *Inscriptions of Orissa,* Vol. III, Part (i), 1960, Bhubaneshwar, p.28.

9 Op cit, vol. III, Part 1, (1960), p.76, No. 60.

10 Ed. A.B. Mohanty, Utkal University, Bhubaneswar, 2nd Edition, 1969.

11 S.N. Rajaguru, op. cit. p.251, No. 224.

12 Barbara Stoller Miller, *The Gītagovinda of Jayadeva,* Delhi, 1977, p.5.

While discussing the historical background of Jayadeva it will perhaps not be irrelevant to understand how he introduced Rādhā and Mādhava and the *daśāvatāra* cult, breaking the stylised tradition. Therefore, we are tempted to conclude that the *Gītagovinda* is a historical text with definite historical relevance through its poetic narration. The cult of Mādhava that was in existence in Orissa from the 7th or the 8th century AD gained momentum from the time of Jayadeva. We come across the first epigraphical evidence of Mādhava in the copper plate grant of Mādhavarāja of the Śailodbhava[13] dynasty where the scribe has particularised the epithet of Cakrāyudha Mādhava. The image of Nīlamādhava[14] installed by the Bhañja monarch at Gandharāḍi (9th century AD) comes next in order of chronology. The village of Santoṣa Mādhava[15] recorded in the Dasapallā copper plates of Śatṛbhañja, Śrī Lokamādhava referred to in the copper plates grant of Indravarman[16] Coḍagaṅga Mādhava in the pillar inscriptions of Rellivalasa[17] at Śrikākuḷam, numerous Mādhava sculptures and temples of Prācī valley clearly reveal the continuing tradition of Mādhava worship in Odisha with wide distribution in Prācī valley, the birthplace of Jayadeva. Jayadeva, as a devout devotee of Mādhava, infused exuberantly in his *Gītagovinda,* the lucid description of Mādhava.

Jayadeva introduced and popularised the cult of Rādhā and Kṛṣṇa through his *Gītagovinda.* Since the society at that time did not approve the association of Rādhā with Kṛṣṇa, the cult of Rādhā could not flourish till the 16th century, but Kṛṣṇa gained wide celebrity in art and literature. The cult of Kṛṣṇa (known as Gopīnātha in Odisha) gained momentum in sculptural representation from the 12th century AD. Although there are profuse descriptions about the image in the literature of an earlier period, due to the influence of *Bhāgavata* and the *Gītagovinda,* the cult of Gopīnātha and the composite figure of Kṛṣṇa-Viṣṇu became quite popular in Odisha replacing the earlier form of four armed Viṣṇu. The composite sculpture of Kṛṣṇa-Viṣṇu in *tribhaṅga* with upper two hands playing the flute in the company of *aṣṭagopī* and cattle (the associative feature of Kṛṣṇa) indicates the amalgamation of two cults at a time, when *Vaiṣṇavism* became the state religion of Odisha.

---

13 S.N. Rajaguru, *Inscriptions of Orissa,* Vol. I Part (ii), 1958, p.162 ff.

14 K.C. Panigrahi, *History of Orissa (Hindu Period)*, Cuttack, 1981, p.384.

15 S.N. Rajaguru, *OHRJ,* Vol. I, No.3 (1952), pp.208-12 ff.

16 S.N. Rajaguru, *Inscriptions of Orissa,* Vol. III, (part i) (1960), p.80.

17 Ibid, p.281, No.244, *Inscriptions of Orissa,* Vol. III, Part II, pp.278-80, No.243.

Although Gopīnātha was accepted as a cult image from the 12th century AD the sculptures representing *Gopīnātha* appeared in the temple architecture from an earlier period. A miniature image of two-armed Gopīnātha with a flute adorns the 11th century temple of Rājārāṇi at Bhubaneswar. The images of Gopīnātha correspond to the *dhyāna* mantra of the *Gopālasahasranāma.*[18]

To popularise the cult, several Gopīnātha temples were erected in Odisha. It was during this time that the construction of a Gopīnātha Temple on the outskirts of a *Brāhmaṇa śāsana* was considered mandatory. Though in course of time many such temples are lost, the idols however survive and are housed in newly built temples.

Jayadeva, in intense devotion, structurised and popularised the ten *avatāra* of Viṣṇu in his poetry. He converted the prevalent scattered narrations into a holistic concept of *daśāvatāra.* This could be a lasting contribution of the poet that influenced later poetry and other visual forms.

Due to the impact of the *Gītagovinda, devadāsī* or the dancing women were dedicated to the temples for performance of dance and music, and the *devadāsī* tradition was institutionalised. Importance of the dancing girls in the temple ritual grew to such an extent that a special architectural structure called *nāṭamandira* or *nāṭamaṇḍapa* was added to the existing *deuḷa* and *mukhasāḷā.*[19]

This continuing tradition of *devadāsī* was epitomised in Padmāvatī, the consort of Jayadeva who was dedicated by her father to Lord Jagannātha as a *devadāsī.*

The above discussion would justify the *Gītagovinda* of Jayadeva as a significant historical text in the ramification of its literary and religious connotation. Jayadeva, while highlighting and systematising the existing traditional cults has aptly introduced his own ideologies through poetic imageries. Such is the greatness of Jayadeva and the *Gītagovinda* and munificence of the illustrious Gaṅga monarchs who immensely patronised art and architecture, religion and literature during the post-Jayadeva period.

18 *Śrī Gopālasahasranāmastotram*, Gita Press Gorakhpur, p.11.

19 K.C. Panigrahi, *Archaeological Remains at Bhubaneswar*, Cuttack, 1981, p.169; Also see Bijay Kumar Rath, "Nāṭamaṇḍapa in Odishan Temple Architecture; A Pavilion for Dance Performance" in *Angarāg*, No. 7, Spring, 2009.

Gopīnātha, with aṣṭagopī, Orissa State Museum.

The King and the Priests: An Analysis of the *Gītagovinda* Tradition

Gaganendra Nath Dash

In Candradatta's *Bhaktamāḷā* written in the 17th century several traditions regarding the poet Jayadeva and his famous work *Gītagovinda* have been recorded. One of these traditions deals with the re-introduction of the *Gītagovinda* in the temple of Jagannātha, Puri after it was prohibited by the king of Odisha. The tradition is as follows:

> The king (of Odisha) composed a *kāvya* imitating the *Gītagovinda* and ordered that the learned people must read and sing this second *Gītagovinda* composed by him (and not the *Gītagovinda* by Jayadeva) and they would be punished otherwise. Nobody dared to read and sing the *Gītagovinda* by Jayadeva because of the royal order. Once the king came to visit Śrī Puruṣottama i.e. Lord Jagannātha and found that Jayadeva was singing from his *Gītagovinda* and dancing. The king asked, "Why do not you recognise my *kāvya*?' The poet replied that he did recognise the *kāvya* written by the king but the *kāvya* written by the king was not as dear to the Lord as his own *kāvya* was and the king was at liberty to test this statement. Then both of them kept their respective *kāvya* in front of Lord Jagannātha; asked him to specify which of the two *kāvya* was dearer to him; went out and closed the door for an instant. When the door was opened it was found out that Jayadeva's *kāvya* had been placed on the top and the king's *kāvya* under it (signifying that Jayadeva's *kāvya* was dearer to the Lord). The king did not touch food out of sorrow. During the night he saw in a dream that somebody in the guise of Puruṣottama told him, "Why are you sorry O' king? There is nothing dear to me like the *Gītagovinda* (by Jayadeva)–and in order to please me–you should propagate it." The king woke up pleased; read the *Gītagovinda* with devotion and propagated it in different countries.[1]

Facing page: Gītagovinda *scribed on circular palmleaf folios, meant to be counted as rosary beads, Orissa State Museum.*

1 Prastavana, *Gītagovinda,* Nirnaya Sagar Press, Bombay, 1949.

The different versions of this particular tradition have been recorded in several other later works such as:

1. *Bhaktamāḷā Ṭīkā* in Hindi by Priya Dāsa[2]
2. *Bhakta Vijaya* in Marāthī by Mahīpatī[3]
3. *Bhaktamāḷā* in Bengali by Śrī Kṛṣṇa Dāsa[4]
4. *Dārḍhyatā Bhakti* in Odia by Rāma Dāsa[5]

All the different versions of this tradition mostly agree though sometimes slight additions and/or alterations have been made which are minor in nature. The only major addition to the version recorded by Candradatta in his *Bhaktamāḷā* is that Lord Jagannātha, in order to console the broken-hearted king, who had earlier discovered that the *Gītagovinda* by Jayadeva was dearer to the Lord, ordered to include twelve *śloka* (according to Hindi *Bhaktamāḷā Ṭikā*, Bengali *Bhaktamāḷā* and Odia *Dārḍhyatā Bhakti,* or twenty-four *śloka* (according to Marāthī *Bhakta Vijaya*) from the *Gītagovinda* written by the king in the *Gītagovinda* written by Jayadeva.

We will now make an attempt to study the historical basis and background of this tradition if any, with the help of both internal and external evidences as that may throw light on 1.) the history of the Jagannātha Cult and 2.) the origin and nature of other traditions regarding the *Gītagovinda.*

Presently we come across an unpublished work named *Abhinava-Gītagovinda* the authorship of which has been ascribed to Gajapati Puruṣottamadeva of solar dynasty of Odisha who reigned from 1466 to 1497 AD at several places and in the long eulogistic colophon of this work.[6]

Most probably the real author of *Abhinava-Gītagovinda* is Kavicandra Rāya Divākara Misra, a powerful Sanskrit poet of Odisha, who in his *Bharatāmṛta Mahākāvyam* had claimed the authorship of this work.[7] It appears he wrote this work under the patronage and perhaps instruction

---

2 K.N. Mahapatra, *Śrī Jayadeva O' Śrī Gītagovinda*, Bhubaneswar, 1973, pp.20, 57-61, 250-251.

3 Ibid., pp. 23, 61-65, 250 See also *Stories of Indian Saints*, English translation of Mahīpati's *Bhakta Vijaya* by J.E. Abbott and N.R. Godbole, Poona, 1933, pp 11-14.

4 Ibid., pp.25, 65-67, 351.

5 *Darḍhyatā Bhakti* by Rāma Dāsa, 55th Adhyāya.

6 K.N. Mahapatra, "*Abhinava-Gītagovinda* by Gajapati Puruṣottamadeva (1466-1497 AD)", in *Orissa Historical Research Journal* (*OHRJ*), 1961, IX, 3 ṛ 4.

7 K.N. Mahapatra, *A Descriptive Catalogue of Sanskrit Manuscript of Orissa, Bhubaneswar, 1960*, Vol.II, Introduction, pp. CIII.

and guidance of Gajapati Puruṣottamadeva and as a token of his gratitude the authorship of the work was attributed to Gajapati Puruṣottamadeva. It seems that this *Abhinava-Gītagovinda* has been alluded to in the above mentioned tradition as the Second *Gītagovinda* or the *Gītagovinda* written by a king of Odisha.

According to Marāthī *Bhakta Vijaya* by Mahīpatī, the second *Gītagovinda* mentioned in the tradition was written by a king named Sātvīk.[8] There is not a single evidence available supporting his thesis which should not be taken seriously. But K.N. Mahapatra thinks that the second *Gītagovinda* mentioned in the tradition and written by a king (of Odisha) in imitation of the *Gītagovinda* by Jayadeva was in fact written by Bhānudeva II of Gaṅga dynasty who ruled from 1309 to 1328 AD. He advanced several arguments in support of his theory which we propose to critically examine.

Firstly, by the time *Rasikapriyā* commentary of the *Gītagovinda* was written by Rāṇā Kumbhakarṇa i.e. before 1468 AD, the date of Rāṇā Kumbhakarṇa's death, 18 verses (*śloka*) had been interpolated into the *Gītagovinda* of Jayadeva because these 18 verses were not mentioned in the earlier *Sarvāṅgasundarī* commentary by Kavirāja Nārāyaṇadāsa. As these verses were not taken from *Abhinava-Gītagovinda* which must have been written after the *Rasikapriyā* commentary, K.N. Mahapatra argues, they must have been taken from some work written in imitation of the *Gītagovinda* after the date of *Sarvāṅgasundarī* commentary i.e. after 1285 and before 1468 AD.[9]

But this argument is completely untenable. The source of interpolation should not necessarily be a work written in imitation of the original work. Moreover the tradition that 12/24 *śloka* from the second *Gītagovinda* i.e. from the royal edition of the *Gītagovinda* were included in the *Gītagovinda* by Jayadeva does not necessarily prove that 18 interpolated *śloka* were from the royal edition of the *Gītagovinda* especially when the number of interpolated *śloka* is neither 12 nor 24. Again as Jagaddhara of Mithila has commented on the above mentioned 18 *śloka* in his *Sāradīpikā* commentary, these verses should not be considered as interpolated verses only because Kavirāja Nārāyaṇadāsa has not commented on them in his *Sarvāṅgasundarī* commentary which was written after *Sāradīpikā* was written.

---

8 K.N. Mahapatra, *Abhinava-Gītagovinda*. P. 56.

9 (a) Ibid, p. 61.
(b) K.N. Mahapatra, *Śrī Jayadeva O' Śrī Gītagovinda*. P. 87.

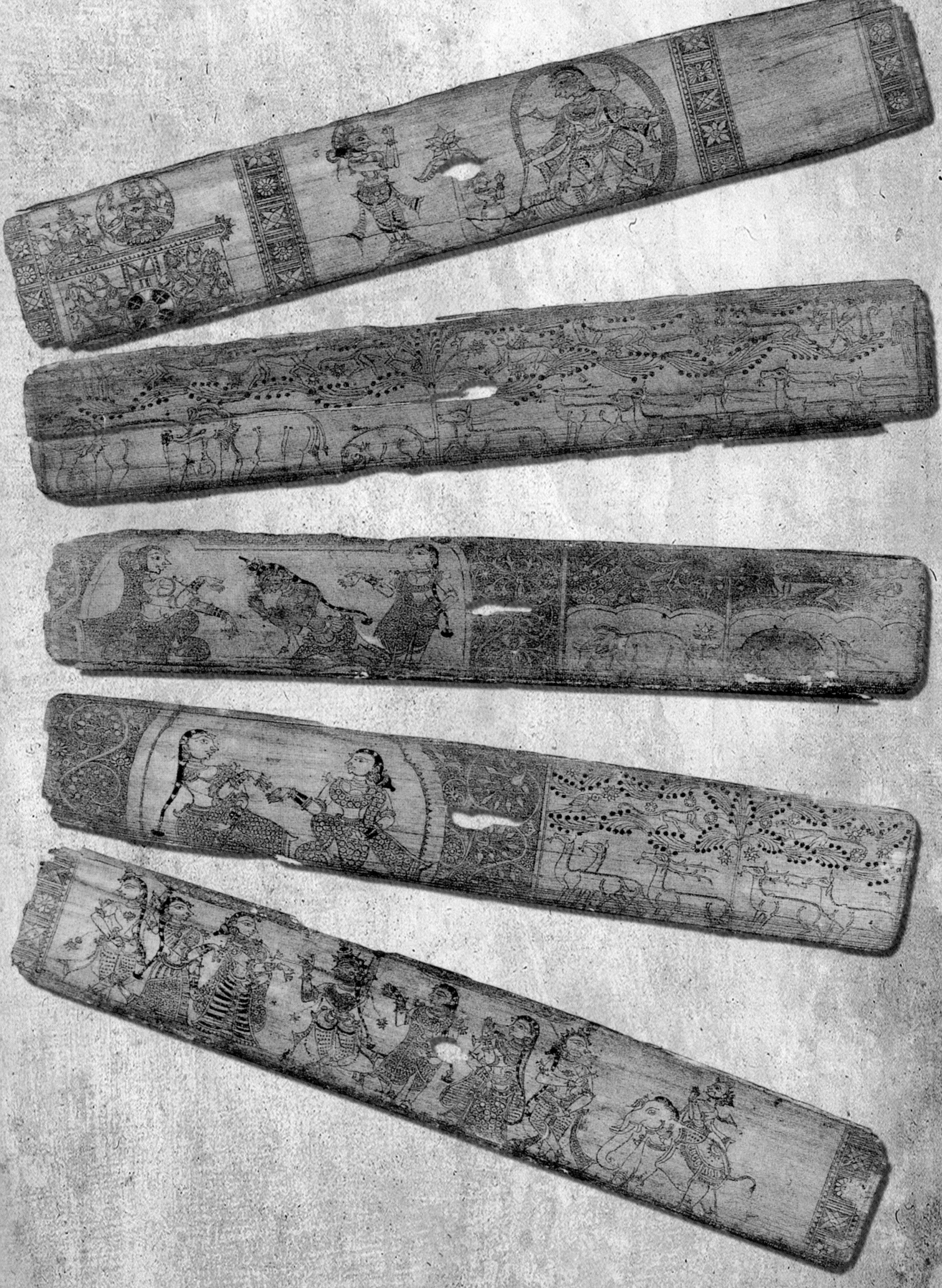

Secondly, according to an Odishan tradition certain Puruṣottamadeva of Gaṅga dynasty imitated the famous *Gītagovinda* by Jayadeva. Though there was no Gaṅga king bearing the name Puruṣottamadeva, in some of the inscriptions Bhānudeva II of Gaṅga dynasty, the *Anka* year of the king have been calculated in the name of Puruṣottamdeva i.e. Lord Jagannātha, as Bhānudeva II declared himself to be the deputy of the Lord Jagannātha. Therefore, according to K.N. Mahapatra, Puruṣottamadeva was taken as the second name of Bhānudeva II "by the common people who were ignorant of the significance of the expression used in the epigraphic records." Thus Mahapatra identifies Puruṣottamadeva of the tradition with the Gaṅga king Bhānudeva II who, according to him, wrote the second *Gītagovinda* mentioned in the tradition.[10]

But the argument is equally untenable. Instead of accepting the complicated theory and the difficult argument that K.N. Mahapatra advances it will be much more reasonable to identify Puruṣottamadeva of the tradition with Gajapati Puruṣottamadeva of solar dynasty. As Gajapati Kapilendradeva, the founder of solar dynasty and father of Gajapati Puruṣottamadeva was, according to a popular tradition of Odisha, believed to have been adopted by the last Gaṅga King–thereby continuing the Gaṅga line–it was quite natural to believe that Gajapati Puruṣottamadeva was a Gaṅga king especially in a similar tradition. But the most important question is if really ever such tradition existed?[11]

Thirdly, according to K.N. Mahapatra, Rāṇā Kumbhakarṇa refers to a work written by a king (in imitation of the *Gītagovinda* by Jayadeva) while commenting on the 13th verse of 4th *sarga* (i.e. at the end of 9th *prabandha*). As *Abhinava-Gītagovinda* was not written by the time Rāṇā Kumbhakarṇa wrote his commentary *Rasikapriyā* it seems that there was another king who wrote a *kāvya* imitating *Gītagovinda* by Jayadeva.[12]

The passage in Rāṇā Kumbhakarṇa's commentary to which K.N. Mahapatra refers is *Prabandha Pṛthivibhartra Prabandha Pritaye Hareh.* But this passage does not refer to a work written by a king in imitation of the *Gītagovinda.* On the contrary this passage has been

---

10 K.N. Mahapatra,
(a) *Abhinava-Gītagovinda.* p.61.
(b) *Śrī Jayadeva O' Gītagovinda*...p. 86.

11 According to K.N. Mahapatra this tradition was first mentioned by Jagabandhu Singh in his book *Prācina Utkaḷa.* But Jagabandhu Singh did not mention such a tradition. See *Prācina Utkaḷa*, Bhubaneswar, 1964, pp. 52-53, 36.

12 K.N. Mahapatra, *Abhinava-Gītagovinda,*..p.62.

quoted from another work of Rāṇā Kumbhakarṇa named *Sangītarāja.*[13] By the expression *Pṛthivibhartra* i.e. the king, Rāṇā Kumbhakarṇa refers to himself. In *Rasikapriyā* commentary Rāṇā Kumbhakarṇa quotes an identical passage again at the end of the 13th *Prabandha* of the *Gītagovinda*–and a similar passage *Prabandha Pṛthivibhartra Hari Bhakten Varnita*, at the end of 10th *Prabandha* from his *Sangītarāja* from which he often quotes in *Rasikapriyā*.

Finally, we have not yet come across any such work other than *Abhinava-Gītagovinda* by Gajapati Puruṣottamadeva. As there is no definite evidence that a royal imitation of the *Gītagovinda* other than *Abhinava-Gītagovinda* was ever prepared, it may be concluded that by the royal imitation of the tradition *Abhinava-Gītagovinda* by Gajapati Puruṣottamadeva is meant.

Again we find that in an order issued in the 4th year and mentioned in Odia inscription installed at the Jaya Vijaya door of the Jagannātha Temple Puri, Gajapati Pratāparudradeva of solar dynasty and son of Gajapati Puruṣottamadeva made the singing of his father's work (i.e. *Abhinava-Gītagovinda*) compulsory in the Jagannātha Temple and prohibited the singing of any other song i.e. *Gītagovinda* by Jayadeva. (It corroborates our earlier thesis that *Abhinava-Gītagovinda* by Gajapati Puruṣottamadeva has been referred in the tradition as the royal imitation of the *Gītagovinda*).

---

13 *Sangītarāja*, ed. Premalata Misra, Varanasi, 1963, p. 578.

Left and pages 46-47: *Illustrated folios from the* Gītagovinda, *palmleaf manuscript, Museum Rietberg Zurich.*

But many scholars, including K.N. Mahapatra, believe that in the said inscription Gajapati Pratāparudradeva in fact made the singing of the *Gītagovinda* by Jayadeva compulsory and prohibited the singing of *Abhinava-Gītagovinda* or any other imitation of Jayadeva's work.[14] As both the virtually conflicting and opposite views largely depend on the different interpretations of the same inscription a detailed discussion of these interpretations will not be considered out of place here.

In 1875 R.L. Mitra provided the reading of the inscription for the first time.[15] This reading was rejected by M.M. Chakravarti who furnished a fresh reading along with the translation and a note in 1893.[16] So far almost all the scholars have accepted the interpretation and translation provided by Chakravarti. The existence of *Abhinava-Gītagovinda,* the authorship of which is ascribed to Gajapati Puruṣottamadeva, was most probably not known to M.M. Chakravarti. Otherwise he might have interpreted and translated the inscription differently. To him, therefore *Gītagovinda* meant only the famous poetical work by Jayadeva and with this preconceived notion he tried to interpret and translate the text of the inscription. The result was a complete artificial analysis of the sentences (especially the first sentence) on which his translation was based and he had to imagine things in order to be able to fill in the gaps left open by this artificial analysis. As for example, the analyses of a part of the first sentence, *baḍaṭhākuraṅka Gītagovinda ṭhākura bhoga bele* (line2-3) may be considered. Instead of analysing it as consisting of two independent noun phrases i.e. *baḍaṭhākuraṅka Gītagovinda* (meaning *Gītagovinda* by *baḍaṭhākura*) and *ṭhākura bhoga bele,* (meaning at the time of offering *bhoga* to the deities) which is natural and clear he analyses it as a single noun phrase in which the head of the noun phrase *bele* (at the time) is modified by *bhoga* (offering) which in turn is modified by two separate noun phrases *baḍaṭhākuraṅka* (Balarām, elder brother of Lord Jagannātha according to M.M. Chakravarti) and *Gītagovinda ṭhākura* (Lord Jagannātha according to M.M. Chakravarti). This is because he could not understand the expression *baḍaṭhākuraṅka Gītagovinda,* as to him *Gītagovinda* meant only the famous work by Jayadeva. Thus he had to create an artificial expression such as *Gītagovinda ṭhākura,* which incidentally occurs nowhere else and

14 K.N. Mahapatra, *Śrī Jayadeva.* p. 89.

15 R.L. Mitra, *Antiquities of Orissa,* Vol.II, PP. 165-167, 1880.

16 M.M. Chakravarti, "Uriya Inscriptions of the 15th and 16th centuries", *Journal of Asiatic Society Bengal* (*JASB*), LXII,I. pp. 96-97, 1893.

imagine that it means Lord Jagannātha. Because of that he had to contradict himself while interpreting the 3rd sentence (lines 5-6) of the inscription and accept *baḍaṭhākuraṅka Gītagovinda* as a single phrase which he sought to reject while interpreting the first sentence (lines 2-3) as shown above.

In 1929 AD the existence of *Abhinava-Gītagovinda* was brought to the notice of the scholars for the first time by Jagabandhu Singh.[17] Later in 1934 H.P. Sastri noticed it in his *Descriptive Catalogue of Sanskrit Manuscript* in the collection of *Asiatic Society, Bengal, Vol. VII.*[18] But even after that scholars never cared to suspect if *Gītagovinda* of the inscription really means *Gītagovinda* by Jayadeva or *Abhinava Gītagovinda* by Gajapati Puruṣottamadeva and invariably accepted the artificial and contradictory interpretation provided by M.M. Chakravarti. Only K.B. Tripathy in 1962 supplied a fresh and different reading with a natural translation of the text.[19] He also suspected, though not entirely certain, if *baḍaṭhākura* of the inscription did not mean Gajapati Puruṣottamadeva and thereby hinted that *Gītagovinda* of the inscription may mean *Abhinava-Gītagovinda.*[20] But K.N. Mahapatra has preferred to accept M.M. Chakravarti's interpretation and translation already rejected by K.B. Tripathy.[21]

Without entering into detailed linguistic analysis of the inscription text—which will undoubtedly support our theory—it will be enough to say that in this inscription the phrase *baḍaṭhākuraṅka Gītagovinda* occurs twice in lines 2-3 and lines 5-6 and always means the same thing i.e. the *Gītagovinda* by *baḍaṭhākura* (*Abhinava-Gītagovinda* written by Gajapati Puruṣottamadeva). Otherwise the expression '*e nāṭa*' (meaning this play) occurring at the end of the first sentence of the inscription (i.e. *e nāṭa hoiba*) will be confusing and it will not be possible to understand

---

17 Jagabandhu Singh, *Prācina Utkala*, Puri, 1929, p. 45.

18 K.N. Mahapatra, *Abhinava-Gītagovinda.* p. 51.

19 K.B. Tripathy, *Evolution of Oriya Language and Script*, Bhubaneswar, 1962, pp. 300-301.

20 Ibid, p. 301 f.n.

21 K.N. Mahapatra, *Śrī Jayadeva O' Gītagovinda*...p.89. Though Mahapatra claims that he has accepted the reading of M.M. Chakravarti the reading given in his book is different from Chakravarti's reading as he adds suffix-*nka* after the expression *Gītagovinda thakura* and before the expression '*bhogabele*' which is not found in Charkravarti's reading (line 3). This suffix is also not found in Tripathy's reading. It may seem that addition of this suffix may support Mahapatras's interpretation. But even if we accept Mahapatra's reading for the sake of argument it will be difficult to accept his interpretation of the text for linguistic reasons.

what it really means and to what it refers. On the other hand if we accept *baḍaṭhākuraṅka Gītagovinda* as a single phrase then *e nāṭa* will refer to *Gītagovinda* by *baḍaṭhākura* and will mean the play based on *Gītagovinda* (by *baḍaṭhākura*) or dramatic performance of *Abhinava Gītagovinda* by *baḍaṭhākura* (Puruṣottamadeva).

It may be mentioned here that to interpret the expression *baḍaṭhākura* as Gajapati Purusottamdeva is in no way inconsistent or inappropriate though the tradition of *ṭhākurarājā* or *caḷanti Viṣṇu*, as we understand it today, might have originated much later.

Both inscriptional and literary instances can be cited to prove that the Odia word *ṭhākura*, meaning king or master, was in constant use in medieval period though its significance varied according to the time and place of its use.[22] In an inscription one of the four Bhānudevas of Gaṅga dynasty of Odisha has been referred as *ṭhākura*.[23] In another inscription Gajapati Puruṣottamadeva has also been referred as *ṭhākura*.[24] Later in another inscription king Govinda Vidyādhara has also been described as Gobindadeo *ṭhākura*.[25] In Rājabhoga section of the Jagannātha Temple chronicle *Mādalāpāñji* and *Cakadāpothī* the uses *ṭhākura* and *rājā ṭhākura* are to be found referring to the *rājās* of Khurdā.[26] In *Prema Pancāmṛta*, a late 17th century poetical text, Gajapati Divyasinghadeva (1688-1716) has been described as *Utkaḷa desara ṭhākura* (king of Utkala).[27] In *Kānci Kāveri*, another Odia poetical text of medieval period, Gajapati Puruṣottamadeva has been referred as *ṭhākura*.[28] In his letters Gajapati Birakesarideva (1733-1793) refers to his father, Gajapati Rāmachandradeva II, as *dadāi ṭhākura*[29] and himself as *Śrī ṭhākura*.[30]

---

22 D.C. Sircar, *Indian Epigraphical Glossary*, 1966, p. 340

23 K.B. Tripathy, *Evolution of Oriya*.... Inscription serial no. 2, line 6, pp 227-228.

24 Ibid, Inscription serial no. 41, line 2, pp, 298-300.

25 Ibid, Inscription serial no. 53, line 5, pp. 317-319m.

26 (a) *Mādaḷāpāñji*, ed. A.B. Mahanty, Cuttack, 1940, pp.47, 68.
(b) *Cakadāpothī O cakada basana ba cayini cakada* ed. Sudhakara Pattanayak, Cuttack, 1959, p.13.

27 Bhupati Pandita, *Prema Pancāmṛta*, 10th Adhyāya.

28 *Puruṣottama Das by Kanci Kaveri* ed. Sukumar Sen and Sunanda Sen, Calcutta, 1957, Ist and 2nd *Chanda*.

29 Chakradhara Mahapatra, *Utkala Itihasara Eka Ajnata Adhyāya*, Cuttack, 1959, pp.305-306.

30 N. Pattanayak, "Administration of Jagannatha Temple in the 18th century." in *Man in India*, 43,3, 1963, p.215.

As in Odishan royal families, the family members are never addressed by their proper names or never referred by normal kinship terminology such as *pua* (i.e. son) as is the case otherwise but by special terms like *Jenāmaṇi* it is quite possible that Gajapati Pratāparudradeva referred to his father as *baḍaṭhākura.* This is corroborated by the fact that Gajapati Kapilesvaradeva has been described as Kapileśvara *ṭhākura* in the said inscription and Birākesarideva describes his father as *daḍaiṭhākura* as mentioned above. Perhaps when Gajapati Puruṣottamadeva was alive he was referred to as *baḍaṭhākura* i.e. the elder master (in Odia *baḍa* means either big or elder) and the crown-prince Pratāparudra as *sāna ṭhākura* i.e. the younger master (in Odia *sāna* means either small or younger) which are quite natural in Odishan context. Therefore it was perfectly logical to refer Gajapati Puruṣottamadeva as *baḍaṭhākura* even after his death, most probably in order to perpetuate his memory immediately after his death.

Taking it for granted that *Abhinava-Gītagovinda* written by Gajapati Puruṣottamadeva and the order simultaneously introducing and making compulsory the singing of *Abhinava-Gītagovinda* (and prohibiting the singing of the *Gītagovinda* by Jayadeva at the same time) in the Jagannātha Temple, provided the basis for the mention of second *Gītagovinda* written by an Odishan king and prohibiting the singing of *Gītagovinda* by the royal order, we now know for certain that there was no historical basis for that part of the tradition which mentions personal confrontation between Jayadeva and the author of the second

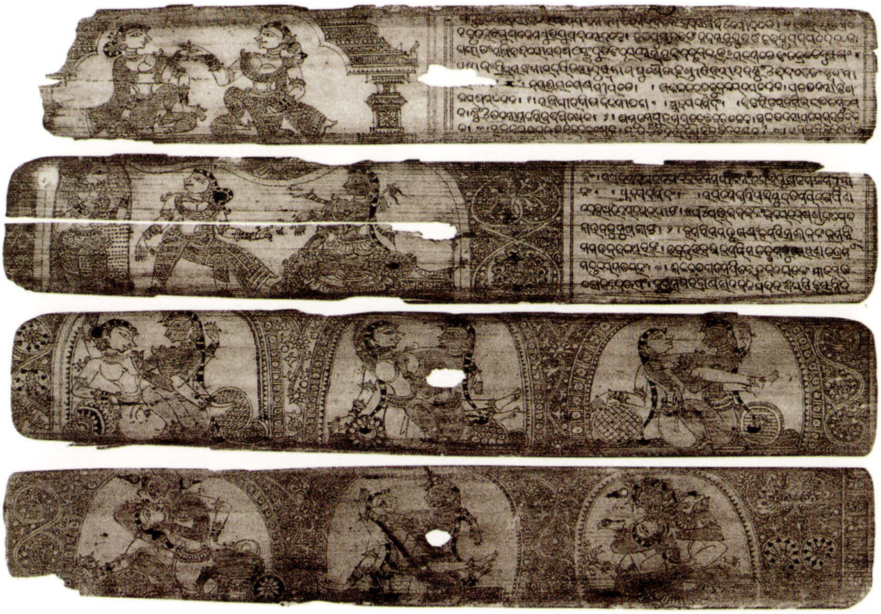

Illustrated folios from the Gītagovinda, *palmleaf manuscript, Museum Rietberg Zurich.*

Gītagovinda, as both Jayadeva and Gajapati Puruṣottamadeva were separated by three hundred years or so. Moreover the controversy as to which of the two *Gītagovinda* was superior or dear to the Lord Jagannātha must have arisen sometime after Gajapati Pratāparudra issued his famous order prohibiting the singing of *Gītagovinda* and introducing and making compulsory the singing of *Abhinava-Gītagovinda* when both Jayadeva and Gajapati Puruṣottamadeva were dead. But there is no doubt that such a controversy arose after the royal order was issued prohibiting the singing of the *Gītagovinda* in the Jagannātha Temple.

The effort to reintroduce the singing of *Gītagovinda* by Jayadeva in the Jagannātha Temple must have been at the root of the controversy as to which of the two *Gītagovinda* is superior and dear to the Lord. In that case the tradition that Lord Jagannātha himself recognised and specified the superiority of *Gītagovinda* over *Abhinava-Gītagovinda* was either created or manipulated with the active connivance of the priests of the Jagannātha Temple who were supporters of the *Gītagovinda* so that Pratāparudra's order could be challenged successfully and the re-introduction of *Gītagovinda* in the Jagannātha Temple could be legitimised. Without the active collaboration of the priests of the Jagannātha Temple it would have been impossible either to create the tradition that *Gītagovinda* was dearer to the Lord and superior to *Abhinava-Gītagovinda* or to manipulate the test of superiority between the two *kāvya*. Because of this controversy several other traditions were created to prove that Jayadeva's *Gītagovinda* was dear to the Lord Jagannātha. These traditions are recorded in the *Bhaktamāḷā* by Candradatta. The priests of the Jagannātha Temple must have contributed and actively participated in the creation of these traditions. Therefore there must have been stiff opposition to Pratāparudra's order from among the priests of the Jagannātha Temple. This opposition again must have been deep-rooted.

Next, the question, what was the reason behind the priestly opposition to *Abhinava-Gītagovinda* and support to *Gītagovinda* should be answered. It seems by that time *Gītagovinda* by Jayadeva had achieved a quasi-scriptural status. We find that only a few years later, when Caitanya was on his South India tour, Rāya Rāmānanda was quoting from *Gītagovinda* in order to prove Kṛṣṇa's deep love for Rādhā and Caitanya accepting the authority of the *Gītagovinda* without any hesitation.[31]

---

31 Kṛṣṇadāsa Kavirāja, *Caitanya Caritāmṛta, Madhya lilā*, Chapter-8.

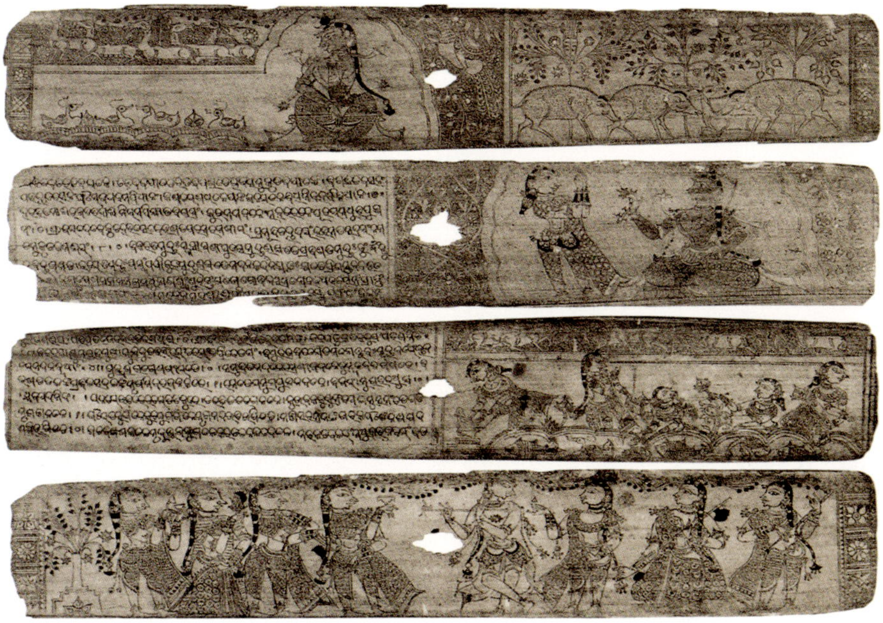

Therefore to the priests the singing of the *Gītagovinda* in the temple was a sort of temple-ritual and Pratāparudra's order prohibiting it was a gross violation of it. Seen in this light the priests were simply fighting to maintain a temple-ritual. But more probably the priests were extra sensitive to any explicit or implicit attempt on the part of the kings to bring the cult under the royal control and they suspected in Pratāparudra's proclamation such an attempt which in the long run would undermine their position in the cult. The tone of the proclamation must have seemed quite aggressive to them.

A comparison of the texts of the *Gītagovinda* and *Abhinava-Gītagovinda* will support the above conclusion. It appears that, as the name indicates, *Abhinava-Gītagovinda* is an imitation of the *Gītagovinda*. Though there are only ten *sarga* or chapters in the former in place of the twelve to be found in the latter in both the texts the theme and the presentation are quite similar. Even the influence of the *Gītagovinda* in naming the *sarga* of *Abhinava-Gītagovinda* is quite evident. But there is an important difference. *Gītagovinda* begins with an invocation to ten *avatāra* or incarnations of Keśava or Harī. Though Kṛṣṇa happens to be the main character or the hero in this *kāvya*, it must be noted that, he has not been listed as one of the *avatāra*. In the beginning of *Abhinava-Gītagovinda* we find a similar invocation to the ten *avatāras* of Lord Jagannātha or more exactly of Nīlagiripati Acyuta. But here Kṛṣṇa has been included in the list of *avatāra* and he takes the place of Buddha *avatāra* of the *Gītagovinda*. It appears, to Jayadeva, Kṛṣṇa was *avatārī*

Illustrated folios from the Gītagovinda, *palmleaf manuscript, Museum Rietberg Zurich.*

or the source of incarnations and not merely an *avatāra*. Therefore from the point of view of the subject matter of the texts *Abhinava-Gītagovinda* should have been more acceptable to the priests of the Jagannātha Temple instead of *Gītagovinda* because it attempted to give a relatively higher status to Lord Jagannātha as the source of incarnations.

If *Abhinava-Gītagovinda* was not accepted by the priests it was not because of its subject matter but because of the fact that it was supposed to have been written by a king and it was sought to be introduced by another king. To the priests these seemed as utter interferences in their prerogative.

Pratāprudra's order prohibiting the singing of the *Gītagovinda* was issued in his 4th *Anka* year corresponding to 1499 AD.[32] Kṛṣṇadāsa Kavirāja in his *Caitanya Caritāmṛta* maintains that once a *devadāsī* was singing the *Gītagovinda* in the *Jagamohana*. Caitanya on his way to the Yamesvara Tota (grove) listened to the song and in consequence was overwhelmed with emotion and ran to the temple.[33] It is clear that here by the word *Jagamohana* the *Jagamohan* or the audience hall of the Jagannātha Temple is meant, as in *Caitanya Caritāmṛta* Kṛṣṇadāsa Kavirāja refers several times to the *Gītagovinda* by Jayadeva[34] and not even once to *Abhinava-Gītagovinda* by Puruṣottamadeva it is equally clear that by *Gītagovinda* he means the famous poetical work by Jayadeva.

In this connection it must be mentioned that, according to Kṛṣṇadāsa Kavirāja, Caitanya in fact loved to read and listen to the singing of the *Gītagovinda* by Jayadeva.[35] Kṛṣṇadāsa Kavirāja places this incident just before the commencement of Caitanya's *divyonmāda* i.e. the last 12 years of his life which he spent in Puri. Caitanya came to Puri in 1535 AD after which he lived for 24 years. So this incident must have happened sometime around 1522 AD which means that *Gītagovinda* by Jayadeva was already re-introduced in the Jagannātha Temple by that time.

We must now take our discussion a little further. Had Pratāparudra's order prohibiting the singing of the *Gītagovinda* by Jayadeva been in force when Caitanya came to Puri in all probability he must have tried

32 Ibid, *Antya Lilā*, Chapter 13.

33 Ibid, *Madhya Lilā*, chapter 2,8,10, *Antya Lilā*, Chapter 15, 17,19,20.

34 Ibid.

35 P. Mukherji, *Gajapati kings of Orissa*, Calcutta, 1953, p. 100.

to get it re-introduced in the Jagannātha Temple because of his deep appreciation of it especially when he accepted it as an authority as we have already seen. Again as Caitanya was held in high esteem by Pratāparudra so much so that Pratāparudra granted clemency to one Gopīnātha Pattanayak an official who misappropriated a large sum of money, in order to please him (Caitanya)[36] in all probability he would have yielded to Caitanya's request. In that event Caitanya's role in getting *Gītagovinda* re-introduced in the Jagannātha Temple must have found mentioned in his biographies. But all his biographies are silent about it. Therefore it must be concluded that the *Gītagovinda* was already re-introduced in the Jagannātha Temple by the time Caitanya came to Puri in 1510.

It seems the strong resistance of the priests forced the king to countermand his order shortly after its proclamation in 1499. We have seen how Rāya Rāmānanda was already familiar with the *Gītagovinda* and quotes it as an authority when Caitanya asked him to prove Kṛṣṇa's deep love for Rādhā. The deep appreciation of Rāya Rāmānanda or people like him for the *Gītagovinda* by Jayadeva must have given moral support to the priests in their resistance to *Abhinava-Gītagovinda.*

Any historical basis for the tradition that 12 or 24 *śloka* of *Abhinava-Gītagovinda* by the order of Lord Jagannātha seems to be lacking.[37] This part of the tradition–not mentioned in *Bhaktamāḷā* by Candradatta–had been created either by the supporters of *Abhinava-Gītagovinda* or by the supporters of the *Gītagovinda.* The supporters of *Abhinava-Gītagovinda* might have created such a tradition to explain the re-introduction of the *Gītagovinda* in the temple without loss of face. On the other hand the supporters of the *Gītagovinda* might have created such a tradition for one or a combination of the following reasons:

1. to explain away the interpolations;
2. not to hurt the feelings of the Odishan kings–after their victory–unnecessarily.

We have so far studied the historical basis of the tradition regarding the singing of the *Gītagovinda* in the Jagannātha Temple, Puri. Now we

36 *Caitanya Caritamāta, Antya Lilā,* Chapter 9, also *Madhya Lilā,* Chapter1.

37 The number of the *śloka* incorporated in the *Gītagovinda* from *Abhinava-Gītagovinda,* according to the tradition, was either 12 as there are 12 *sarga* in the *Gītagovinda* the calculation being one *śloka* per *sarga* or 24 as there are 24 *prabandha* in *Gītagovinda* the calculation being one *śloka* per *prabandha.*

will try to study and interpret the same tradition both in context and terms of different forces interacting with each other centering round Lord Jagannātha in a bid to reconstruct the general historical background of this tradition.

This tradition may be compared with some other similar traditions recorded in the *Rājabhoga* section of *Mādalāpāñji*:

(a) Once this king (Niśankabhānudeva of the Gaṅga dynasty) came to visit Lord Jagannātha. The worshipper (*paśupāḷaka*) found nothing to give the king as oblation because there was neither flower nor *tuḷasī* on the body of Jagannātha. There was a garland of *dayanā* flowers on the head of this priest worshipper. He brought it from his head secretly and gave it to the king as oblation. The king found a strand of hair in the oblation of flower garland (and became suspicious). He enquired how it was possible to find a hairstrand in the oblated flower garland. The priest became nervous and replied that it was the hairstrand on the head of Lord Jagannātha. On hearing this, the king got angry and got the priest taken into custody and ordered the priest to show the hair on the head of Lord Jagannātha. (In fact there is no strand of hair on the head of Lord Jagannātha). Lord Jagannātha knew the nervousness of the priest and ordered the king in a dream, "Why do you trouble my priests (*sevaka* = servant)? You yourself will see the strand of hair on my head at the time of morning decoration." The king woke up and came to *darśana* at the time of morning decoration. He saw the hair hanging from the head of Lord Jagannātha. He was surprised and rolled down at the feet of Lord Jagannātha. He got the priest released and consoled him a lot.[38]

(b) The king (Puruṣottamadeva of solar dynasty) found out that the priests (*sevakas* = servants) were worshipping Lord Jagannātha not properly sanctified. Therefore the king asked the priests to work in accordance with the prescription of the *ācārya*. So the priests brought this to the notice of Lord Jagannātha with due respect. This very night the *ācārya* was ordered (in a dream), "Do not poke your nose regarding the affair of the priests of this *Kṣetra* i.e. Puri. You are granted the Kūrma Kṣetra (Śrīkūrmam) from today. You will stay

38 Rāma Dāsa, *Mādalāpānji*, p.39. This tradition has also been recorded in *Darḍhyata Bhakti*, 20th *Adhyaya*.

there'...The same night the king was ordered (in a dream), "These priests are my companions. During Kṛṣṇāvatāra they were playing with me as milkmen and milkmaids. Were they practising any purification rites in those days! I cannot leave them.'[39]

(c) ...The king became very angry at the sight of the cake in his hand and got this *Dāsamuduli* (the temple priest) arrested. The next day he (the king) got the *bhoga* prepared by another priest. That night Lord Jagannātha said to him (the king) in a dream, "You have imprisoned my *Mahāsuāra* (the chief cook). I was not at all satisfied with the cakes (prepared by the new cook)." The king woke up, held the *Dāsamuduli* in great esteem and awarded him the title of *Mahāsuāra*. He presented him a turban as a token of this new title. He ordered him to prepare the cakes as usual.[40]

It is highly interesting that all these traditions have a common thematic pattern running through them:

1. The king (of Odisha) interferes in the affairs of the Jagannātha Temple.
2. Lord Jagannātha opposes this interference by the kings.
3. The king at last yields to the wish of Lord Jagannātha and the matter comes to an end.

---

39 *Mādalāpāñji*, pp. 49-50. This tradition has also been recorded in *Prapannāmṛta* by Anantacarya where *Acārya* of this tradition has been identified with Rāmānuja. See also *Life and Teaching of Śrī Rāmānuja* by C.R. Srinivas Ayangar, Madras, 1908.

40 This tradition has also been recorded in a medieval *kāvya* (poetical work) *Kānci Kāveri* by Puruṣottama Dāsa. See *Kānci Kāveri*, ed. Sukumar Sen and Sunanda Sen, Calcutta, 1957. See also 'Genealogy of the King of Oḍradeśa' Local Records, Vol.60, Telugu Manuscript, Oriental Manuscript Library, Madras.

Kṛṣṇa in the form of Viṣṇu sitting in a lotus maṇḍala, *talking to Laḷitā, a parrot sitting nearby.*

This thematic similarity is rather striking. What are the reasons underlying this thematic similarity?

As we have already seen–in the case of the tradition regarding the singing of the *Gītagovinda* in the temple of Jagannātha–all these traditions–are neither completely fictitious nor completely based on facts. There is a substratum of truth in all these traditions running like an undercurrent.

Generally the beginnings and the ends of these traditions–the traditions invariably begin with the interference of the king in the affairs of the temple of Jagannātha and end when the interference of the king comes to an end–are more or less based on facts or contain the germ of historical truth. But Lord Jagannātha's crucial opposition was either fabricated or cleverly and carefully manipulated by the priests of the Jagannātha Temple, who must have opposed and resisted the interference of the kings.

It appears that in the fight between the kings and the temple priests, Lord Jagannātha–completely monopolised by the priests–serves as the rallying point for the priests and is portrayed as the great supporter of the cause of the priests. Not only the priests could offer a strong resistance in the name of Lord Jagannātha to the kings but using Lord Jagannātha as a supporter of their cause they were able to muster public sympathy. No wonder they won invariably in the test of strength and the kings always surrendered to popular pressure.

On the whole we find quite a good number of traditions based on the conflict between the Odishan kings and the priests of Jagannātha Temple, Puri of which the present tradition serves as an example. It appears both the Odishan kings and the temple priests tried to monopolise the Jagannātha Cult and in the process clashed with each other from time to time.

Kṛṣṇa seated on a padma maṇḍala *listening to a* sakhī *sent by Rādhā.*

One of the severest clashes occurred at the time of Gajapati Pratāparudra and this internal conflict might have contributed greatly to Pratāparudra's weak position at home and his inability to resist aggression from outside resulting in his defeat at the hands of Kṛṣṇa Deva Rāya of Vijayanagar. Therefore the patronisation of the Caitanya Cult by Pratāparudra can be viewed as a political expedient–an effort to create counter balancing force to the Jagannātha Cult completely monopolised by the priests. This internal dissension most probably influenced the subsequent political decline of Odisha.

The Village Kenduvilva and the Area Around

Prafulla Kumar Tripathy

The village of Kendubilva is located in Pratāparudrapur gram-panchāyat that comes under Bāliantā police station in the district of Puri. The river Prācī, revered as the Gaṅgā in Odisha flows on the north and the river Kusabhadrā of mythological importance flows on the south of Kendubilva. These two rivers besides making the soil fertile accentuate the holiness of the place. The vast extensive shady groves of *kendu* and *bilva* trees stretching along the village boundary justify the name Kendubilva. The village is divided into three parts, namely Kenduli, Kenduli Pāṭṇā and Kenduli Śāsana.

Proceeding from the Hansal crossway on the National Highway between Cuttack and Bhubaneswar one has to cover a distance of about twelve kilometres on the north embankment of the river Kusabhadrā to reach Kenduli through Pratāparudrapur. Similarly by proceeding from Fulnakharā crossway on the road leading to Mādhava, one has to cross the river Prācī near Kantāparā or Adāspur to reach Kenduli, the birthplace of Jayadeva.

On entering the village from the west, the temple of Nṛsiṁhanātha first comes to sight. The temple, built of sandstone, is about 20 feet high having a *jagamohana* (*mukhaśāḷā*). The architectural features of the temple lie concealed under a thick coat of lime plaster. Inside the temple are two granite images of Nṛsiṁhadeva. Of these two images, one is Lakṣmī Nṛsiṁha with the goddess Lakṣmī on the lap and the other the incarnation figure tearing open the bowl of the demon king Hiraṇya-Kaśipu. In the sanctum there is an image of Mādhava with the attributes of conch, wheel, mace and lotus adorned in four hands. Close to the temple is a branch of Trimāli or Tirumalla monastery of Puri. Lakṣmaṇa Sūri, a courtier in the court of Tirumalla Ray, the king of Vijayanagar, (1565-1580 AD), has earned wide reputation all over India due to his commentary, *Śrutiranjani* on the *Gītagovinda*. Most probably Tirumalla Ray along with his courtier Lakṣmaṇa Sūri had come to Śrīkṣetra (Puri) and established

Facing page: *Padmavatī, the presiding deity of the Caṇḍi Temple, Kenduli. principal deity at Kendubilva.*

the Trimāli monastery. Legends reveal that Tirumalla Ray had visited Kendubilva, and established a monastery in the village. The pilgrims from the south on their visits to Kendubilva used this monastery as a shelter. Evidences of these visits are available at the Trimāli Maṭha at Puri.

From a tank adjacent to the monastery a stone box had been discovered, which contained a copper plate inscription. The inscription recorded that in his 8th regnal year Narasimha IV of Gaṅga dynasty, had in *Śaka* era 1305 (1383 AD) gifted the village Kinri Śāsana situated in between Vārāṇasi Kaṭaka and Kalmora Uttarakhaṇḍa to Mahapātra Naraharidāsa Praharāja after renaming the village as 'Vijaya Narasimhapura'. The copper plate also indicates the boundaries of the village and depicts the glory of the Gaṅga dynasty. Some of the villages mentioned in the inscription still exist. Of all the copper plate inscriptions discovered so far in Odisha it is the biggest one. It is said that the homestead land, tank, etc of Mahapātra Naraharidāsa Praharāja were in this village. Legends reveal that a little away from the monastery was a sacrificial altar guarded by granite stone pillars where Jayadeva used to perform sacrifices. In commemoration of this, on the auspicious day of *Akṣaya Tṛtīya*, sacrifices are performed. It is believed that the mounds in the groves at the south of the sacrificial altar was the ancestral home of Jayadeva.

Standing sculpture of a hermit said to be of Jayadeva in Pratāparudrapur village.

The temple to the south of this altar enshrines a black granite image of a goddess seated in *padmāsana* with the seven-hooded *nāga* over her head. Beautiful carvings of flowers and creepers adorn both sides of the goddess. On the left there is a figure of a lion ready to attack while on the right side is a devout couple meditating in kneeling position. The lower part of the pedestal contains figures of dancing girls. The face of the goddess looks calm and composed. She has a crown over her head and is adorned with delicate ornaments like necklaces, bracelets and anklets on her body. A sacred thread passes in between her breasts. and she holds in her left hand a full blown lotus. However, the stem of the lotus is damaged. On her right shoulder hangs a bunch of five mangoes. The other image is almost identical with this. Researchers are of the opinion that both the images were carved at the same time. The followers of the Vajrāyāna sect might be worshipping the images as their goddesses. Some historians identify these images as Caṇḍī but the local people venerate them as Jāgeśvarī and Padmāvatī.

Daśāvatāra place names around Kenduli village

Map not to scale

Insides the temple complex one finds the lower part of a temple containing the *Śakti* of Mukteśvara *Liṅgam*. The other granite image of Mādhava holding conventional *āyudhas* belonging to this temple is now displayed in the local museum.

Close to the temple in a vast area measuring about six acres, a museum named after Jayadeva has been established to perpetuate the memory of the great poet. Inside the museum the images of Mādhava and Lakṣmī Mādhava have been displayed. The stone inscription kept in the museum is badly defaced making it difficult for decipherment. It probably belonged to the Gaṅga period. The opulence of trees and creepers somewhat confirms to the descriptions in the *Gītagovinda*. Here the birth of Jayadeva (Jayadeva Jayanti) is celebrated annually.

In the past several villages around Kenduli had flourished and were named after the ten incarnations of Viṣṇu. The following is a detailed discussion on those villages.

(i) Matsyapura

Matsyapura under Balipātṇā police station in the district of Puri is now known as Māchapur. It is about a kilometre south of Kenduli. The Nimāparā-Koṇārka route which originates from Uttarā crossway passing through Basant Māla in a southernly direction reaches Māchapur.

The stone image of Nṛsiṁha.

Bordering the village is a thatched *maṭha* where the wooden image of Lord Jagannātha is worshipped. On the south of the village, the old brick temple of Bhuvaneśvara is dedicated to Śiva. The temple is in a dilapidated state with images of Mādhava and Buddha embedded in the wall. Inside the temple, the granite image of Nṛsiṁha, tearing open the gut of Hiraṇya-Kaśipu is worshipped. The niches on the western and southern sides are empty. This image of Mādhava uncommon as an attending deity in a Śiva temple might have been brought from some other place and installed here later. One kilometre away from Māchapur on the east one comes across another brick temple with lime plastering called Fula Bilas. The images of Trivikrama and Nṛsiṁha occupy the niches on northern and southern sides. There is a Śiva temple named Beleśvara at Karunjapur near Sāna Māchapur on the west of Māchapur. It appears that the Śiva temples in the village are later constructions whereas the Viṣṇu temple whose remains and sculptures have been used in the Śiva temple seems to be of older date. The priests of the Viṣṇu temple have been granted landed property. The *Gītgovinda* used to be recited in the Viṣṇu temple in its daily ritual which now has become occasional only on festive occasions.

(ii) Kūrmapura Śāsana

At a distance of about two kilometres to the west of Kenduli is a *Brāhmaṇa* settlement named Kuanarpur. It is close to the way leading from Fulṇakharā on National Highway No. 5 towards Mādhava. Kūrmapura, now known as Kuanarpur, belongs to the Govindpur police station in the district of Cuttack. Close to the northern border of Kuanarpur *Brāhmaṇa* settlement, there is a village named Bhaghalpur in the memory of Bhaghal Devī, the queen of Aniyankabhīmadeva (1190-1198 AD) of the Gaṅga dynasty. In between Kuanarpur and Bhaghalpur, there is a muddy tank full of weeds known as Tara Pokhari. On the way leading to Mādhava through the village Bhaghalpur, there is a temple dedicated to Dakṣineśvara Śiva. Only a few yards away from this Dakṣineśvara Śiva temple, is the temple of Dadhivāmana with constructed stones of about 70 feet high with a covered porch (*mukhaśāḷā*). Inside the porch there are granite images of Nṛsiṁha, Varāha and Vāmana. Niches earlier occupied by incarnation sculptures are now vacant. At the entrance to the porch is a Garuḍa pillar with a black granite image of Garuḍa mounted on it. A wall of rough stones surrounds the temple. The style of the temple appears to be of Gaṅga period. The *Gītagovinda* is recited here on festive days.

On the north-west corner of the Bhaghalpur village amidst extensive cornfields, Kūrmapur is situated under the jurisdiction of the Sadar police station of Cuttack district. Here the stone temple of Śītaḷeśvara with no notable architectural features is situated. The images of Kārtikeya, Gaṇeśa and Pārvatī made of granite stone are placed as side deities. The stones lying scattered lead to the conclusion that an earlier temple existed here and the present temple has been built atop its ruins. On the west, at a distance of about two kilometres, there is a place called Nagari where the granite image of Kṛṣṇa is worshipped as Gopīnātha. Among the incarnations, the idols of Vāmana and Nṛsiṁha are also worshipped here. The elderly villagers refer to a lofty Gopīnātha Temple which now is in ruins. A new temple has come up with the remains of the old one and the image has been removed.

(iii) Varāhapura

At a distance of about one kilometre on the north along the banks of the river Prācī is the Varāhapura *Brāhmaṇa Śāsana*. This village under the jurisdiction of Govindpur police station of the district of Cuttack is just on the wayside route from Fulnakharā to Mādhava branching off National Highway No. 5. On the south of the village, close to the road leading to Mādhava, there is a large tank, named Gupta Māṇika considered holy for a ritual dip. In a monastery close to this tank, images of Kṛṣṇa and Jagannātha are worshipped. The monastery perhaps belongs to the 18th century. At Adaspur on the east, very close to Varāhapur, Varāha-Viṣṇu and Lakṣmī-Nṛsiṁha are worshipped together as Varāha-Nṛsiṁha. Inside the temple are images of Rādhā and Kṛṣṇa venerated by the villagers. At the centre of Adaspur village in a monastery Mādhavānanda Viṣṇu is worshipped. People believe that Jayadeva often came here to propitiate this image. The architectural remains of Adaspur and Varāhapura might belong to the Gaṅga period. Adaspur is probably named after Aṭṭahāsadeva, the younger son of Coḍagaṅgadeva, who founded the Gaṅga empire. But opinions differ and a few others ascribe its origin to Uḍḍiśa of the Vajrayāna sect of Buddhism. The Śiva temple of Svapneśvara and the Jaina statues of Tīrthankara Ṛṣabhadeva also abound around the place.

(iv) Bijaya Narasimhapur Śāsana

On the south of the village Kenduli, while excavating the Nṛsiṁha temple tank, a large stone container with thirteen copper plates was discovered. The plates are a gift deed made by the Gaṅga emperor Narasimhadeva IV in his 8th regnal year in the *Śaka* year 1305. The deed informs that the village Kinri lying between Kalamore and Uttarakhanda was renamed as Bijaya Narasimhapur Śāsana and was gifted to Mahāpātra Naraharidās Praharāja. The local people believe that the high mound near the tank was his property on which his house once stood.

It is learnt from the gift deeds that on the western border of the Bijaya Narasimhapur Śāsana, there were two *śāsana* villages called Ulaṭapur and Aṭṭahāsapur presently identified with Oltapur and Adaspur. Villages of Bhakarsahi and Mohulunda mentioned in the copper deeds are the present Bhākarsahi and Muhukhandā within the borders of Kenduli. Of all the villages mentioned in the copper

Temple of Sobhaneśvara where the tradition of māhārī *dance was prevalent. The descendants of* māhārī *used to live in a nearby village.*

plate only one remains unidentified. Probably the area around the Nṛsiṁha temple is the earlier Kenduli within the Bijaya Narasimhapur Śāsana of yesteryears.

(v) Dadhivāmanapur Śāsana

It is located on the east of Kenduli at a distance of six kilometres along the side of a canal leading to Nialī under Bālipātnā police station of Puri district. Dadhivāmana is worshipped in a thatched monastery on the outskirts of the village.

(vi) Bhārgavpur

It is perhaps buried in the river bed of Bhārgavī, a branch of the river Kuākhāi which has its source in Kāthjori. The village Bhārgavpur derives its name from the river Bhārgavī which reverberates in a glorious memory. The village Baudhakhanda is situated to the east of this place. It is under Bāliantā police station in Puri district and is located at a distance of about seven kilometres from Kenduli in a south-west direction. In a modern building, an early stone image of Mādhava is worshipped as Vāsudeva with recital of *Gītagovinda*. From the stylistical considerations the image can be dated to the 8th or the 9th century. Every evening, the *Gītagovinda* is recited in the presence of the deity.

At a distance of one kilometre to the south of the source of the river Bhārgavī is Purba Śāsana (Pūrva Śāsana) from where an image of Gopīnātha was discovered which is now kept in the Orissa State Museum. The image could probably be assigned to the 13th century.

(vii) Rāmchandrapura

Covering a distance of eight kilometres, on the National Highway No. 5 (Cuttack-Bhubaneswar), from Fulnakharā approaching Mādhava and then taking a south turn from Kurāṅga Śāsana on the metalled road one comes across Rāmachandrapura. The village is under the jurisdiction of Bāliantā police station in Puri district and is about six kilometres from Kenduli.

At a place bordering the village at Duduravasta, people worship two images of Hanumān Mahāvīra as the presiding deities. However people allege that the image of Rāmacandra, their venerated idol, has been removed elsewhere. Further away from the place where Mahāvira are worshipped is the Bakreśvara Śiva Temple with an old tank bounded on the two sides by bricks and stones. Half a kilometre to the east froṃ the altar of Mahāvī ra there is the famous Gaṅgeśvara Gada. Coḍagaṅgaḍeva, the founder of the Gaṅga dynasty used to frequent this place and the Śiva Liṅga then worshipped by him is now known as Gaṅgamaṇi. Coḍagaṅgadeva was initially a devotee of Śiva. The temple dedicated to Gaṅgamaṇi is built of stones with lime plaster. Old bricks found in the construction point to an earlier brick temple. A broad road locally called Bhetta connects Cudaṅga Gaḍa to Gaṅgeśvara Gaḍa. Even now the road between Gaṅgeśvara to Sarveśvara, nearly eight kilometres in length, remains undamaged. Some settlements of colonies have sprung up by its side. The legendry heroine of the famous Kaliṅga war Janguliki Dhamilla, with flowing long hair and an expert in black magic was of this locality and a village on the side of this historic road refreshes her memory.

(viii) Balabhadrapura

Balabhadrapura is under Bālipātna police station in Puri district and is four kilometres away to the south-west of the village Kenduli. On proceeding from the Uttarā crossway through the village of Bālakāti it lay at a distance of one kilometre to the south of Bālipātnā on the Nimāparā-Koṇārka route. In a small modern temple in this *śāsana* a two handed image of a goddess is worshipped as the village deity. In a thatched house close to the temple the image of Balabhadra is being worshipped. The village named Baudhakhaṇḍa in the west, Buddhanātha in the north-west and Kaliyuga Bhaghalpur in the south-east of this village are situated within a radius of two kilometres.

(ix) Baudhakhaṇḍa

Baudhakhaṇḍa now known as Bodhakhaṇḍa is under the jurisdiction of Bālipātṇā police station in Puri district. It is about five kilometres from Kenduli in a south-west direction and one kilometre south of the Sishilo Chak on the Nimāparā-Koṇārka route. Adjacent to this is another village called Budhapara. To the north of the village Baudhakhaṇḍa in the village of Gāredi Pāñcāṇa there is the famous Śiva temple of Budhanātha. In between the Baudhakhaṇḍa village and the Budhanātha Temple a small village named Shisilo is situated. Apparently the name Shisila is derived from Śriśaila. The stone images of Ananta, Vāsudeva and Subhadrā have been discovered during the excavation of the village tank. The stylistical attributes of the sculptures ascribe them to the Gaṅga rule. The architectural features of the Śiva temple of Budhanātha places it in the Soma dynasty. The village Gāredi Pāñcāṇa and the deity Budhanātha have been closely linked. The name of the deity was Gāreḍi Pāñcāṇa, which was probably transformed to Budhanātha. Initially it belonged to the village Bodhakhaṇḍa and this Śiva Liṅga was the community god of the surrounding villages. This was probably the cause for naming the god as Budhanātha. Half of the temple has collapsed. On the eastern wall of the inner shrine of the temple there is a beautiful image of Mādhava. An inscription containing the words *Bṛhat prasta dhavena* is engraved on it in Prākṛt. The other part of the inscription is illegible. In the temple niches there are the images of Gaṇeśa, Kārtikeya and Pārvatī. On the western facade there is a sculptured panel depicting the royal court.

Varāha sculpture, Denua.

(x) Kalipura or Kaliyuga Bhaghalpur

A Śiva temple constructed of bricks is seen at Bhaghalpur by the side of the road leading to Nimāparā. It originates from Uttarā Chak and passes through Bālakti. On a broken altar one sees the images of Ananta, Vāsudeva and Subhadrā-Ekānaṃśā. The incarnation images of Varāha and Nṛsiṁha are placed aside on the altar. The old Viṣṇu temple as well as the Śiva temples are now in a dilapidated condition. Close to the temples there is a huge muddy and swampy tank covering an area of about twelve acres. At the advent of Gaṅga rule Viṣṇu and Śiva were worshipped together and these temples testify to this new religious synchronism. The village Bhaghalpur has been named probably after Bhaghal Devī, the queen of Aniyankabhīmadeva (1190-1198 AD), who had established this village. The recital of the *Gītagovinda* in the daily ritual of this shrine is significant in the context of a legend that boasts of Jayadeva's association. Towards the north-west of the village Kenduli there is another village of Bhaghalpur belonging to the district of Cuttack.

It is not just an accident that Kenduli is surrounded by these villages bearing the names of incarnations of Viṣṇu. The kings and queens who established these villages with *Brāhmins* as inhabitants had a great design in their mind to boost the religious fabric of this place keeping in tune with the local traditions. The Viṣṇu and Śiva temples and the numerous images of Mādhava, Ananta, Vāsudeva, Ekānaṃsā as well as the archaeological evidences proclaim the presence of Jayadeva and the tradition of the *Gītagovinda.*

The Homeland of Jayadeva, Orissa

Banamali Rath

A few scholars[1] are of the opinion that the poet Jayadeva belonged to the court of king Lakṣmaṇa Sena of Bengal and he was born in the village Kenduli situated on the bank of the river Ajaya in the district of Birbhum. In support of their opinion they have advanced several arguments which warrant attention and demand a thorough examination.

It is generally argued that Jayadeva in his *Gītagovinda* refers[2] to himself along with a group of poets like Umāpatidhara, Śaraṇa, Ācārya Govardhana and Dhoyī. As these poets belonged to the court of Lakṣmaṇa Sena, very likely, Jayadeva also adorned Sena's royal court and was a contemporary of these poets. But this is only a supposition because excepting Dhoyī[3], no historical data is available to support that the other three belonged to the court of Lakṣmaṇa Sena. The supposition gives rise to a chronological problem concerning Lakṣmaṇa Sena and his court poets.

On the basis of *Saduktikarṇāmṛtam*[4] of Sridharadāsa, the reign of Lakṣmaṇa Sena is approximately fixed between 1184-1205 AD. The poet Umāpatidhara[5] is known to be the writer of *Deopārā* a record of king Vijaya Sena (1125-60 AD). So the possibility of his associtation with the court of Lakṣmaṇa Sena, the grandson of Vijaya Sena is doubtful. Also

---

1 Nihar Ranjan Ray, *Bāṅglāra Itihāsa; History of Bengal*, Dacca University; Macdonell's *History of Sanskrit Literature.*

2 *vācashpallavayatyaumā patidharaḥ sandarbh śuddhim griām, jānite jayadeva eva śaraṇaḥ slāghyoduruha dṛteh. dhoyī kavi kṣmāpatiḥ*

3 Dhoyī in his *Pavanadūtam* refers to '*Lakṣmaṇam Kṣauṇīpālam*', *J.A.S.*, 1905, pp. 41-71.

4 The *Saduktikarṇāmṛtam* was compiled in *Śaka* year 1127 — "*Saka saptaviṁśatyadhika śatopeta daśaśate*". i.e. in AD 1205 in the 21st regnal year of king Lakṣmaṇa Sena "*Śrimallakṣmaṇa Sena Kṣitipasya tasyaikaviṁśebde*". This indicates that King Lakṣmaṇa Sena was ruling from AD 1184 to 1205.

5 *Inscriptions of Bengal*, Vol. III, p. 49.

Facing page: Sakhī *beseeching Rādhā in a wooded* kuñja, *palmleaf painting.*

the date of the composition of the *Gītagovinda* (1150 AD)[6], as accepted almost certainly, does not tally with the time of Lakṣmaṇa Sena. The poet Śaraṇa makes a vague reference to a '*Senakulatilaka*' in one of his stray verses[7] preserved in the *Saduktikarṇāmṛtam*. The name of this king is not known. Moreover the authorship of the different verses is ascribed to Śaraṇa Deva. Śaraṇa Dutta and Cirantana Śaraṇa, are not probably identical. Acārya Govardhana has been established[8] as a resident of Niāli Śāsana in the district of Puri. It is known from a commentary that his mention of a "*Senakula Tilaka Bhūpatī*" in his *Āryāsaptaśati* refers to Pravara Sena, the author of *Setubandhakāvyam*. Again it is noteworthy that not a single stanza from *Āryāsaptaśati* is preserved in the *Saduktikarṇāmṛtam*. Thus the poets Umāpati, Śāraṇa and Govardhana have nowhere mentioned the name of Lakṣmaṇa Sena, as has been done explicitly by Śridharadāsa,[9] Dhoyī[10] and Halāyudha[11] in their respective works.

Moreover some scholars[12] expressed doubts about the genuineness of the otherwise controversial verse. The verse[13] amounts to mocking at the illustrious poets and appears to be somewhat improper on the part of a poet and devout person like Jayadeva. Even Rāṇā Kumbha also known as Kumbhakarna in his *Rasikapriyā* commentary expresses his grave doubts over the authorship of this particular verse.

Further, nowhere in the *Gītagovinda* do we find any direct or indirect reference to king Lakṣmaṇa Sena or any other king. On the other hand, we come across two references in the *Gītagovinda* that it was written for the propitiation of Lord Jagannātha[14] only.

Again the verse under reference gives only the poet's own estimate of himself and four other poets. But it does not imply directly or

---

6 *Souvenir on Jayadeva*, pp.13-18, ed. N.K. Sahu, Jayadeva Sānskṛtika Pariṣad.

7 *Sevabhiryadi senavamśa tilakadasadaniya śriyah.*

8 *Orissa Historical Research Journal* Vol. VII April, 1958. and *Govardhanācārya and Udayanācārya* by K.N. Mahapatra.

9 *Sa śri Lakṣmaṇa ekaṇirpati.*

10 *Pavanadutam-saduktikar-ṇāmṛtam.*

11 *Vijaya rasikamate Lakṣmaṇa kṣauṇibhartuh, Brāhmaṇa Sarvasvam.*

12 N.K. Sahu in Souvenir on Jayadeva p. 10; See also Introduction to *Pīyūṣalaharī*, ed. K. Kar, p.292.

13 *Gītagovinda*, Verse No. 4, *Vācah pallavayatyumā-patidharaḥ*, etc.

14 "*Prītyai śripuruṣottamasya racitam Śrigovindakam.*" It is quoted from a manuscript copied in the Ist regnal year of Vīrakesarideva. See also *Gītagovinda*, the last verse "*Vyāpārāh puruṣottamasya dadatu sphitāmmudam sampadam.*"

indirectly that the said poets were contemporaries and were associated with the same court. Besides it is also well-known to the students of Sanskrit literature that it was a traditional practice[15] with Sanskrit poets to compare the merits of one's own work with those of the others. Thus due to the paucity of plausible and authentic evidences, it will be historically unsound to arrive at a definite conclusion that the five poets referred to in the verse were contemporaries and adorned the same royal court.

In order to prove Jayadeva's association with the court of Lakṣmaṇa Sena, the following traditional verse is often cited, where Jayadeva alongwith the above four poets has been enlisted as the jewel of the court of Lakṣmaṇa Sena i.e. "*Govardhanaśca Śaraṇo Jayadeva Umāpatih Kavirājaśca ratnāni samitau Lakṣmaṇasyaca*".

This verse is alleged to have been noticed[16] for the first time by Rūpa and Sanātana Goswāmi, at Navadvīpa three hundred years after Lakṣmaṇa Sena and the report of which came to us after four hundred years. As the verse lacks the authenticity of any kind, it has been accepted by the scholars as spurious or one based on hearsay.[17] Hence it need not be discussed here at length.

Another vexed issue is Jayadeva's birthplace. All the commentaries of the *Gītagovinda* have accepted Kendubilva as the birthplace of Jayadeva, though the location and the identification of the village Kendubilva has become a matter of long-standing controversy among scholars. A few Bengali critics have tried to identify Kendubilva with the Kenduli village situated on the bank of the Ajaya river in the Birbhum district of Bengal, while their colleagues in Odisha locate the place Kendubilva near the Pratāparudrapura Śāsana between the rivers Prācī and Kuśabhadrā in the district of Puri.[18]

The advocates of the Bengal origin of the poet, refer to a Bengali book entitled *Jayadevacarita* by one Banamāli Dāsa which presents strange accounts about Jayadeva. According to it when the father of Padmāvatī arrived at the village Birbhum Kendubilva with his daughter in search of the God-ordained groom Jayadeva, the villagers told him that they knew

---

15 See Aihole inscription of Pulakeśi II by Ravikīrti; Rājaśekhara's Bālarāmāyaṇa, P.V. Kane, History of Sanskrit Poetics, p.203.

16 *Vīrabhum vivaraṇa* e.g. *Śri Rūpa Śri Sanātana śridhama navadvīpe Lakṣmaṇa Sener sabhā gṛhadvāre nimnokta ślokati ankit dekhiyā chilen*".

17 *O.H.R.J.* Vol. VII, Oct. 1958 & Jan. 1959, Nos. 3 & 4, p. 195-96.

18 *Gītagovinda*, 3rd canto: *Varṇitam Jayadevakena hareridam pravaṇena Kinduvilva samudra sambhava rohiṇi ramaṇena*".

nothing about Jayadeva or his parentage; but, however, they had seen a lunatic named Jayadeva in the village. The very basic fact that the co-villagers did not know anything about the great poet and his parentage demolishes the theory advocated on that basis.

The authenticity of the *Jayadevacarita* is challenged[19] by scholars. This work has been published by Bangiya Sāhitya Parishad, Calcutta, from a single manuscript of the work in 1803 AD. Nothing is known about the original manuscript nor has a second manuscript of this work been discovered anywhere in Bengal.[20]

Further, to support this identification, the association of poet Jayadeva with the temple of Rādhāvinoda, and a *Vaiṣṇava maṭha* at Kenduli is persistently asserted. It is also said that an annual fair on the full-moon day of *Māgha* is held at Birbhum Kenduli in honour of the poet. However, the argument does not hold ground. The image of Rādhāvinoda whom Jayadeva is said to be worshipping daily, as well as the temple, was constructed by the mother of Mahārājā Kīrticandra of Burdwan in *Śaka* year 1614 (1692 AD)[21] while the *Vaiṣṇava maṭha* was established there early in the 18th century AD by Brajavāsi Rādhāmohana whose 9th successor is now the pontiff of the *maṭha*. Had this Kenduli been the birthplace of Jayadeva, Caitanya would have surely visited the place and the extensive *Vaiṣṇava* literature of Bengal written in post-Caitanya period would have been vociferous in the glorification of the shrine. The conspicuous silence in this matter on the part of the great *goswāmin* proves that the advocacy in the favour of Birbhum Kenduli as the alternative and in course of time authentic place of birth of Jayadeva started after the construction of the Rādhāvinoda Temple here at the fag end of the 17th century.

From the above analysis it appears that the attempts, in some quarters, made to identify the Kendubilva of *Gītagovinda* with the Kenduli of Bengal on the basis of the hyped myth described in the *Jayadevacarita* are of little historical significance and even rarer authenticity by supporting literary evidences.

Here it may be mentioned that the Kenduli of Birbhum was not known in Bengal up to the 18th century AD. Because the Bengali *Bhaktamāḷā* of

---

19 K.N. Mahapatra, *Souvenir on Jayadeva*, pp.22-4.

20 *Vīrabhum Vivaraṇa*, H.K. Mukhopadhyay, 1323 Sal, p.201. "*Kon ādarśa puthi haite iha grantha nakala karāhaya, tāhā jānā jāya nāi/grantha anya kothāo pāoya jāya māin //*".

21 S. Sen, *Banglā Sāhityera Itihāsa*, p.41.

Kṛṣṇa Dāsa[22] of the 18th century bears ample testimony to Puri Kendubilva as the birthplace of the poet. In this connection the following observation of William Jones, who was interested in ascertaining the birthplace of Jayadeva, is remarkable, since it points to a place in the south beyond Bengal. As he had earlier denounced the south i.e. South India, by this south he meant south of Bengal, that is, in Odisha. William in his article written in 1784 and published in 1799 remarks[23]:

> "I had hope of procuring the original music (of Jayadeva), but the pandits of the south referred me to those of the west and the *Brāhmaṇas* of the west would have sent me to those of the south while they, I mean those of Nepal and Kashmir, declared that they had no ancient music, but imagined that notes to the *Gītagovinda* must exist if anywhere in one of the southern provinces where the poet was born".

Jones again in the Preface to his English translation[24] of *Gītagovinda* goes on to observe:

> "...*Gītagovinda*; it was the work of Jayadeva, who flourished, it is said, after Kālidasa and was born, as he tells us himself, in Kenduli, which many believe to be in Kaliṅga; but since there is a town of similar name in Burdwan, the natives of it insist that the finest lyrical poet of India was their countryman".

From the above citations it is clear that Jones, a Judge of the Supreme Court, tried for ten years to collect correct information about the poet and concluded that Jayadeva was born in one of the southern provinces. Further he recorded the belief of the people that Kenduli, the birthplace of the poet was in Kaliṅga (presently Odisha). It is also evident from his statement that by this time attempts were made in Bengal to claim the "finest lyrical poet of India as their countryman" on the grounds of similarity between the names of Kenduli in Burdwan and Kendubilva mentioned in the *Gītagovinda*.

---

22 Published by Vasumati Sahitya Mandir in 1922 AD.

23 "On the musical modes of the Hindus" in *Asiatic Researches*, Vol. III 1799, pp. 83-84.

24 Preface to the *Gītagovinda*, translated by Sir William Jones and published by Upendralal Dās, Calcutta, 1894.

It is a mockery of history that at the time of William Jones, Orissa was not annexed to the British Empire[25], neither could Jones visit Puri nor was he able to procure the correct information through British officers. Thus the village Kenduli in Burdwan as mentioned in the Musical Modes of Hindus by Jones, was repeated in the *Lyrical Drama*, a Latin translation of the *Gītagovinda*, by the French scholar Lassen in 1837. Though Lassen referred to Burdwan as the birthplace of Jayadeva, he expressed his doubts and was not firm in his convictions because for him "the locality was doubtful." But Edwin Arnold, notwithstanding Lassen's doubtful premise, recorded in his *Indian Song of Songs* (1857) that the poet Jayadeva belonged to Bengal. The later scholars have indiscriminately repeated what Arnold had said without caring for its authenticity.

As an alternative to an erroneous point often repeated we would like to quote Sukumar Sen, an authority on the cultural history of Bengal as well as Sanskrit Literature.[26] Sen declares the earlier assumptions as baseless. Sen opines:

> "There might have existed a village called Kenduli in Bengal in the past, but it does not exist at present. Though the place where the *melā* or annual fair is held in honour of Śrī Jayadeva is vaguely called Kenduli, it has got no connection with any village. The *melā* is held on the sandy strip of land on the bank of the Ajaya river on the day of *Pauṣa Sankrānti* for taking bath in its water. The name of the adjoining village is not Kenduli. There is no evidence regarding the existence of the Kenduli village in this locality. Only the *melā* held on the occasion of taking a dip in the holy water of the river by a vast crowd of people on the first day of the auspicious month of *Makara* is known as 'Jayadeva-Kenduli' or simply 'Kenduli'. Investigation is to be made to find out whether the word Kenduli is more commonly used in this region for denoting a *melā*. There is no mention of Jayadeva nor is there any reference to Kenduli or any other place as the birthplace or place of residence of Jayadeva in the literature of the day of Caitanya. The birthplace of Nityānanda is not very far from this place. So the silence of the biographer of Caitanya about the existence of Kenduli is really surprising. The history of the temple and sacred precincts starts only from 1694 AD. (Supposed to be the year of construction of the temple)".

25 For the first time, Orissa was ruled by the British in 1803 AD.

26 *Bāṅgāla Sāhityera Itihāsa*. Vol. I-Part I, 1967 edn., p.41. The English rendering of the Bengali passage is taken from *Souvenir on Jayadeva*, p.33.

The historical accounts presented by Sen in the passage cited above establish beyond doubt that no village named Kenduli ever existed or is now existing on the bank of the Ajaya River in the district of Birbhum and thus the gratuitous assumptions regarding the birthplace of Jayadeva in Bengal appear to be set effectively at rest.

On the other hand the Kenduli Śāsana on the Prācī river in Odisha can easily be identified with the Kendubilva of Jayadeva, based on a series of plausible and convincing grounds.

Candradatta, a scholar of Mithilā, in his Sanskrit *Bhaktamāḷā* records:

Jagannāthapurīprānte deśe caivotkalābhidhe
Kinduvilva iti khyāto grāmo Brāhmanasamkulaḥ
Tatrotkale dvijo jāto Jayadeva iti śrutaḥ
Vidyābhyāsarataḥ śāntaḥ puruṣottamapūjakaḥ[27]

The accounts given by Candradatta appear to be based on first hand information as his personal presence at Puri is ascertained by his repeated reference to the glory of Lord Jagannātha and to the extraordinary religious practices[28] prevalent only at *Puruṣottama Kṣetra.*

The *Brāhmaṇa* village Kendubilva referred to by Candradatta as the birthplace of poet Jayadeva is located, undoubtedly, near the Pratāparudrapura Śāsana located between the Prācī and Kuśabhadrā rivers under the Bāliantā police station in Puri district in Odisha. The Kendubilva Śāsana is now divided into three parts i.e. Kenduli Śāsana[29] (a *Brāhmaṇa* settlement), Kenduli Deuḷi (seat of temples) and Kenduli Pāṭnā (village inhabited by a group of people belonging to various castes).[30]

The statement of Candradatta is further corroborated by a more authentic evidence furnished by Nārāyaṇadāsa, the great grandfather of the famous rhetorician Viśvanātha Kavirāja of Odisha. Nārāyanadasa, in the late 13th century, wrote his *Saravāngasundarī* commentary on the *Gītagovinda* where he has clearly stated that the Kendubilva[31] of

---

27 *Bhaktamāḷā* published by Kṣemarāja Śrī Kṛṣṇa Dāsa, Venkatesvara Press, Bombay, *Sarga* 39. p.61.

28 *Anyatra dvija samspṛṣṭam bhoktum na jāyate manaḥ Jagannāthapureśnāti sarvaśreṣthadvijopi hi, Bhaktamāḷā*, 149 *Sarga*, p. 214.

29 In Odisha, *śāsana* specifically means a village given by kings for *Brāhmaṇa* to reside.

30 Sheet No. 73/H/16 one inch Topo map.

31 *Gītagovinda*. 3rd canto: *Kenduvilva-samudra-sambhava-rohiṇīramaṇena.*

the *Gītagovinda* is none other than *Kendu vilvākhya śāsana.*[32] Also in this connection the evidence supplied by Rāṇā Kumbha, the author of the *Rasikapriyā* commentary on the *Gītagovinda*, is very revealing. In the middle of the 15th century the learned commentator records that *Kenduvilvam tat śāsanam.*[33]

The authentic statement of the commentators noted above, convincingly establish the identification of Kendubilva with the *Brāhmaṇa* village Kenduli Śāsana on the Prācī River near Puri, whereas the so called Kenduli on the Ajaya River loses its ground as it was never a *Śāsana* or a *Brāhmaṇa* village known to the students of history.

Śāsana has a great significance in the cultural history of Odisha. Right from the Somavaṃśi Emperor Yayāti Keśarī (9th century. AD) a number of *śāsana* villages as the cultural centres were established throughout Odisha from time to time by the rulers. Kenduli is undoubtedly one of them which bears the testimony to that tradition. The cultural and devotional environment of the *śāsana* situated in the Prācī River valley and in the adjacent area is beautifully recorded in Śobhaneśvara[34] and Megheśvara[35] Temple inscription composed by Udayana Ācārya, the younger brother of Govardhana Ācārya in 1180 AD. The descriptions aptly reveal the cultural heritage of the area where the Kenduli Śāsana is situated.

Another glorious facet of the village Kenduli on the Prācī River in Odisha is that it is rich in its archeaological wealth and has a longstanding tradition to justify the village as the birthplace of the poet. The village is surrounded by old brick as well as stone temples and sculptures belonging to *Śaiva*, *Vaiṣṇava*, and *Śākta* faiths, some of which are attributed to the 10th and the 11th century AD. Interestingly a two armed image (both

---

32 Quoted from the manuscriptof *Sarvāṅgasundarīṭīkā* preserved in the Orissa State Museum, Bhubaneswar.
"*Kinduvilvākhyam śāsanam tacca mahattvāt samudratven rūpitam tadevam kinduvilvaśāsanājjātaḥ tasyaivonnatikārako yathā sāgarājjātah candraḥ sāgaravṛddhikāraka ityarthaḥ.*"

33 *Rasikaprīyā* published with the *Rasamanjarī*, a commentary on the *Gītagovinda* in the *Kāvyamālā* series.

34 *J.B.O.R.S*, Vol. XVII, 1931., p. 119-135. *Kvaciddevedīpā kvacidapi taḍāgāhkvacid drumāḥ, mathā pūjā kvāpi kvacidapi tathā mandapacayāḥ / prapāh kvāpi pratipadamudā kṛṣitiraho, bibhānti Kṣmācakre jaladhi valaye yasya paritāḥ //*

35 *J.A.S. Bengali Vol. LXVI, 1897, pp. 18-24. "Apāmsālāmālāḥ pathi pathi taḍāgāḥ pratipuram, pradīpāḥ sampūrṇāḥ pratisuragṛham yasya vimalā. maṭhā vedādīnāṃ dvijapuravihārāḥ pratidiśaṃ, birājante satrāṇyapi ca paritaḥ setunivahāḥ"*

the arms broken) with heavy matted locks is worshipped by the local people as the sage Jayadeva. The two goddesses—Ambikā and Jāgeśvari beautifully chiselled out of black chlorite, are the objects of interest and veneration in the locality and they are regarded as the presiding deities of the village. It is said that Jāgeśvarī was originally installed under a *kendu* tree and Ambikā under a *bilva* tree, because of which the place was named as Kendubilva. A peculiar ritualistic practice is still in vogue in the temple. *Durgā Saptaśati*, commonly recited before the goddess, is replaced by the recitation of the *Gītagovinda*. This undoubtedly is an indication of the popularity of the *Gītagovinda* in that locality. About two miles south-east of the village is the confluence of three rivers, the Prācī, the Kuśabhadrā and the Dhanuā. The confluence is regarded as *Triveṇī* with a halo of sacred traditions. The Viṣṇu worshipped here is named Triveṇī Mādhava and an annual fair is held here on the *Amāvāsyā*, new moon day of the month of *Māgha*[36]. Triveṇī Mādhava, and the *Triveṇī* fair held in his honour are attributed to the Gaṅga period and are referred to by late medieval literature including the *Kapila Samhitā* and the *Prācī Mahātmaya*.[37]

The poet Jayadeva was a great devotee of Mādhava.[38] A number of old Mādhava temples attributed to the pre-Gaṅga era[39] are seen around the village Kenduli Śāsana. The Mādhava images beautifully carved in

36 *Kapila Samhitā* published by Ratnākara Gargavatu pp. 105-106. *Triveṇi saṅgamam tatra mahāpuṇya pradāyakam, tatra snānam mahīpāla māghamāse prakīrtitam. Sarvatra sukhasancāre vidvajjanamanohare, tatra vilveśvaro nāma vilvamūlāśrito haraḥ.*

37 *Prācī Māhātmaya* gives an elaborate description of all the temples and other sacred places existing on the banks of the river Prācī.

38 *Gītagovinda.* 1st verse "*Rādhāmādhavayorjayanti*" ....

39 *The History of Kaliṅga*, Subba Rao, pp.180-182.

Nilamadhava worshipped at Kantilo, Rasika Haravali palmleaf painting, 18th century, Museum Rietberg Zurich.

chlorite stone and the famous Mādhavānanda Temple nearby the place in the Prācī River valley show the richness and the glorious tradition of the place in Mādhava faith. The beautiful Nīlamādhava[40] image of 9th century is still worshipped at Gandharāḍi near Baud town. This was the cultural and religious milieu of the place where Jayadeva was born and brought up. This inspiring environment with Mādhava-centric faith perhaps provided him with the required incentive and accentuated his rapturous feelings to sing the glory of his Mādhava who is none other than the Jagannātha or Jagadīśa[41] enshrined in Puri.

Thus the Kenduli Śāsana on the Prācī River, rich in historical, archaeological and devotional temper and verve, should be accepted as the birthplace of Jayadeva in preference to any other place in India.

In Odisha we find the names of a number of villages originated from the names of the familiar trees grown in that area. Owing to the preponderance of *kendu* trees, a series of village have, accordingly, assumed the names like, Kendupadara, Kendujhara, and so on. This has also been evidenced by epigraphical records of Gaṅga Era.[42] Likewise the names of Belagunthā and Vilveśvara etc, came into existence. Further Odisha is noted for its extensive forests of *kendu* trees, the leaves of which form an important source of income to its exchequer. In fact the Kendubilva or Kenduli village on the Prācī River must have been so named because of its surroundings, full of *kendu* and *bilva* trees, the remnants of which can be seen even today. Thus the very name militates against the supposition of Bengal origin of the poet, as there is no fruit or tree with the name of *kendu*, known anywhere in the State of Bengal.[43]

One of Liṅgarājā Temple inscriptions[44] is relevant for a discussion. It is specially important that the epigraphical record speaks of a famous venerable *sādhu* named Jayadeva who was living near Jagannāthā Puri in the 12th century. The presence of the saintly poet was required on the occasion of presenting a *Mahādīpa* in the temple of Kīṛtivāsa by an old and aristocratic lady named Meḍamā Devī. As the date of inscription tallies with the period of the saintly poet Jayadeva, the *Sādhupradhāna* Jayadeva of the inscription, can

40 Jagannātha is well known as Nīlamādhava in *purāṇas* and in tradition.

41 *Gītagovinda. "Jayajagadīśa Hare"*

42 *J.A.S.B.*, Vol. LXV (1896), Pt. I, ed. N.N. Basu.

43 In Bengal it is called '*Gaba*' (*Galava*).

44 *Inscriptions of Orissa* Vol. III, p.294

easily be identified with our poet of repute, and thus our argument is further corroborated.

The ten incarnations[45] of Kṛṣṇa as described in the *Gītagovinda* were very popular in Odisha prior to the advent of Jayadeva. The two Viṣṇu images[46] with side figures of the ten incarnations belonging to the 8th century AD discovered at Saintalā in the district of Bolangīr of Orissa, are the earliest and finest representations of ten incarnations. Apart from this, the *daśāvatāra* images of the 7th century preserved in the Tīrthamaṭha, under the jurisdiction of Erasamā Police Station of Cuttack district, the images of ten incarnations ascribed to the 9th century, found in a temple of Kākaṭapur in the district of Puri, the existing *daśāvatāra* images in Odisha, had perhaps, inspired Jayadeva to compose the famous hymn to Jagadīśa Hari or Jagannātha of Puri. This long standing tradition of ten incarnations in Odisha, which has been faithfully preserved in the *Gītagovinda*, indirectly supports our conclusion of the poet's Odishan origin.[47]

The immense popularity of the *Gītagovinda* in Odisha, brought about a remarkable change in Odishan iconography. In the post Jayadeva scenario we notice Jagannātha, the state deity of Odisha, began to be regarded as another form of Kṛṣṇa, which has been evidenced by epigraphical records[48] right from 1278 AD. The earlier images of four handed Viṣṇu with conch, disc, mace, lotus began to be replaced by the image of the two handed Kṛṣṇa standing in a *tribhaṅga* pose, playing on the flute and surrounded by *gopī*. This historical phenomenon is substantiated by the availability, throughout Odisha, of a number of Gopīnātha images attributed to the Gaṅga period[49],

45 *Gītagovinda*. Verse 5 "*Daśākṛtikṛte Kṛṣṇāya tubhyam namaḥ*".

46 *J.K.H.R.* Society Vol. II, Nos. 2 & 3, pp. 124-125.

47 P.C. Bagchi opines that the *Vaiṣṇavism* in Bengal contributed largely to the systematisation of the theory of *daśāvatāra*. This dictum does not stand scrutiny in view of the ample archaeological evidences found in Odisha. *History of Bengal*, Dacca University p.403.

48 *E.I.*, Vol. XIII, p.150. Kṛṣṇa is substituted for Jagannātha in the inscription of Candrikā Devī in the Ananta Vāsudeva Temple of Bhubaneswar dated AD 1278.

49 *O.H.R.J.*, Vol, Oct. & Jan, 1959, No. 3 & 4.
(i) The Gopīnātha image discovered from Dharmaśālā police station.
(ii) Three Gopīnātha images of Alāpur, Hirāpur and Sarakana villages of Orissa. (AD 1278-1307).
(iii) Gopīnātha images of Remuṇa, (c. AD 1278-1307). Balasore district.
(iv) Gopīnātha images of Someśvarapur (AD 1264).
(v) Gopīnātha images of Bageśvarapur, near Pipili (AD 1264-1278).

whereas, according to R.D. Banerjee, "No images of Kṛṣṇa earlier than the 15th century has been discovered anywhere in Bengal or Bihar"[50]. This should be considered as no less weighty in strengthening our conclusion.

Moreover the *gīta* (songs) of Jayadeva are exclusively meant for Govinda. This Govinda is none but Lord Jagannātha of Puri. The significance of the sanctified *mantra*,[51] traditionally uttered in the worship of Lord Jagannātha, bear ample testimony to this conclusion.

It is remarkable that the earlier commentaries on the *Gītagovinda* are written by the Odishan authors. Udayana Ācārya, the younger brother[52] of Govardhana Ācārya and a junior compere of Jayadeva had written a commentary entitled *Bhāvavibhāvinī*[53] while Nārāyaṇadāsa wrote his *Sarvāṅgasundarī*[54] commentary in 13th century AD.

Further the earliest imitations of the *Gītagovinda* have also been written by Odishan scholars. The *Abhinava-Gītagovinda*[55] of Puruṣottamadeva (15th century AD) have been accepted on all hands to be the earliest imitations. Apart from the two referred above, we have 29 more works of this type, which were written by the scholars of Odisha.[56] This glorious tradition of preservation and dissemination of Jayadeva's music and genre in Odisha, and nowhere in any province of India, confirms Odisha's claim of the poet as her own.

Mediaeval Odia writers have taken advantage of all the musical *rāga* (notes) used in the *Gītagovinda*. This is amplified in the poetic creations of Upendra Bhanja, a 17th century poet whose work heralds the beginning of Odia poetry in its popularity. In general, the impact of the *Gītagovinda* in the later Odia literature is immense.[57] The Bengali literature certainly is devoid of such *Gītagovinda* nuances.[58]

---

50 R.D. Banerjee. *Eastern India School of Mediaeval Sculptures.*

51 *Om Klim Kṛṣṇāya Govīndāya Gopījanavallabhāya Svāhā.*

52 Dasgupta and De, *History of Sanskrit Literature.* p. 666.

53 *Aryāsaptaśati*; colophon. "*udayana Balabhadrābhyām saptaśtī śiṣyasodarābhyām namaḥ*"

54 The manuscript is preserved in the Orissa State Museum, Bhubaneswar, No. L/129.

55 *O.H.R.J.*, Vol, IX, 1960, Nos. 3 & 4. pp. 51-68.

56 A paper - "Contribution of Orissa to the field of Sanskrit *Gītakāvyas*" has been contributed by the present writer to the proceedings of the Inernational Sanskrit Conference, New Delhi, 1972.

57 See the Article of K.C. Panigrahi in *Jhankāra* Vol. XXI., No. 10, Jan. 1970.

58 Maydhar Mansingh, *History of Oriya Literature*, (*Odia version*), pp. 130-138.

Another significant point that should not be missed here is that Caitanya (1509 AD) for the first time discovered the jewel of *Gītagovinda* in Puri and came to realise the religious merit of the work from Rāya Rāmānanda on the banks of the Godāvarī when the Master was on his peninsular pilgrimage.[59] Had it been written in Bengal the Master would have known it before his sojourn to Puri.

It is quite interesting to note that a manuscript (No. 225) dated 1794 AD preserved in the Bodlin Library of Oxford University, London, gives a clear reading as "*Utkaliyena Jayadeva.*" Moreover the palmleaf manuscripts of the *Gītagovinda* are found in plenty in every village in the nook and corner of Odisha which show its tremendous influence and immense popularity in Odisha. Apart from this, the correct reading and the exact number of genuine verses of the *Gītagovinda* are conveniently ascertained[60] from the literary records traditionally available only in Odisha.

Very recently a few poems, the authorship of which is attributed to the celebrated poet Jayadeva, have been discovered by two Odishan scholars.[61] The poems are written in proto Odia language mixed with Sanskrit style. Some striking similarities in the tenor and manner of the *Gītagovinda* are conspicuously seen in the poems. The colophons are more akin to that of the poet's *aṣṭapadī* found in the *Gītagovinda.* However before embarking on any conclusion these poems need careful consideration.

The *Gītagovinda* is an inseparable part of Odisha's uninterrupted religious tradition. The earliest reference to the *Gītagovinda* is found in the *Mādalāpāñji* or the Jagannātha temple chronicle which describes[62] that Kavi Narasimhadeva (1278-1306 AD) the son of illustrious Lāṅguḷā Narasimhadeva introduced the recitation of the *Gītagovinda* into the liturgy of Jagannātha temple of Puri. This has been re-ordained epigraphically by Gajapati Pratāparudradeva (1504-1532 AD) through an Odia inscription belonging to the Jaya Vijaya series. The tradition of dancing and recitation of the *Gītagovinda* before the Lord inspired others to follow, and as a result the *Gītagovinda* recitation has become a

---

59 "Śrikṣetra" *Bengali*, p. 243.

60 A paper - "A study in the imitations of the *Gītagovinda*" has been contributed by the present writer to the All India Oriental Conference XXVI Session held in Ujjain, 1972.

61 Bansidhar Mohanty in *Jhankār*, April, 1969; See also N.N. Pradhan, *Oriya Sāhityare Jayadeva* in the Appendix VII, pp. 215-219.

62 *Mādalāpāñji*, p.36. "*Euttara kavi Narasimha Deva Rāja hoile. Gītagovinda silou kale" (Śubhadele).*

tradition in almost all the Viṣṇu temples in Odisha. Thus the role played by the *Gītagovinda* in the religious tradition of Odisha cannot just be underestimated. From the cultural and literary history[63] of Odisha we come to know that there were great authors in different subjects whose surname was 'Deva'. Thus we find 'Deva' has been suffixed to the hisorical names Jīva, Bhāva, Bāma, Gopāla, Vasu, Jaya, etc. A number of copper plates issued by the Bhaumakara kings reveal a number of names like this. Many royal preceptors, *Brāhmaṇa* by caste, bear the surname 'Deva'. Besides this, many learned poets of the illustrious family of the famous *Kaviḍiṇḍima Jīvadeva,*[64] were having the same surname 'Deva'. Thus most likely Jayadeva came of such a family in Odisha.

That Odisha was the land of Jayadeva, has been unequivocally supported by a series of literary evidences, recorded in the works, written in different parts of India beginning from the 12th century to the present era. The *Alaṃkāraśekhara* of Keśava Miśra preserves a verse as an instance of literary blemish, the authorship of which is attributed to Ācārya Govardhana. The verse,[65] under reference, states clearly that the poet Jayadeva belonged to Utkala. The *Sampradāyapradīpa* of Gadādhara Dvivedi (1533-54 AD) explicitly states that Jayadeva belonged to Utkala.[66] Mahīpatī of Maharashtra in his *Bhaktavijaya* speaks of the celebrated poet Jayadeva and records that the poet was an inhabitant of village Tinduvilva[67] near the sacred city of Jagannātha. Nāvāji of Gwalior in his *Bhaktamāḷā* in Hindi assigns Jayadeva to Utkal.[68] Candradatta of Mithilā, already referred to above, mentioned beyond all doubts, that Jayadeva belonged to a *Brāhmaṇa* village named Kendubilva near Jagannātha Puri. Even the modern writers like Sāmbaśiva, the author of a work on music the great composer, the

---

63 Binayaka Misra, *Orissa under the Bhumakara kings,* pp. 4-7.

64 A Das, *Catalogue of Sanskrit manuscript of Orissa,* Vol. II, Preface p. XCIII.

65 *Bāṅglā Viśvakoṣa,* Nagendranatha Vasu ed. p.663;
Alamkāraśekhara, Keśava Miśra, 2nd Ratna,
Prāk pratyak pṛthivīvṛtopariṣadi
Prakhyāta samkhyāvatāṃ
ahnāyādbhutatarkakarkaśatayā
vicchidya vidyāmadaṃ
ye kepyutkalabhūpate tava sabhā
sambhāvitāh panditāḥ
pattram Śrījayadevapanditakavis
tan mūrddhni vinyasyati.

66 P.V. Kane, *History of Dharmaśāstra Literature,* Vol. I. p.660.

67 *Tindu, Kindu* and *Kendu* are synonyms in Sanskrit.

68 *J.K.H.R.* Society Vol. I- pp. 243 & 245.

Maharashtrian critic Hirācand[69], the historian V. Varadachary, Sukumar Sen,[70] Parasuram Chaturvedi[71] and Malani Suryanarayana Sastry, the author of *Kavijivani Carita* are of the opinion that Jayadeva was a poet of Odisha. To conclude, we would like to gladly quote the unequivocal remarks of Ashutosh Bhattacharya, Professor of Bengali, Calcutta University, who almost gives a verdict that Jayadeva was an Odishan and in reality the annual festival observed at the Kenduli of Birbhum, is a *Baul Melā* and it has no relation to the birthplace of Jayadeva. The assumption that the poet belonged to the court of Lakṣmaṇa Sena of Bengal is not acceptable because of his unchallengeable affinity to Odisha and its deity Lord Jagannātha.[72]

---

69 *Gītagovinda*, H. Hirachand ed. Introduction, Bombay, 1865.

70 *Sekh Subhodaya* ed. Sukumar Sen, Introduction, p.7, Asiatic Society, Calcutta.

71 *Uttarabhārat ki Santha Paramparā*.

72 *Yugavani* 7th June, 1969 (A Bengali Weekly).

Gopīnātha and Jayadeva

Thomas E. Donaldson

Although many of the early rulers of Odisha professed to be "devout followers" of Viṣṇu (*Paramavaiṣṇava*),[1] the earliest extant Vaiṣṇava temples date only from the 10th century. Examples of *Kṛṣṇa-līlā* scenes and several *avatāra* do appear in the iconographic programme of earlier *Śaiva* temples, however, including images of Rāma, Paraśurāma and Balarāma on the Siṃhanātha Temple to suggest that already by the late 9th century Balarāma and not Kṛṣṇa was considered as the eighth *avatāra* of Viṣṇu, that Kṛṣṇa was considered as equivalent to Viṣṇu. This is also evident on two broken images of Viṣṇu at Saintalā, in Bolangīr district, dating to the early 10th century, where the *daśāvatāra* are carved on the back-slab, Balarāma, being the eighth *avatāra*. The iconographic programme of the brick Indralāṭh Temple at Rāṇīpur-Jhariāl in Bolangīr district, the earliest surviving *Vaiṣṇva* temple, combines *Śaiva* and *Vaiṣṇava* imagery with Lakulīśa, Naṭarāja and Cāmuṇḍā appearing along with Nṛsiṁha, Varāha, *Pūtanā-Vadha* and Hanumān among the identifiable images, suggesting that *Vaiṣṇava* iconography is in its incipiency. Although the niches on the Nīlamādhava Temple at Gandharāḍi in Baudh-Phulbani district, also dating to the early 10th century, are now empty, there are detached and fragmented images within the compound of several *avatāra*, including Matsya, Kūrma, Varāha and Vāmana to suggest that all ten were probably included within the iconographic programme as *āvaraṇa-devatā*. In that all of these earliest examples appear in western Odisha, it is probable that introduction of the *daśāvatāra* is associated with the Somavaṃśi-Keśari rulers moving into Odisha at this time from the upper Mahānadī valley. By the mid-10th century Vaiṣṇava temples with *daśāvatāra* were even being constructed in eastern Odisha, as evident on the Pañca-Pāṇḍava Temple at Ganeswarpur. Though most of the iconographic programme is missing,

Facing page: *Kṛṣṇa expecting the arrival of Rādhā, palmleaf painting, Museum Rietberg Zurich.*

1 See Prabhat Mukherjee, *History of Medieval Vaiṣṇavism in Orissa* (Calcutta, 1940), pp. 7-13.

the niches on the north-west corner shrine are filled with *Kṛṣṇa-līlā* scenes, while other examples appear on the sides of the platform where they alternate with erotic motifs. Only two images survive from the niches of the main shrine, one of Buddha and the other of Kṛṣṇa Yāmalārjuna, suggesting that the iconographic programme probably combined *Kṛṣṇa-līlā* motifs with *daśāvatāra*, though it is not known if all ten *avatāra* were included. By the 11th century, Vaiṣṇava temples were even being constructed at Bhubaneswar, as attested by the small temple within the compound of the Paramaguru family adjacent to the Śiśireśvara Temple, where the *daśāvatāra* served as *āvaraṇa-devatā*. Eight of the *avatāra* are in situ with only Buddha and Paraśurāma missing.

Thus, by the mid-10th century, *Kṛṣṇa-līlā* scenes depicting Kṛṣṇa defeating various demons were gradually being replaced in popularity by the *daśāvatāra* theme of the incarnations of Viṣṇu. Also emerging at this time is the motif of Kṛṣṇa as Gopīnātha, Kṛṣṇa playing his flute and sporting with *gopī,* cowherdesses, in the forest, a theme stressing love rather than battle. Although there is a small scene of Kṛṣṇa and Balarāma with *gopī* on the Siṃhanātha Temple, along with possible scenes of Kṛṣṇa sporting with the *gopī* in the forest, the earliest surviving example of Kṛṣṇa playing a flute is a small image carved on one of the balcony balusters of the Kośaleśvara Temple at Baidyanath in Bolangir district, dating to the late 9th or early 10th century. Perhaps the most important large images of this new concept of Kṛṣṇa is the detached images in the Biriñchi-Nārāyaṇa Temple at Pālia, in Balasore district, dating to the late 10th century. The theme is Kṛṣṇa Govardhana with Kṛṣṇa lifting up the mountain with one of his left hands. He is four-armed and holds a *cakra* in one of his right hands. The other two arms embrace a female on either side, a pose possibly influenced by images of Kāma embracing Ratī and Prīti. The female figures probably represent *gopī* and the scene most likely alludes to the upcoming *rāsa* dance in which Kṛṣṇa multiplies himself so as to stand between each two damsels.

Although the official faith of the Somavaṃśi-Keśarīs was Śaivism, they were cosmopolitan in their religious outlook and even revived the *Vaiṣṇava* shrines of Jagannātha at Puri. In the 12th century, with the conquest of Odisha by Coḍagaṅga and the establishment of the Gaṅga period, *Vaiṣṇavism* comes to the forefront. Although Coḍagaṅga was originally a *Śaivite*, after his conquest he adopted *Vaiṣṇavism.* He had close connections with the Coḷas and Cāḷukyas of South India as attested in the Garteśvara Temple inscription of 1136 AD where endowments were made by a brāhmin named Kāmāṇḍi who belonged to the Coḷa country.[2] It was about this time that the philosophy of *Viśiṣṭa-advaitavāda* was being propagated in South India, by *Śrīvaiṣṇava* teachers, many of whom including Rāmānuja, Viṣṇu Svāmī, Madhvācārya and Nimbārka, made Puri the centre of their activities and established *maṭha* there for the propagation of their religious faiths. Of these four great reformers of Vaiṣṇavism, only Nimbārka proclaimed Rādhā as the Śakti of Kṛṣṇa and his spouse in divine sport. It is quite probable that the exaltation of Rādhā as espoused by the Nimbārka school at Puri inspired the erotic mysticism developed by the poet Jayadeva in his *Gītagovinda*.[3] From the Antirigam copper-plates of Jayabhañja we know that *Śrīvaiṣṇavism* was popular even with feudatoy rulers in Odisha and it was probably due to this receptive climate that the South Indian reformers moved to Odisha.[4]

In his invocation in the *Gītagovinda*, Jayadeva addresses all ten incarnations of Viṣṇu while describing Lord Kṛṣṇa as Jagadīśa-Haré, thus associating Hari with Jagadīśa who is responsible for these incarnations, Jagadīśa being a synonym of Jagannātha. The *gīta* of Jayadeva are meant exclusively for Govinda, none other than Jagannātha, and it was a hymn to Govinda which was solely intended to be sung before the deity, certainly not to gain the goodwill and favour of any patron.[5] In the third canto the author states:

> This, of Hari alone, is a song by the famed Jayadeva, who arose, as out of the ocean the moon, from the village of Kendubilva.

Many scholars identify this Kendubilva as a site of the Ajaya river in the Birbhum district of Bengal. More convincing, however, are arguments of Odisha scholars, such as K.N. Mahapatra and B. Rath, who identify it with the village of Kenduli in the Puri district of Odisha, between the Prācī and Kusabhadrā rivers and close to Pratāparudrapur Śāsana. In that the arguments of the Odisha scholars appear mainly in the small journal

---

2 See K.C. Mishra, *The Cult of Jagannātha* (Calcutta, 1971), p. 40.

3 Kedarnath Mahapatra, "New Light on Poet Jayadeva, the Author of the *Gītagovinda*", *OHRJ*, VII, No. 3/4 (1958-59), pp. 201-02.

4 *Epigraphia Indica* XIX, pp. 43-44. K.C. Mishra (*op. cit.*, p. 56) dates the Inscription to the 11th century to suggest Śrī-Vaiṣṇavism was popular even prior to Rāmānuja. Snigdha Tripathy (*Inscription of Orissa*, VI, Bhubaneswar, 1974, p. 214) dates the Inscription to the 13th century.

5 K.N. Mahapatra, *op. cit.*, p.192.

produced by the Orissa State Museum, little known outside Odisha, it includes the most salient arguments here.

In the 18th century the Englishman Sir William Jones tried unsuccessfully to procure the original music of the *Gītagovinda*.[6] Later, in the preface to his English translation of the work, he informs us that many people believe Kendubilva to be in Kaliṅga, "But since there is a town of similar name in Burdwan, the natives of it insist that the finest lyrical poet of India was their countryman," suggesting that attempts were being made in Bengal to claim Jayadeva as belonging to their state. The village Kenduli in Burdwan as mentioned by Jones in *Asiatic Researches* (Vol. III, pp.185-207) was repeated in the *Lyrical Drama*, a Latin translation of the *Gītagovinda* by the Frenchman Lassen in 1837 AD, though he doubts its authenticity as the birthplace. Edward Arnold, in his *Indian Song of Songs* (1857 AD), states that the poet belonged to Bengal and this view is repeated in almost all later works.[7] Present advocates of the Bengal origin of the poet generally refer to a Bengali book, of doubtful authenticity, entitled *Jayadevacarita* by Vanamālidāsa, which records that when the father of Padmāvatī arrived at the village of Kendubilva with his daughter in search of Jayadeva, the villagers told him that they knew nothing about Jayadeva or his parentage, though they had seen a lunatic named Jayadeva inside the temple of Rādhāvinoda and a *Vaiṣṇava maṭha* at this Kenduli, along with the annual fair held in honour of the poet. This temple was constructed in 1962 AD, however, while the *maṭha* was established only in the 18th century. According to the Bengali scholar Sukumar Sen, the *melā* or fair held in honour of Jayadeva has no connection with any village. It is held on the sandy strip of land on the bank of the river and the name of the adjoining village is not Kenduli; in fact, there is no evidence regarding the existence of any village by this name in this area, only the *melā* being known as Jayadeva-kenduli.[8] Nor is there any mention in the biographies of Śrī Caitanya of the village of Kenduli in Birbhum as the birthplace of Jayadeva, even though his own birthplace is not far away. Though there may have been a village named Kenduli at this spot at one time, it certainly was not known up to the 18th century as even the Bengali poet Candradutta of Mithilā, in his *Bhaktamāḷā*, does not claim Jayadeva for

---

6 Odisha not yet being annexed to the Empire, Jones could neither visit Puri nor was he able to procure information from British officers.

7 Banamali Rath, "Orissa, the Land of Jayadeva" *OHRJ*, XXII, Nos. 3/4 (1977), pp1-18. See also *Souvenir on Jayadeva*, ed. by N.K. Sahu (Bhubaneswar).

8 Banamali Rath, *op. cit.*, pp.7-8.

his own land, but mentions definitely that he belonged to a *brāhmaṇa* village named Kendubilva near Jagannātha Puri.[9] It appears then that the association of Jayadeva with this site in Bengal begins sometime in the 18th century. Other literary references which place Kendubilva in Odisha include the *Sampradāpradīpa* of Gadā Dvivedi (1533-1554 AD) which states that Jayadeva belonged to Utkala; the *Bhaktavijaya* of Mahīpatī of Maharashtra which speaks of Jayadeva as an incarnation of Vyāsa belonging to a village named Tinduvilva near the sacred city of Jagannātha; and the *Bhaktamāḷā* by Nāvāji of Gwalior which assigns Jayadeva to Utkala.[10] Perhaps the earliest reference to the homeland of Jayadeva is the verse attributed to Govardhana Ācārya, preserved in the *Alamkāraśekhara* of Keśava Miśra, which states that Jayadeva was the greatest of the poets that adorned the court of the king of Utkala.[11]

Whereas the site referred to as Kenduli in Bengal has no antiquities earlier than the 17th century, the Kenduli on the Prācī river in Odisha, surrounded by *kendu* and *vilva* trees, is of great antiquity. It is an area teeming with *Vaiṣṇava* ruins and temples, perhaps more than any other site in India. At nearby Niāli alone there are a dozen large Viṣṇu images from the sanctum of collapsed temples at Mādhava. On the lintel of the Caṇḍī Temple at Kenduli is an inscription with the figures of 112 in the margin which can be read as "*Jaya Jaya deva hare* 112" suggesting the temple may have been built in commemoration of poet Jayadeva in *Śaka* year 1112, or 1190 AD. The recitation of the *Gītagovinda*, rather than *Durgā Saptaśati*, is still in vogue at the temple.[12] There are many other images housed within the recently constructed Archaeological Museum, the museum and surrounding grounds being called the Jayadeva Culture Centre. Recently discovered from the tank adjacent to the Nṛsiṁha Temple within the village is a set of copper-plate grants of the Gaṅga king Nṛsiṁha IV (1407-1435 AD). In the compound of the Ākhaṇḍaleśvara Temple at Pratāparudrapur, only three km away, is an image of Gopīnātha and another of a standing male which the local populace refers to as Jayadeva. About three kilometres south-east of Kenduli, at the confluence of the Prācī, Kuśabhadrā and Dhanuā rivers, is the famous

---

9 Kedarnath Mahapatra, "Jagannātha Puri as a Centre of Culture through the Ages", *OHRJ*, VI, No. 4 (1958), p.301.

10 K. Mahapatra, "New Light on Poet Jayadeva", pp. 199-201.

11 Kedarnath Mahapatra, "Śrī Jayadeva was not a poet of the Court of Lakṣmaṇa Sena", *OHRJ*, XXII, No. 2 (1976), pp. 43-44.

12 Banamali Rath, *op. cit.* p. 11.

Triveṇī Saṅgama where a big festival is held every year on the day of *Amāvasyā* of the lunar month of *Māgha*. According to tradition, Jayadeva used to take his bath here every day and worshipped the deity of Mādhava called Triveṇī Mādhava. The antiquity of the festival (*Triveṇī Amāvasyā*) probably dates to at least as early as the 13th century.[13] An inscription in the Liṅgarāja Temple at Bhubaneswar, dated 1163-1164 AD during the reign of Rāghava, records the name of one Jayadeva Sādhu Pradhān who lived at Śrikūrma and stood witness for a purchase of land.[14] It is possible that this record refers to the poet Jayadeva. Śrikūrmam, situated in the Śrīkākulam district of Andhra Pradesh, bordering the Ganjam district of Odisha, was an important seat of *Śrī-Vaiṣṇavism* and was considered as the *Gurupīṭha* (sacred place of gurus) of the Gaṅga kings of Odisha and attracted other famous poets, including Vilvamaṅgala and Kavikarnapura.[15]

Kendubilva Śāsana today is divided into three parts, *i.e.* Kenduli Śāsana (a *Brāhmaṇa* colony), Kenduli Deuli (seat of temples), and Kenduli-Pātnā. In the *Sarvāṅgasundarī Tikā* of Nārāyaṇadāsa, a commentary on the *Gītagovinda* written in the early part of the 14th century, it is clearly stated that the Kendubilva of Jayadeva is *Kenduvilvākhya śāsana*, while in the *Rasikapriyā Tīkā* of Rāṇā Kumbha of Chittor, a 15th century commentary on the *Gītagovinda*, it is recorded as *Kinduvilvam tat Śāsanam*. In both cases Kenduli is thus described as a *śāsana*, or *brāhmaṇa* village, which can only refer to the Odishan Kenduli as the so-called Kenduli in Bengal was never a *śāsana* or *brāhmaṇa* village. Here it may be mentioned that the *Śāsana* is a village granted by the Odishan kings only to *brāhmin*. So such usage is restricted to Odisha only. At other places the word with above meaning is known as *agrahāra*.[16]

Bhojadeva's heir, Ramādevī's son, Jayadeva,
Expresses the power of poetry
In the *Gītagovinda*.
Let his poem be in the voice
Of devotees like Sage Parāśara.[17]

---

13 K.N. Mahapatra, "New Light on Poet Jayadeva", pp.196-98.

14 S.N. Rajaguru, *Inscription of Orissa*, III, part II, p.294.

15 K.C. Mishra, *op. cit.*, p.58.

16 Banamali Rath, op. cit. p.9-10.

17 B. Miller, *Gītagovinda*, p.125.

The legendry accounts of Jayadeva's life identifies Bhojadeva as a *brāhmaṇa* of Kanauj who migrated to the village of Kendubilva. This can easily be accommodated with Odishan tradition, according to which Yayātī-I performed ten *Aśvamedha* sacrifices to which he invited ten thousand *brāhmaṇa* from Kanauj. Most of the *brāhmaṇa* in Odisha still trace their origin to these ten thousand.[18] In all the versions of the legend that sanctifies Jayadeva's life, it is stated that he was born in a *brāhmin* family and became an accomplished student of Sanskrit as well as a skilled poet but that he abandoned scholarship at a young age and adopted an ascetic life. His life as a wandering mendicant supposedly ended when a *brāhmaṇa* of Puri insisted that Jagannātha himself had ordained the marriage of Jayadeva with Padmāvatī, the *brāhmaṇa*'s daughter who was dedicated as a dancing girl in the temple: "Padmāvatī served her husband and he shared her devotion to Jagannātha. As Jayadeva composed, she danced—thus the *Gītagovinda*".[19] Thus, even in these legendary accounts whether born in Odisha or elsewhere, his actual writing of the *Gītagovinda* is associated with Puri and the Jagannātha cult appears to have provided the context for the composition whereby Kṛṣṇa is identified with Jagannātha.

With respect to the *Gītagovinda*, nowhere is there a reference to any king, yet scholars invariably associate Jayadeva with the court of Lakṣmaṇa Sena (1184-1205 AD), primarily on the basis of the third verse of the first *Sarga*:

> Umāpatidhara is prodigal with speech,
> Saraṇa is renowned for his subtle flowing sounds,
> But only Jayadeva divines the pure design of words.
> Dhoyī is famed as king of poets for his musical ear,
> But no one rivals master Govardhana
> For poems of erotic mood and sacred truth.[20]

In this verse, however, Jayadeva only gives his own estimate about himself and four other poets who might, "at best be taken to be his elder contemporaries", a common practice by poets of this period who had to prove their worth in the gatherings of pandits. Bāṇabhatta, for example, in the introduction to his *Harṣacarita*, after giving his own

---

18 K.C. Panigrahi, *Chronology of the Bhauma-Karas and the Somavamsis*, p.15.

19 Barbara Stoller Miller, *Gītagovinda*, p.3.

20 *Ibid*, p.69.

estimate with respect to eminent works and authors, including Bhāsa, Kālidāsa, Guṇādhya and others, speaks of his own achievements in verse 19. Rājaśekhara, a court poet of Mahendra Pāla and Mahīpāla of Kanauj, compares himself with Vālmīki, Bhartṛphauri Menṭha and Bhavabhūti in his *Bāla-Rāmāyaṇa*; while Kavirāja Sūri, a court poet of Kāmadeva II (1182-1187 AD), a chief of the Kadamba family of Jayantipura, near Goa, proclaims himself in an introductory verse as on par with Subandhu and Bāṇabhaṭṭa; and in a similar vein Govardhana Ācārya refers to Vālmīki, Vyāsa, Guṇāḍhya, Kālidāsa, Bhavabhūti, Bāṇabhaṭṭa and others in the introductory stanzas of his *Āryāsaptaśati.*[21] Jayadeva thus was only following poetic tradition speaking about four other notable poets of his age.

Jagaddhāra of Mithilā (circa 1330 AD), one of the earliest commentators of the *Gītagovinda*, while interpreting the verse in his *Sāradīpikā*, clearly states that Jayadeva has deprecated the poets of the court of Lakṣmaṇa Sena by establishing the superiority of his work. In the *Sarvāṅgasundarī Ṭīkā* (circa 1300 AD), a textual commentary on the *Gītagovinda*, Kavirāja Nārāyaṇdāsa interprets the verse as follows:

> Poet Umāpatidhara, a minister for peace and war can no doubt make the words sprout, *i.e.* he is proficient in the use of bombastic and florid words, but his knowledge of the use of words is only superficial and not deep. Śaraṇa is praiseworthy only in quick and difficult composition but in nothing else. Ācārya Govardhana is unrivalled in the composition of faultless erotic verse, but he has no mastery in other "*rasa* except *śṛṅgāra.* Kavirāja Dhoyī can remember what he hears once, which implies that he has a strong memory and imitativeness, but he lacks in originality. But Jayadeva alone had profound mastery over use of words and had originality and spontaneity.[22]

Rāṇā Kumbha in his *Rasikapriyā Ṭīkā*, Mahāmahopādhyāya Śaṅkara Miśra of Mithilā in his *Rasamañjarī Ṭīkā*, and Caitanyadāsa of Bengal in his *Bālabodhinī* commentary, all interpret the verse as Jayadeva praising himself and none of these commentators associate the poet with Bengal or with the court of Lakṣmaṇa Sena. Thus the verse in no way implies that all the poets belonged to Bengal or that they adorned the same court.

---

21 K.N. Mahapatra, *Jayadeva was not a Poet of the Court of Lakṣmaṇa Sena*, pp. 28-

22 *Ibid*, p.31.

Govardhana Ācārya, spoken respectfully of by Jayadeva, had no connection with the court of Lakṣmaṇa Sena and, in fact, hails from Niāli Śāsana in Puri district, only a short distance from Kenduli, and his brother, Udayana Ācārya, wrote the *Bhāvavibhāvinī*, the first commentary on the *Gītagovinda* (circa 1190 AD), as well as the Megheśvara and Śobhaneśavara Temples' inscriptions as indicated earlier.[23] Govardhana speaks eloquently about the scholarship and poetic talent of his two younger brothers, Udayana and Balabhadra, who helped him improve the composition of his *Āryāsaptaśati.* Even in the *History of Bengal,* published by the Dhaka University, it is suggested that this Udayana may be identical with Udayana Kavi who composed the *praśasti* of the Megheśvara Temple.[24] It is also possible that a commentary on the *Naiṣadhacarita* of Śrī Harṣa, called *Udayakarī,* was written by Udayana Ācārya, brother of Govardhana.[25]

Umāpatidhara definitely worked at the court of Vijaya Sena (1125-1160 AD) and may possibly have worked for his grandson, Lakṣmaṇa Sena. Although Śaraṇa was patronised by a Sena king, as attested by a verse of his in the *Saduktikarṇāmṛtam* (1205 AD) of Śrīdharadāsa, the name of the king is not mentioned. As regards the poet Dhoyī, on the other hand, there is definite evidence that he was patronised by Lakṣmaṇa Sena, in whose honour he composed the *Pavanadūtaṃ.*[26] Thus, of the five poets, only Dhoyī can be definitely placed in the court of Lakṣmaṇa Sena without reservation. Śaraṇa and Umāpatidhara worked for the Sena court and possibly for Lakṣmaṇa Sena while Jayadeva and Govardhana Ācārya were both from Odisha. In that Jayadeva is also praising Govardhana, it is plausible that his intention was to champion the poets of the court of Odisha over those of the Sena court.

One last argument associating Jayadeva with the court of Lakṣmaṇa Sena is a verse, listing Govardhana, Śaraṇa, Jayadeva, Umāpati and Kavirāja as the jewels of the court of Lakṣmaṇa Sena, supposedly inscribed on the gate of his assembly hall in Navadvīpa. There is no contemporary epigraphic or literary evidence to prove that Nadiyā was ever the capital of either Lakṣmaṇa Sena or his forefathers and

---

23 Kedarnath Mahapatra, "Govardhana Ācārya and Udayana Ācārya", *OHRJ,* VII, No. 1 (1958), pp.40-48.

24 Ibid, p.46.

25 Kedarnath Mahapatra, "Studies in the *Naiśadhīya Caritam* of Śrī Harsa", *OHRJ,* VIII, No. 1 (1959), pp.65-74.

26 Kedarnath Mahapatra, *New Light on Poet Jayadeva,* pp.193-194.

successors, the grants always being issued from Vikramapura or, in the case of the later ones, from Dharyagrāma and Phalgugrāma. Similarly, in no Sanskrit work written during the Sena period is Nadiyā mentioned as the capital of Lakṣmaṇa Sena. In the *Pavanadūtaṃ* of Dhoyī, the capital of Lakṣmaṇa Sena is called Vijayapura. Only in the *Tabaqat-i-Nasiri*, written in 1260 AD, is Nadiyā described as the seat of government. It is not a reliable account, giving the king a reign of eighty years and narrating fanciful stories about his birth and the destruction of Nadiyā. According to it, Muhammad-i-Bakhtiyar destroyed the city and left it in desolation suggesting there was no trace of the palace left standing, though the verse supposedly was discovered on the gates some three hundred years later. Thus, according to Mahapatra, "The story of the discovery of the so-called inscription describing the connection of five poets with Śrīdhara Navadvīpa originated and was circulated in the post-Caitanya period when Nadiyā came to prominence due to the birth of the great reformer Caitanya in that holy place".[27] There is little evidence, literary or archaeological, that the *Gītagovinda* was popular in Bengal prior to the advent of Caitanya. In fact, Caitanya first "discovered the jewel of *Gītagovinda*" when he visited Puri in 1509 AD, and came to realise the religious significance of the work from Rāya Rāmānanda on the banks of the Godāvarī when he went on pilgrimage to the south.[28]

In Odisha, on the other hand, the popularity of the *Gītagovinda* was almost immediate and the two earliest commentaries on the poem were produced there, the *Bhāvavibhāvinī* by Udayana Ācārya (circa 1190 AD) and the *Sarvāṅgasundarī* by Kavirāja Nārāyanadāsa. The latter was a court poet of the Gaṅga king Nṛsiṁha II (1279-1307 AD) and it was through his efforts that the recitation of the *Gītagovinda* in Jagannātha temple enhanced its prestige and no doubt helped its rapid circulation outside Odisha by pilgrims hearing it on their visit to Puri, its popularity already discernible in the stone inscription of Maharāja Sāraṅgadeva Vaghela of Anahillapattan (Gujarat) dating to 1291 AD which opens with Jayadeva's invocation to Kṛṣṇa in his *daśāvatāra* forms.[29] The earliest imitation of the *Gītagovinda* so far known was also written in Odisha, by Kavichandrarāya Divākara Miśra, known as *Abhinava-Gītagovinda*. Its recitation was introduced in the Jagannātha temple by Puruṣottamadeva

27 *Ibid.*, pp. 194-95.

28 B. Rath, *op. clt.*, p. 16.

29 See M.R. Majumdar, "The Gujarati School of Painting and Some Newly Discovered Vaiṣṇva Miniatures", *JISOA*, X (1942), p. 15.

(1446-1497 AD) but it was, according to tradition, disliked by Lord Jagannātha. Pratāparudradeva (1497-1540 AD), the son of Puruṣottama, strictly ordered in an inscription not to sing any other song before the deity except the *Gītagovinda*. The relevant portion reads:

> "Dancing will be performed thus at the *Bhoga* time of the elder *ṭhākura* Balarāma and *Gītagovinda ṭhākura*, i.e. Jagannātha. This dancing will be held from the end of the evening *dhūpa* upto the time of *Baḍasingāra* (bed-time) *dhūpa*. The batch (of dancing girls) of *Baḍa ṭhākura*, the fixed female dancers of Kapileśvara *ṭhākura*, the old batch, the *Telanga* batch, all will learn no other song than the *Gītagovinda* of *Baḍa ṭhākura*. They will not sing any other song. No other kind of dancing should be performed before the god. Besides the dancing, there are four *Vaiṣṇava* singers; they will sing only the *Gītagovinda*. Hearing in one tone from them, those who are ignorant will learn the *Gītagovinda* songs; they should not learn any other song. That superintendent who knowingly allows other songs to be sung, and other dancing to be performed, goes against Jagannātha".[30]

A second early imitation of the *Gītagovinda* is the *Jagannātha Vallabha Nāṭakam* which was composed by Rāya Rāmānanda Pattanāyaka, the Odia governor of Rāja Mahendri, under the Gajapati king Pratāparudradeva, sometime between 1497 AD and 1509 AD. There are in addition twenty-nine more *kāvya* written in imitation by Odishan authors. The earliest commentaries and imitations of the *Gītagovinda* were thus written in Odisha, at least two of each prior to the time of Caitanya, whereas it was Caitanya who popularised the *Gītagovinda* in Bengal, after his visit to Odisha.[31] In fact, from the 16th century onward, numerous commentaries in Odia script were written in other parts of India, including the *Rasika Raṅgadā Ṭīkā* by Lakṣmaṇa Bhaṭṭa and the *Śrutirañjanī Ṭīkā* by Lakṣmaṇa Sūri. This phenomenon of copying into Odia commentaries written in other parts of India, as pointed out by Kapilā Vātsyāyan, "speaks of the pervasive popularity of the text and the active dialogue between different parts of India".[32] In addition it suggests an association of the *Gītagovinda* with Odisha in the minds of these authors.

---

30 *JASB*, Vol. L XII (1998), pp.96-97.

31 K.N. Mahapatra, *New Light on Poet Jayadeva*, pp. 301-23.

32 Kapila Vātsyāyan, "The Illustrated Manuscripts of the Gita Govinda from Orissa", *Madhu*, ed. by. M.S. Nagaraja Rao (Delhi, 1981), p.275.

From the end of the 15th century, dramas based on the *Gītagovinda* also began to appear which were markedly different from the lyrical versions, a genre of dramatic performance called the *saṅgītanāṭaka* which served as the precursor of the better known *Kṛṣṇayātrā* tradition of Odisha. In the 16th century another type of drama evolved, a one-act play, such as the *Pīyūṣa laharī* attributed to Jayadeva II which was staged in the compound of the Jagannātha Temple at Puri, while several other dramas, including *Vaiṣṇavāmṛtam*, were likewise enacted in the courtyard.[33] It is also noteworthy that all the musical notes (*rāga*) used in the *Gītagovinda* are fully utilised with greater dimensions by old Odia writers whereas these *rāga* are rarely met with in old Bengali literature. Hundreds of palmleaf manuscripts of the *Gītagovinda* are found in villages throughout Odisha to attest its tremendous influence and popularity.[34] Included among these are some forty illustrated manuscripts scattered in public and private collection. In keeping with Odishan tradition, these are generally more erotic in nature than those elsewhere in India. In summary, as pointed out by Vātsyāyan, "There is no gainsaying that Odisha is the richest repository of the tradition of the *Gītagovinda* in the literary, pictorial and the performing arts alike."[35]

The impact of Jayadeva and the *Gītagovinda* is almost immediate in sculpture also. Already in the inscription of the Megheśvara Temple, composed by Udayana Ācārya, younger brother of Govardhana, in the last decade of 12th century, it is mentioned that Kṛṣṇa is the favourite of the Gopāla clan, in comparing Svapneśvara with Viṣṇu, "who is the consort of Lakṣmī, destroyer of Bali in the Vāmana incarnation, favourite of the Gopāla clan, doer of every exploit and who held the earth up in the Viśvaksena and Varāha incarnations". It is doubtful, however, that the scene on the temple identified by Panigrahi as the Godhanaharaṇa by Brahmā[36] actually represents Kṛṣṇa. The major figure is seated with legs bound by a *yoga-paṭṭa* and has dishevelled hair, suggesting probably it to be a form of Bhairava, while the cows on the pedestal possibly suggest a hermitage. The female figures are *dākini* or *yoginī* rather than the *gopī*. A similar scene appears on the Śobhaneśvara Śiva Temple at Niāli, identified by P.K. Ray as illustrating the Sunahsepha episode from the *Rāmāyaṇa*.[37]

---

33 *Ibid.*, p.276.

34 Banamali Rath, *op. cit.*, pp. 15-16.

35 Kapila Vatsyayan, *op. cit.*, p.275.

36 Panigrahi, *Archaeological Remains at Bhubaneswar, p.85.*

37 P.K. Ray, *Praci Valley : Archaeological Survey Report* (1974-75), p.34.

Two large sculptures of Viṣṇu-Kṛṣṇa, one in the Jagannātha-Ballava Maṭha at Puri[38] and the other, from Dharmaśālā, in the Orissa State Museum,[39] dating to the late 12th or early 13th century, poignantly illustrate, the ideology propounded by Jayadeva in the *Gītagovinda*, that Jagadīśa-Hari is responsible for the *daśāvatāra*, that Kṛṣṇa is identical with Viṣṇu and not one of his *avatāra*, an ideology already noticed in the Megheśvara Temple inscription. In the Dharmaśālā image, the *daśāvatāra* are carved on the pedestal and the back-slab. Viṣṇu-Kṛṣṇa is four-armed and stands with his right leg crossed in front of his left in the manner of Gopīnātha images and likewise holds a flute in his front two hands, the flute now missing. His uplifted back hands hold a *cakra* and a conch. He is richly ornamented and wears a long *vanamālā* while his coiffure is arranged in a tall *kirīṭa-mukuṭa*. Next to his left foot, on the right edge of the *viśvapadma* cushion, is a diminutive image of Viṣṇu Anantaśayana while to its right, on a small lotus pod, is a small kneeling figure with hands folded in *añjali*, possibly Bhūdevi.[40] At the base of the back-slab on either side of Kṛṣṇa-Viṣṇu are two female figures standing in front of a *khakharamuṇḍi*. The inside set of figures represent Śrīdevī and Sarasvatī while the outside figures are probably Rukminī and Satyabhāmā, the consorts of Viṣṇu and Kṛṣṇa respectively. The pedestal is decorated with a herd of cows along with three *avatāra*, Kūrma in the centre with Matsya and Varāha at the corners. The remaining *daśāvatāra* are carved on the back-slab, beginning on the proper right, above the *khākharamuṇḍi*, with Nṛsiṁha and ending in the corresponding area on the left with Kalki. The images of Vāmana, Paraśurāma, Rāma, Balarāma and Buddha are placed around the *makara-toraṇa* (arch) framing the head of Viṣṇu-Kṛṣṇa. Even though Viṣṇu-Kṛṣṇa has one leg crossed, the overall pose is quite rigid and suggests an experimental stage, combining the rigid and hieratic *samabhanga* (without bends) pose of conventional Viṣṇu images with the relaxed pose of Kṛṣṇa playing the flute (Gopīnātha or Veṇugopāla). There is also a small four-armed image of Kṛṣṇa within the compound of the Varāha Temple at Jajpur. The back left hand holds a conch while the back right hand is broken off. He is flanked on either side by a cow and *gopī*.

Kṛṣṇa, stone sculpture in Akhandaleśvara Temple, Pratāparudrapur.

38 K.C. Mishra, *op. cit.*, p.57.

39 See P.K. Ray, "A Unique image of Viṣṇu-Kṛṣṇa in the Orissa State Museum" *OHRJ*, IX, No. 4 (1963), pp.255-59.

40 *Epigraphia Indica*, Vol. XXXIX, pp. 125-31. See also *JASB* (old Series), Vol. L. XVII (1998), part I, pp.317-

Four-armed images are generally associated with the Govardhana motif with the back hands holding the mountain, as at Palia or in a *paga* niche on the Cāteśvara Temple at Kisenpur dating to the early 13th century. The latter possibly represents the earliest example of Kṛṣṇa serving as an *āvaraṇa-devatā* on a Śiva temple. The temple was built on the site of an earlier temple which contained an extensive series of *Kṛṣṇa-līlā*, many of the scenes haphazardly inserted into the *Jagmohana* of the present temple, though most of the decorative programme is covered with plaster. The iconographic programme of the *deuḷa* is intact, however, and is unique for a Śiva temple with the *anartha* niches of both storeys housing *Vaiṣṇava* themes, including Yaśoda rebuking Kṛṣṇa, Kṛṣṇa carried across the river, *Ariṣṭāsura-vadha-mūrti*, *Cāṇura-vadha-mūrti*, two scenes with Rāma, and two images of Gopīnātha. In one of the latter images, the one we are concerned here with, the Gopīnātha motif is combined with the *Govardhana-dhāraṇa*. Kṛṣṇa stands in a pronounced *tribhaṅga* pose with his right leg crossed and playing the flute with his two major hands. His back two hands are lifted holding Mount Govardhana up. Several cows are in the lower left corner of the niche and possibly *gopī* in the opposite corner though the images are indistinct due to accumulated coats of whitewash. The religious synthesism of the iconographic programme is also apparent in the images enshrined in the upper *rāha* niches, above the *pārśvadevatā*. On the south, for example, the centre niche is occupied by Lakulīśa while the flanking niches are filled with Kārtikeya and Gaṇeśa a programme stressing the *Śaivite* nature of the temple. On the north side, on the other hand, the centre niche has an image of Vārāhī, stressing *Śākta* ideology, with the flanking niches housing a male embracing a female on either side and an enigmatic scene with four figures arranged in a circle. On the west side the centre niche is occupied by Bali seated in *lalitāsana* while the flanking niches are filled with Trivikrama and Vāmana, stressing *Vaiṣṇava* influence. According to the inscription on the temple, consisting of 25 lines lauding the exploits of Anaṅgabhīma III (1211-1238 AD) against the Muslim and the Kalacurīs, the temple was erected by Viṣṇu Ācārya, the *Brāhmaṇa* minister and commander-in-chief of Anaṅgabhīma III.[41] This is the same Viṣṇu Ācārya who was only a royal preceptor in the time of Anaṅgabhīma II (1190-1198 AD) though it was at his behest that the poet Udayana Ācārya, brother of Govardhana Ācārya as mentioned in the latter's *Āryāsaptaśati*, composed the Megheśvara Temple inscription. It is possible, as Mahapatara suggests,

41 Kedarnath Mahapatra, *Govardhana Ācārya and Udayana Ācārya*, pp. 40-46.

that Viṣṇu Ācārya belonged to the family of the famous Nīlāmbara Ācārya and thus was related to Udayana and Govardhana.[42]

The popularity of Kṛṣṇa as the favourite of the Gopāla continues throughout the 13th century with large independent images appearing particularly along the Prācī river, the homeland of Jayadeva, and coastal Odisha, long before such images became popular in Bengal or elsewhere in India.[43] Such images, created either for special shrines or as presiding deities have been found at Alarpur (now moved to Baliāntā), Antarvedi Maṭha, Bāgesvarapur, Bārdhapur, Bhingarpur, Dharmsālā, Hirāpur, Jāipur Jānakdevīpur (Patna Museum), Kuranga Śāsana, Manikarṇika Maṭha, Nivārana, Nuagaon (Radhākanta Maṭha), Pāndavakuda, Pratāpanagara, Pratāparudrapur, Puri, Pūrbaśāsana, Purānasatang, Remuna, Sarakana, Somesvarpur and Viṣṇupur. The images are generally carved of chlorite and depict Gopīnātha standing in a *tribhaṅga* pose with his right leg crossed in front of the left. He is two-armed and holds the flute near his right shoulder. Iconographically he conforms to the description of Kṛṣṇa as the supreme *Brāhmaṇa* as found throughout the *Brahma-Vaivarta Purāṇa.* A tree branches out above his head and he is generally flanked by his *aṣṭapāṭṭavamśi* or eight chief consorts. Despite the popularity of the *Gītagovinda* and its influence on Odishan sculpture, however, there are no examples of Rādhā with Kṛṣṇa either as his favourite *gopī* or as his divine consort. According to Mahapatra, Rādhā could not be deified singly or in the company of Kṛṣṇa as her worship "was not sanctified by the *Bhāgavata Purāṇa* which had gained popularity in Odisha before the days of Jayadeva", nor was she recognised by the *Smṛti* writers, who were moulding the religious life of the people in those days with the support and patronage of the kings. The cumulative effect of these trends of religious thought of that age was that Jagannātha was regarded as another form of Śrī Kṛṣṇa and the worship of only Gopījanavallabha Śrī Kṛṣṇa and not Rādhāvallabha Śrī Kṛṣṇa got the royal sanction.[44]

Caitanya, in the *Caitanya Bhāgavata* (III.2), recites a *śloka* in honour of Jagannātha conceived as Gopīnātha and during the *Herā-Pañcami* festival Jagannātha is regarded as Kṛṣṇa. It is said that

42 See Rakhal Dās Banerji, "Eastern India School of Medieval Sculpture", *ASI*, XL VII (Delhi, 1993).

43 Kedarnath Mahapatra, *New Light on Poet Jayadeva*, pp. 200-201. In the Alarpur plates of Narasimha II, for example, we learn that three Gopīnātha temples were erected in Garakana-Śāsana.

44 P. Mukherjee, *History of Medieval Vaiṣṇavism in Orissa*, p.67.

Jagannātha Kṛṣṇa longs at that time for the "disport of Vṛndāvana. So he repairs to the Gundicā house, which resembles, the abode of *gopī*."[45]

In that these hieratic images of Gopīnātha were placed in the sanctum for individual worship, it is likely that the worshipper himself is playing the role of Rādhā, that the votary "serves Kṛṣṇa as a lover, offering him his or her own person".[46]

In the evolving Gauḍiya-Vaiṣṇava doctrine of *bhāva*, the devotee, consciously imitates the *gopī* by devoting his whole mind and being to becoming a *gopī* in an attempt to transcend the phenomenal world of custom and tradition...When man expresses himself in devotion to Kṛṣṇa, when he sports with Kṛṣṇa in ecstatic bliss, all desires are fulfilled. Man becomes rapt in the intoxicating beauty of Kṛṣṇa...The essential nature of all men is that of a *gopī*. 'In truth every finite being is essentially an emanation or phase of Rādhā, to wit, a *mañjari* or a milkmaid on Eternal Vṛndāvan in the prime of perennial youth.'[47] There is thus no need to represent Rādhā with Gopīnātha. According to the *Sahajiya* doctrine, the "*Jīva* is a *Gopī*, or Rādhā. One is, and should consider oneself, a woman, in relation to the sole male of the universe, Kṛṣṇa."[48]

The depiction of Kṛṣṇa enchanting many *gopī* with his flute, rather than just Rādhā, is also in keeping with earlier tradition revolving around the *Bhikṣāṭana* motif of Śiva in the Pine forest exciting the wives of the *ṛṣi*. In each motif the setting is a forest, the females are married, and the deity displays a maddening, lustful and unorthodox behaviour. Whether in the Pine forest or Vṛndāvana, "True devotion is a mad, intoxicating affair that needs such a setting to express itself fully. The normal world is inhibiting, full of obstacles and distractions."[49] Although the wives of the *ṛṣi* may be unaware of who the intruder is and the husbands display their anger, the females become uninhibited and lust after Śiva as the *gopī* do after Kṛṣṇa.

Even more than the lust of the females, however, the emphasis in both motifs focuses on the virility of the deity, his ability to satisfy many women, a theme particularly popular in later Odishan temples where the king or guru assumes role of the deity, and no doubt equally popular

45 *Ibid*., pp. 67-68.

46 D. Kinsley, *The Sword and the Flute* (1977), pp. 63-65.

47 Edward C. Dimock, *The Palace of the Hidden Moon*, (1966), p. 158.

48 D. Kinsely, *op. cit*., p. 62.

49 See H. Wilson, *Viṣṇu Purana*, p.425.

with the male populace in the aristocratic, hedonistic society responsible for erecting the temples.

Throughout the history of temple construction in Odisha, characterised by religious synthesism, there has been a tendency to correlate the activity of Kṛṣṇa with that of Śiva and pictorially this is accomplished in these two motifs. It is also in these two motifs, where the deity has only two arms and thus appears human, that the king (or guru) can most easily become identified with, or serve as a surrogate for the deity. Though he can be represented as a great warrior or hunter, for example, he cannot be visually depicted defeating demons, nor, from a temporal framework, be represented practising severe penance for thousands of years as he has the affairs of state to attend to. He can, however, display his sexual potency, whether deified in the iconographic programme of the temple, eulogised in inscriptions or poetry, or actually practised in the confines of his palace or pleasure gardens.

In addition to these hieratic images intended to be enshrined in a sanctum, there are also a few examples where major images, of Gopīnātha are incorporated into the iconographic programme of Śiva temples. On the Chitrakāriṇī Temple at Bhubaneswar, for example, dating to the late 13th century, the motif is carved on the *gavākṣa* lintel on the north side of the *Jagamohana*. Kṛṣṇa is seated on a cushion with his right leg crossed over his left. He wears a *vanamālā* and holds the flute to his lips. Two *gopī* stand in front of him while three more stand behind him in the forest along with several cows. The same lintel on the south side is decorated with a long frieze depicting the marriage of Śiva, suggesting, an attempt as indicated, to correlate the activities of Kṛṣṇa with Śiva. A similar juxtaposition may have appeared on the collapsed Somanātha Temple at Viṣṇupur, dating back to the 14th century, though here they were placed on panels of the upper storey or *gavākṣa-maṇḍana*, immediately above the lintel. In the Kṛṣṇa panel, Gopīnātha assumes the conventional pose with a tree branching above his head. He is flanked at the base on either side by his consorts and two rows of *gopī*. A row of six additional *gopī*, smaller in size, appears below with some of them dancing. Also at Viṣṇupur is a detached panel decorated with an eight petalled lotus-medallion which may have decorated the ceiling of the destroyed *nāṭa-mandira* or possibly served as a window-grill. The top petal contains an image of Kṛṣṇa playing his flute while the other seven petals are each decorated with a dancing *gopī*. Kṛṣṇa is again depicted in, the pericap, this time dancing, so that the theme represents the *Rāsa-maṇḍala* as described by the commentator on the *Harivaṃśa*:

> Between each two damsels was Mādhava, and between each two Mādhava was a nymph; and the son of Devakī played on the flute; for, in fact, Kṛṣṇa is not only dancing with each, but also by himself in the centre.[50]

Kṛṣṇa does not duplicate his image to appear between each *gopī*, however, due to the limited amount of space available. The obvious inspiration for this medallion is the earlier one from Koṇārka which has sixteen outer petals, each with a dancer, while the pericarp contains an image of Surya.[51] Another panel from Viṣṇupur, now in the Orissa State Museum, illustrates the *Vastra-haraṇa* motif narrated in the *Bhāgavata Purāṇa.* (X 22.7-22). Kṛṣṇa is visible in the branches of the tree while the naked *gopī* are standing below on the banks of the Yamunā.

Although the placement of Gopīnātha in niches of a *Vaiṣṇava* shrine, as on the Jagannātha temple at Puri, or on *gavākṣa*-balusters as on the Ananta-Vāsudeva at Bhubaneswar, is to be expected, the insertion of two images of Gopīnātha in the upper *anartha* niches of the Sāri Deuḷa, a *Śaiva* temple from the late 13th century, at Bhubaneswar, is unique. The *anartha* niches on the lower storey all contain secular themes, either of the king or the queen, while the remaining niches of the upper storey, along with the *anurāha* recesses, are filled with female figures. Generally by this time the iconography is standardised and, including the *dikpālapatnī*, all of the images of this upper storey, except one, are of female figures or *maithuna* motifs. The lone exception is usually, a male weighing his *liṅgam*, as indicated earlier, or, in the case of *Śākta* shrines such as Gaṅgeśvarī Temple at Bayālīsbāṭi, Ekapāda Śaiva. An earlier harbinger for the images of a male in the upper recesses is that of Kāma on the Candeśvara Temple near Tāṅgi.[52] The lone male figure is thus serving as a guardian, as in the case of Ekapāda, or is inciting the females with lust as in the case of the male weighing his *liṅgam* (the king or guru as a symbol of Kāma/virility) or Kāma. On the Sārī Deuḷa the images of Gopīnātha, one on the north and the other on the east (back), are thus symbolically identified with Kāma and the *gopī* are identified with celestial damsels. Whereas the king and the queen

---

50 Debala Mitra, *Konark*, pl. XXIV.

51 On the Rājārāni Temple the lone male is naked and carries a child on his shoulder.

52 See Hermann Kulke, "Some Remarks about the Jagannātha Trinity" *Indologen-Tagung*, 1971 (Wiesbaden, 1973), pp. 126-39.

are one with Śiva and Pārvatī on the lower storey, serving as *āvaraṇa-devatā*, on the upper storey, they are one with Kṛṣṇa/Kāma and the *gopī/apsarā* in the overall secularisation of the iconographic programme of the temple.

The hieratic concept of Kṛṣṇa, synonymous with Viṣṇu (Vāsudeva), reaches a climax in the latter part of the 13th century in its placement, along with an image of Balarāma, as the presiding icon in the sanctum of numerous temples, including the brick Vaiṣṇava temple in the compound of the *Sūrya Deuḷa* at Koṇārka, the Ananta-Vāsudeva Temple, and the Anantesvara Temple in the Liṅgrāja compound.[53] In the Ananta-Vāsudeva Temple inscription composed by Umāpati, where Candrikā, the patron, is described as a devout worshipper of Kṛṣṇa and as one expert in music and dance, it is explicitly stated (verse 15-16) that the temple was dedicated to two portions of Hari, that the images within the sanctum represent Ananta and Vāsudeva.[54] At a later date, influenced by the emerging popularity of the Puruṣottama/Jagannātha cult, the images of Ekānaṃsā (Pārvatī) was inserted between these two brothers to transform the icon into a trinity. Eventually these images were replaced by those of Balabhadra, Subhadrā and Jagannātha to form a new trinity with their iconographic form being based essentially on the earlier images of Puruṣottama, included in early trinities worshipped by Nṛsiṁha I (1238-1264 AD), which closely resembles tribal pillar deities carved in wood, such as Stambheśvarī, several examples of which appear on the *Sūrya Deuḷa*. By this time the worship of Kṛṣṇa, as well as other cult deities, became synthesised with that of Jagannātha cult which became the state religion of Odisha.

53 P. Acharya, *OHRJ*, Vol. 1, No. 4 (1953), pp. 274-88.

54 See Hermann Kulke, "*King Anangabhima III, the Veritable Founder of the Gajapati Kingship and of the Jagannātha Trinity at Purī*", pp. 26-39.

Kṛṣṇa Viṣṇu, stone sculpture.

The *Gītagovindasevā*

Mahesh Prasad Dash

The *Gītagovindasevā* was being performed by *devadāsī* or *māhārī* in the Jagannātha Temple at Puri. The tradition of *devadāsī* is very ancient in India, the earliest reference is available in the cave inscription at Yogīmaṭh on the hills of Rāmgarh, now in Madhya Pradesh during the 3rd century BC. An indirect evidence is also found in the Udayagiri cave inscription of Mahāmeghavāhana Khāravela in the 1st century BC. In course of time performances of the *devadāsī* were institutionalised in different religious systems in India and were treated as an integral part of temple rituals. Later the ritual was given sanction and status by *Purāṇa* and *Dharmaśāstra*. This prompted appointment of *devadāsī* in temples and religious institutions. *Devadāsī* or the female servants of the divine, god or goddesses or girls dedicated to temples became a class of their own, who made a living singing and dancing for the deities.

Historically speaking, after a long interval, the appointment of *devadāsī* has been mentioned in the inscriptions of Brahmeśvara Temple (1061 AD) which was built by Kolāvatī Devī, the mother of the king Udyotakeśari of Soma dynasty. Following this we get several inscriptions which record the appointment of temple dancers or *devadāsī*, *gaṇikā*, *dārikā*, *bhāvinī* in different temples of Odisha beginning from the Madhukeśvara Temple (1082 AD) inscription to the Jagannātha Temple inscription (1500 AD) promulgated by the king Anaṅgabhīma Codagaṅgadeva of Gaṅga dynasty and Gajapati Pratāparudradeva of Gajapati dynasty respectively.

In Odisha, *devadāsī* were known as *māhārī*. The word *māhārī* was perhaps derived from the Sanskrit *mahati*, the noble or great lady. *Māhārī* is a local term used specifically for the woman who performed music and dance in the temple.

Māhārī is first mentioned in *Caryāpada* composed in Odia by Kanhupā or Kanhupāda (950 AD). In a copper plate grant of Karṇadeva, the grandson of king Udyotakeśari (1040-65 AD) the word *māhārī* has

Facing page:
Rādhā escorted by a Sakhī *approaching Kṛṣṇa seated inside a* kuñja *palmleaf painting Museum Rietberg Zurich.*

been used for the woman-dancer. The *Gītagovinda* was composed by Jayadeva and was simultaneously performed by his spouse Padmāvatī who was none else than a *māhārī* or *devadāsī*. After the establishment of the Jagannātha Temple at Puri, nine categories of *sevaka* (temple functionaries) were appointed. Gradually the number of categories increased and Anaṅgabhīmadeva introduced *catiśāniyoga* or the thirty-six order of temple functionaries. *Gītagovindasevā* was an important ritual and was included in the thirty-six order.

It is recorded in the *Mādalāpāñji*, the temple chronicle of Puri, that Kavi Narasimhadeva accorded permission for the recitation of the *Gītagovinda* for the first time in the temple. Kavi Narasimhadeva has been identified with Gaṅga king Narasimhadeva II who ruled from AD 1278-1309. The recitation of the *Gītagovinda* continued for sometime until it was prohibited by Pratāparudradeva (1497-1540 AD) who, ignoring the longstanding convention, introduced the recitation of *Abhinava-Gītagovinda*, supposed to have been written by his father Puruṣottamadeva. But the priests and devotees strongly resisted this change and demanded re-introduction of the *Gītagovinda* of Jayadeva. Under their pressure Pratāparudradeva had to withdraw his previous order within a short period.

After the death of Pratāparudradeva, the last great Gajapati king, Odisha passed through a period of political uncertainty which had tremendous impact on the ritual tradition of Jagannātha Temple. The following years were the years of strife, bloodshed, intrigues, conspiracy and civil war. The sons of the Gajapati king were put to death by his treacherous minister Govinda Vidyādhara who symbolised in him the vices of an age of decay and degeneration. When the Sūrya dynasty thus extinguished, Govinda Vidyādhara ascended the throne as the Gajapati king. During his brief rule Odisha disintegrated speedily with independent small principalities coming into existence in inaccessible hill tracts of Odisha. His worthless successors were removed from the scene and a brave general named Mukunda Haricandana ascended the throne and tried desperately to save a disintegrating kingdom.

Kṛṣṇa and Rādhā in love play inside the kuñja *arbour, palmleaf painting, Museum Rietberg Zurich.*

Mukundadeva ruled for nine years (1559-1568 AD) while external invasions and internal dissension became the sad tale of the time. After Mukundadeva was killed in an internal battle, there was complete anarchy and nobody was there to look after the gods and *brāhmaṇa*. Kalāpāhār, the Afghan general, captured Puri and plundered the treasure-trove of Jagannātha. It is said that he also took away the image of Jagannātha and burnt it down. In the subsequent years the image of Jagannātha was kept hidden a number of times by the priests in the inaccessible places of south Odisha. Afghans took a hostile attitude towards the Hindu religion and the Jagannātha Temple suffered immensely during this period. The situation changed when Rājā Mānsingh, the famous Mughal general, defeated the Afghans in 1590 and installed Rāmacandradeva as the ruler of Khurdā and the Superintendent of the Jagannātha Temple. Rāmacandradeva was an able and popular administrator. He was known as the "Second Indradyumna" and completed the renewal ceremony of the Jagannātha trinity sometime in 1591. He systematically reorganised the administration of the Jagannātha Temple.

He established around Puri new *brāhmaṇa śāsana* and invited the leaders of those new *śāsana* with those of the older *śāsana* villages to take seat in the *Muktimaṇḍapa Sabhā* in the Jagannātha Temple which became the highest religious authority of Odisha. The sanctity of the ritual worship was restored and different temple functionaries performed their respective roles according to established custom and convention. Primary sources for the study of temple establishment are the royal letters (*cāmu ciṭāu*) issued by the *rājā* of Puri through the *deuḷa karaṇa* to different institutions and individuals connected with the temple of Jagannātha. These *cāmu ciṭāu*, royal letters, after adequate investigation will throw new light on the *Gītagovindasevā*.

Although there had been a temporary setback in the ritual worship of the temple during the Mughal period, it had to be restored to its previous conditions to save the temple from the loss of pilgrim tax ensuing from the fall of pilgrim visits. The *rājā* of Khurdā played a major role.

In Odisha, Muslim army no doubt overran the land, but they could not do away with its presiding deity Jagannātha because Jagannātha was not like Somanātha and Viśvanātha–idols enshrined in temples–but a living God reflected in the hearts of the devotees of the land. During Marāṭhā rule the powers of the temple administration were concentrated in the hands of the government. The old records in *modi* script in the temple office of Puri when properly deciphered, will reveal many interesting facts on the *Gītagovindasevā*.

Odisha came under the British rule in the year 1803. The first report on the temple functionaries is the report of C. Grome, Collector, addressed to Commissioner at Cuttack on the 10th June 1805. The main report is available in Odisha State Archives but unfortunately its enclosures are missing. Grome mentioned in his report that, "The establishment of the temple of Jagannātha consisted of thirty-six orders and they were in consequence called the *Chattes Neyoog*." He further stated that, "From a period of at least two hundred years others have been added to those original *sevaka* and now these orders belonging to the temple accounts to two hundred fifty". A list of temple functionaries engaged in the temple was also furnished by him wherein the important *Gītagovindasevā* finds mention along with other *sevā* of the temple. It appears that the *Gītagovindasevā* gained much momentum under the patronage of the *Rājā* of Khurdā and continued to be popular during Marāṭhās and the British period. This *sevā* was considered a great honour extended to the talented artists and they used to enjoy certain privileges in the ritual role of the temple. According to established custom and long standing convention only he who received *sāḍhi* from the *rājā* of Puri to perform this *sevā* was recognised as a *Gītagovinda Sevaka* of the temple. A copy of the *cāmu ciṭāu* was kept with the *deuḷa karaṇa* for official reference. The *sevā* appeared to have been made hereditary as recorded in the Record of Rights. By the time the Record of Rights was compiled, it was no longer the practice of issuing formal *cāmu ciṭāu* to the *sevaka* and the responsibility of continuance of *Gītagovindasevā* was entrusted with the Jagannāthavallabha Maṭha and Rāghavadāsa Maṭha. One Śrī Nārāyaṇa Ācārya was engaged by them to recite the *Gītagovinda* in the temple.

Kṛṣṇa decorating Rādhā with flowers (left) and putting ornaments (right). Kṛṣṇa in supplication massages Rādhās's foot (extreme right). Symbol of fighting cock and hen indicates that the couple have settled their differences palmleaf painting, Museum Rietberg, Zurich.

The *sevā* is usually performed during *Sandhyādhūpa* at the Jaya Vijaya gate. *Ārati* is performed and this is followed by a change of dress. The deities are worshipped according to *ṣodaśopacāra pūjā*. During this *pūjā*, *ārati* is performed four times. After the *sandhyādhūpa* the deities are dressed in silken garments and sandal paste is applied over them. This is called *candanalāgi*. Then there is the recitation of the *Gītagovinda* accompanied with the melody of *vīṇā*, followed by the *badasiṇhāraveśa*. The special feature of this ritual is that a special silken cloth called *bāralāgipāṭa*, bearing a verse from the *Gītagovinda*, is offered to the deities by a temple functionary known as *cāngaṭāmekāpa*. The Britishers, whose basic policy was not to interfere in the internal affairs of the temple, had always taken keen interest to know in detail about the ritual custom of the temple in support of which there are quite a good number of documents in the Odisha State Archives. They were specially interested to know something about the *Gītagovindasevā* and *māhārī sevā* in the temple of Jagannātha and one Bengali pandit was asked to furnish a report on the ritualistic proceedings. The pandit reported that earlier there were many handsome nautch singers of some ability, who were in the habit of learning certain books, so the pilgrims had some regard for them, but the situation was changing. He stated that "those who were singing then, were totally ignorant and had no desire to learn anything." The report of Tārākānta Vidyāsāgar on the *Gītagovinda māhārīsevā* appears to have been based on a weak foundation when we study the role of different temple functionaries of the period on the basis of available records. Although it cannot be denied that the normal discipline of the temple organisation had run down by the time the report was furnished by Tarākānta Vidyāsāgar, the sanctity of different *nīti* was maintained and *sevaka* were also punished by the temple authority for causing deviation from the established custom.

Basically *māhārī* were of three orders. They were known as *patuāri*, *sampradā* and *gāuṇi māhārī*. They exchanged *sevā* or service among themselves. For their *sevā* they enjoyed land grants and received *khei* from the temple. There were another class of functionaries known as *mādeli* who made arrangements for the dance performance of *māhārī*.

Mādeli was another associate in the dance performance of *māhārī*. The word *mādeli* is derived from *mādala* and it denotes a percussionist who plays on *mādala*. The *mādeli* did not form a separate class as far as their services in the Jagannātha Temple were concerned. They were considered one with the *māhārī* and were treated like their adopted sons. Locally the *mādeli* were also known as *bhāradā*.

The *māhārī* were also known as *nācuṇī*. They rendered services to the temple depending on their *bāḍa*. The names of the *māhārī* are given below:

> Pārvātī Devadāsī of Bāśeli Sahi, Tārā Devadāsī of Mārkaṇḍeśvara Sāhi, Ratanī Devadāsī, Dukhī Devadāsī and Mahanā Devadāsī of Maṭimaṇḍapa Sāhi, Lāvaṇya Devadāsī, Hīrā Devadāsī and Phakīrī Devadāsī of Bāli Sāhi, Śaśimaṇi Devadāsī of Kuṇḍheiveṇṭa Sāhi and also Haripriyā Devadāsī of Kuṇḍheiveṇṭa Sāhi.

From among the *māhārī* listed above, most of them are dead by now. Only two, Śaśimanī Devadāsī and Haripriyā Devadāsī, are surviving. The *māhārīsevā* has almost died down. The last surviving *māhārī* Śaśimaṇi is in her late 70s, ill and even unable to stand, nevertheless being showcased in several public functions as the sole representative of the glorious divine damsels. (Dinanath Pathy, "Why Deny the Lord?" in *The Telegraph*, Monday, 9 May, 2011.)

The *māhārī* performed several duties as mentioned below:

1. Dance at the time of morning *dhūpa*.
2. Dance in the *jagamohana* during *candana yātrā* (sandal festival).
3. Dance during *cāpa* and *cāpa bāhuḍā*.
4. Dance during *Rukuṇī vivāha*.
5. Singing and sounding *huḷahuḷi* during the time of *ciṭāu lekhā* (letter writing) in the *jagamohana* of Lakṣmī Temple.
6. *Cāmarasevā* at the time of Goddess Lakṣmī's entry into the Vimalā Temple.
7. Dance procession (*paṭuāranāṭa*) during the time of *snānapūrṇimā* (bathing festival on the full moon day).
8. To accompany the Goddess Lakṣmī's procession at the time of return car festival.
9. Dance procession (*paṭuāranāṭa*) from second day onwards in the Gundicā Temple.

10. To tease (*daṇḍamaṇḍa*) the *daitāpati* and to symbolically break a piece of wood from the chariot during *Herāpaṇcamī.*
11. Dance procession (*paṭuāranāṭa*) in the *Jhulaṇa maṇḍapa.*
12. *Rohiṇī Yaśodāsevā* during *Kṛṣṇajanma.*
13. Dance procession (*paṭuāranāṭa*) during *ṣoḷapūjā* in the Vimalā Temple.
14. To accompany the *brāhmaṇa* as the messenger of Goddess Lakṣmī on the day of *Rukmiṇīharaṇa*
15. *Rohiṇī Yaśodāsevā* during *Nandotsava.*

In lieu of the above services the *māhārī* received the following from the temple:

1. *Māṭhapulibhoga.*
2. *Māṇḍuabhoga*—two *pāṭa*—each day for twenty one days during the sandal festival.
3. For cremation they are permitted to use the *vaiṣṇava agni* from the kitchen of Śrī Jagannātha Temple.

Sāḍhibandhāṇa

Their *sevā* was hereditary. But before a *māhārī* was accepted, the *niyoga,* an investiture ceremony was done which was known as *śāḍhibandhāṇa.* They had to appear for a test in the *Muktimaṇḍapa* in the presence of *brāhmaṇa* and *Rājaguru.* After they prove successful in the test, conducted on an appointed auspicious day either the *rājā* of Puri (*Ṭhākura rājā*) or the *Mudiratha* tied a *śāḍhī* on their heads at the foot of the *Ratnasimhāsana.* They painted their heads with *tilaka* with the help of clay from the Gaṅgāmātā Māṭha and put on a garland (*ajṇmālā*) from Jagannātha. They also received a *sanad* wherein their duties and their receipts from the temple were recorded.

Costume for Sevā

They wore *pāṭa,* tied *kāṇculi,* painted *ketaki citā* on their forehead, used *notha, guṇā, deśidaṇḍi, badapeṇḍi, mallakaḍi, bauli, phāsiā* and *lavaṅga,* etc. Sometimes they used *muktājāli* instead of *citā.* Mostly the hair was done in a chignon. There was no tradition to fashion the hair in a plait in Odisha. The chignon was done in two ways: one was *ardhavataka* and the other was *puṣpajuḍā.* A stick (*goikāthi*) was tucked in the chignon. They wore *cāpasari* around the neck, *ananta, bāju, tāḍa, vida* on the arms, *bāhicuḍi khaḍu* on the wrist, *goḍa khaḍu, pāunji, bāṅkiā*, or *pāhuḍa* on the leg. This costume was for the morning *dhūpa*. They dressed themselves at home and arrived at the temple accompanied by elderly *māhārī*.

The *māhārī* dressed in gaudy costumes, used sandal, camphor and wore *dayaṇā*, *maruā*, *jui* and *campak* flowers. This was known as *candanaveśa*, a costume for the *candana yātrā*. When the *māhārī* came to the Narendra pond the pilgrims and the gathering crowd prostrated before them.

Candanasevā

We get details about this *sevā* from *Nilācaḷa Mādhuri* of Chandrasekhar Patnaik. He was a *Vaiśṇava* devotee and had a team of boy dancers (*gotipua*). During the morning *dhūpa* a partition (*ṭerā*) is raised. Dance is performed in *nāṭamaṇḍapa*. Gongs are sounded and pipes are blown. The dance does not accompany singing. The dancer would offer flowers after taking five steps forward with a handful of flowers. The dancer would then dance in rhythmic beats. Unrhythmic steps would be given up. *Rājaguru* would be standing with a golden cane. *Pradhāni* also would be standing with a cane. *Minanāhaka* would be there watching.

After offering the flowers, the dancers recede five steps backwards and start dancing. Near the *simhāsana*, *pandās* would be sitting with *calu* in hand. When the image of Jagannātha is reflected in *calu*, then offerings are made.

After offering of water *pandās* do *japa*. In the meanwhile, the man beating the cymbals (*jhāṇja*) would circumambulate the temple. The partition (*ṭerā*) is lifted. The *pandās* get down from the *simhāsana*. This *sevā* is still in vogue in the temple but the tradition of *māhārī sevā* as mentioned above is no more performed in the temple.

Bhitara Gāyeṇīsevā

The *devadāsī* who performed the *bhitara gāyeṇī sevā* lived in the Bāseli Sāhi and Markaṇḍesvara Sāhi situated close to the temple, because they had to leave the temple quite late, past midnight. The *gāyeṇī māhārī* resided just behind the temple because of the same reason.

The following were the *bhitara gāyeṇī devadasī* some forty years ago. They were Kundamaṇi Devadāsī, Kokiḷapriyā Devadāsī, Tārāmaṇi Devadasī, Vasanta Devadasī, Paraśmaṇi Devadasī, Binodini Devadasī, Śrīmatī Devadasī, Subhāsini Devadasī of Bāseli Sāhi and Indumatī Devadasī of Markaṇḍeśvara Sāhi.

Devadāsīsevā

They sang songs in the morning *dhūpa*. In necessary cases they also performed dance. Each night after *badasinghāra*, the deities are laid to rest and the *śayanaṭhākura* is brought into the main temple. The *devadasī* stood at the *nandavarta* and sang the *Gītagovinda*. The *devadasī* also accompanied the *sayanaṭhākura* by singing songs. They would be standing at the Jaya Vijaya entrance and sang till the *sayanaṭhākura* rested in the sanctorum. They sang during the time of *bāladhūpa* in the month of *Kārtika*. During the forty-two days of the *Candana* festival, they sang near the *Ratnasimhāsana* from the *aṇasara piṇḍi*. They sang *bhajana* for the first twenty-one days and the *Gītagovinda* for the rest of the days. They performed dance in the *jagamohana* of the Jagannātha Temple during the twenty-one day *cāpa*. The dance is also performed in the *cāpa* of *Madanamohana*. They sing *maṅgaḷa gāna* during the marriage of Rukmiṇi inside the Lakṣmī Temple. They accompany the bride and bridegroom up to the *Rājā*'s palace on *Campaka Dvādasi* day. They would accompany Lakṣmī to *bheta maṇḍapa* during *Niḷādri vije*. On the first day of *Guṇḍicā* they would perform dance in the *Guṇḍicā maṇḍapa*. During the month of *Āśvina*, they would dance in the Vimaḷā Temple at the time of morning *dhūpa*.

At the time of *Pahudamājaṇā* of the goddess Vimaḷā they would be singing *māḷaśrī*. Only *devadāsī* are allowed into the Vimaḷā Temple, during the sixteen day ritual in the month of September/October. In the palace they do arrangements for *paṭuāra* in the *Kanaka Durgā Pūjā* on the *puṣyābhiṣeka*.

Legends

Pramila Mishra

The ancient poets rarely left references about them in their works. Occasionally they mentioned names which were not enough to build up a literary history or a historical chronology. Therefore research tends to depend largely on the legends flourished and accumulated centering the poet and his work. Legend and history complement each other. Sometimes history is framed on the merits of legends and legends are fabricated out of the hard facts of history.

Therefore to reconstruct a convincing history about Jayadeva and his work the *Gītagovinda*, we have to rely on several legends and stories in vogue in Odisha and other parts of the country. The traditions figuring the poet in different regional traditions are sometimes similar and at times variable. These legends thus collected from various sources are incorporated in several books such as Sanskrit *Bhaktamāḷā* by Maithili Pandit Candradutta, Oriya *Dārdhyatā Bhakti Rasāmṛta* by Rāma Dāsa, Hindi commentary of Nāvāji Goswāmī's *Bhaktamāḷā* by Priya Dāsa, *Jayadevacarita* of Banamāli Dāsa, *Bhaktamāḷā* of Śrī Kṛṣṇa Dāsa and story on Jayadeva in *Seikh Subhodaya* in Bengali, Marathi *Bhaktī Vijaya* of Mahīpatī, etc.

In collaboration with the above mentioned works, the legends regarding Jayadeva and *Gītagovinda* prevalent in Odisha are presented below and their relevant versions mentioned as footnotes.

Early Life

Jayadeva was born in the village Kenduvilva or Kenduli near Puruṣottama Kṣetra (Puri) in Odisha. He acquired proficiency in different branches of Sanskrit learning. He lost his parents when he was barely eleven years old. Earlier his parents had to mortgage their house to a neighbour to clear a debt. After their death the neighbour demanded the house from Jayadeva as per the agreement and Jayadeva parted with the parental house without hesitation. But while the neighbour was taking

Facing page: Sakhī *inplores Kṛṣṇa inside a wooded* kuñja, *palmleaf painting, Museum Rietberg Zurich.*

possession of the house all of a sudden his own house caught fire. At the sight of the incident the young Jayadeva instantly ran inside the house and recovered the household belongings. At this benevolent gesture a great change occurred in the mind and heart of the neighbour and he wished to return back the house to Jayadeva. But Jayadeva was firm in his decision and renouncing the property he left for Puruṣottama Kṣetra where he first lived as a *sādhu* (mendicant) under a tree and then shifted to a thatched cottage around *Śrīkṣetra*, and spent time in religious pursuits.

A childless *brāhmaṇa* named Devaśarmā came to *Śrīkṣetra*, begged for a child before Lord Jagannātha and promised to dedicate the blessed child in the services of the Lord after he/she grew up. In course of time he was blessed with a beautiful girl child whom the parents named Padmāvatī as the child appeared to them like Lakṣmī.

When the child grew up and attained puberty the devoted Devaśarmā visited *Śrīkṣetra* with his family and was directed in a dream by the Lord to find out his devotee Jayadeva who would be the suitable groom for Padmāvatī. Jayadeva at that time was living as a recluse under a tree deeply engaged in study and meditation. Obeying the dictates of the Lord, the couple left Padmāvatī near Jayadeva in spite of the latter's strong unwillingness to accept her as his wife. They then returned back to their native village. Jayadeva too received the orders of Jagannātha in a dream and Padmāvatī served Jayadeva with sincere devotion. Immensely pleased at Padmāvatī's behaviour, he accepted her hand as his wife. After his marriage with Padmāvalī they shifted to a thatched cottage at a sacred place where the images of Śrī Rādhā-Mādhava were installed. As time passed feelings of deep love and inseparableness developed within their hearts. They sang songs and danced together in the service of Lord Kṛṣṇa.

In other accounts, it was mentioned that after their marriage the couple went to Kenduli where they worshipped Rādhā-Mādhava in the local Viṣṇu Temple.

Yet in some accounts Devaśarmā forgot his vow to dedicate his daughter to the Lord. As soon as the daughter attained puberty, once all of a sudden, one day, she suffered from high fever which appeared difficult to be cured. In a period of utter remorse his past memory flashed across his mind. The parents were also ordered by Śrī Jagannātha in a dream to fulfil their vow and acquire 'Jaya'.

Thereafter, the parents started off to *Śrīkṣetra* with Padmāvatī. They performed the necessary rituals for dedicating their daughter to the Lord and returned home leaving her inside the Jagannātha Temple complex. Unfortunately it was a rainy night. While Padmāvatī stood silently not knowing what to do she met an old priest of the temple engaged in philosophical discussions with Jayadeva. She fell at his feet and earnestly requested him to save her life. It had so happened that the old priest had lost his only daughter a few days ago. As such he took pity on her and requested Jayadeva to marry her. But Jayadeva, being shocked at the unexpected offer, ran away to his cottage in that heavy rain. Padmāvalī followed him, instructed by the priest, and went inside his cottage completely drenched. Bewildered at the situation Jayadeva prayed to Lord Jagannātha. Candra, the nephew of Jayadeva, was however charmed to have a glimpse of the beautiful face of Padmāvalī in that darkness: Addressing her as aunt he welcomed her with much hospitality. Subsequently Jayadeva married her in accordance with the Vedic rites.

Rest of the Life

While staying in his āśrama at Puri, Jayadeva started composing the *Gītagovinda* for the satisfaction of Lord Jagannātha. He sang his poems before the Lord with devotion while his wife Padmāvatī danced. Once, while the composition of *Gītagovinda* was in progress, he went for bath, stumped and confused about a particular phrase in a song of the tenth canto. He hesitated to write down the idea, purporting to be a request of Lord Kṛṣṇa to Rādhā, to place her feet on His head as a mark of His intense love for her. Jayadeva used to take his bath daily in the sea which was about a mile away from his residence. While he was away for his bath, Lord Śrīkṛṣṇa came in the guise of Jayadeva and scribed the line "*Dehi padapallavamudāraṃ*" on the palm-leaf manuscript. On his return from bath Jayadeva was pleasantly amazed to read the mysteriously written lines. His wife narrated the uncommon event. Jayadeva was bewildered. On that very night, Lord Puruṣottama Jagannātha visited him in a dream and Jayadeva was overjoyed to realise that his wife was indeed fortunate enough to have *darśana* of Śrī Kṛṣṇa in person. Once again it so happened that Śrī Kṛṣṇa himself repaired the straw-roof of the cottage of Jayadeva in disguise. *Sādhu* Jayadeva's devotion towards God was intensified from those events and he offered his poetie creation, the *Gītagovinda* to Śrī Jagannātha.

The glory of the work and the fame of the poet spread far and wide. The king of Utkala was pleased to realise the value of the work and was inspired to prepare a similar work, and titled it *Abhinava-Gītagovinda.* He even ordained that only the songs of *Abhinava-Gītagovinda* should be sung during the daily rituals of Lord Jagannātha. But Jayadeva used to sing his *Gītagovinda* before Śrī Jagannātha as usual. This created a controversy and meant defiance of the king's order. Then in order to weigh both the works they were kept inside the sanctum of the temple at night and the doors were sealed. The next morning, to the utter surprise of everybody present, the *Gītagovinda* of Jayadeva was found kept above the other. The same night the desperate king was also directed in a dream by Śrī Jagannātha to give publicity to the glory of Jayadeva's *Gītagovinda*.

Padmāvatī, the ideal devoted wife, decided to copy out the entire *Gītagovinda* on *tulasī* leaves with sandal paste and offer the leaves to the Lord. She tried her best but it seemed as if the work could not be completed within the stipulated period. She became intensely worried. One night two *sādhu* approached her and copied out the rest of the text. She was delighted and went to the temple to offer the garland of *tuḷasī* leaves with the *Gītagovinda* scribed on them to the Lord, but was not allowed to do so by the temple priests. In despair she took back the garland and threw it into the sea. To the great astonishment of all, the next morning when the temple doors were opened, the same garland was seen adorning the neck of Lord Jagannātha. Thus the *Gītagovinda* was declared as dear to the Lord and Padmāvatī as a true and sincere devotee.

Once a village woman, while plucking brinjals in her kitchen-garden, was singing the melodious songs of the *Gītagovinda*. Lord Jagannātha, moved by her song, left the temple and followed the woman listening and enjoying her melodious tune. Because of this the Lord's cloth was torn by the thorns of the brinjal plants. He returned to the temple hurriedly soon after the woman's departure. The torn clothes were detected by the chief priest the next morning and he was confused how that could have happened. The priest and the *rājā* of Puri were told about the whole incident in a dream that night. Thereafter the village woman was sent for and was appointed by the king to sing the verses of the *Gītagovinda* while the temple rituals were performed before Lord Jagannātha.

At the same time, as a precautionary measure, the king prohibited the singing of the *Gītagovinda* outside the temple premises. Violating the king's order one Muslim youth recited a few of the songs from the *Gītagovinda* while passing by the temple on horseback. Śrī Jagannātha, enchanted at the melody of his favourite songs, appeared before the youth to listen to his renderings. The Muslim singer thus could get the *darśana* of the Lord and was liberated.

Twelve pieces of sacred cloth, each one woven with a canto of the *Gītagovinda* were later introduced in the temple ritual for use of the Lord. The expert weavers of the Kenduli village were assigned the work of weaving the *Gītagovinda.* It was also then decided that Jayadeva would sing the songs while they were at their looms. Thus the work continued uninterrupted and one day while they were on the seventh *sarga,* Jayadeva became overwhelmed with emotion and went into a state of ecstasy and eventually the weavers stopped their work. A strange thing happened. Mysteriously, a *sādhu* appeared in front of the weavers' houses and sang the remaining lines of the canto, as a result of which the weavers could finish the weaving.

Once, in order to test the chastity of Padmavati, as well as her love for her husband, the queen sent her a false news of the sudden death of Jayadeva who had accompanied the king to the temple. Garments dipped in blood were also displayed before Padmāvatī. Unable to cope with the tragedy, she fell down unconscious and died instantly. The queen was utterly shocked and was in panic. The king and Jayadeva learnt the whole affair after their return from the temple. The angry king ordered punishment for the queen immediately. The saint Jayadeva, being very compassionate towards the queen, prayed for pardon, sat in deep meditation and was soon immersed in singing the songs of the *Gītagovinda.* To the astonishment of the entire crowd Padmāvatī regained consciousness as if woken up from a swoon.

Another day, Jayadeva, invited by some of his disciples visited them in a far off village. His disciples honoured him and presented him with valuable jewellery and clothing. On his way back through a jungle he was attacked by a group of robbers. To get rid of the robbers, he handed over the entire wealth to them, but still the cruel robbers chopped off his hands and feet and deserted him in that helpless condition. Unperturbed even at the grievous physical injury, he, in rare composure, prayed to his Lord and was rescued from the great disaster.

Fortunately he was found by the king during his hunting expedition and was brought back and left under the care of Padmāvatī. After a few days the same set of robbers once again appeared at his house but were received cordially by Padmāvatī. Though Jayadeva could recognise the thieves, yet he requested the king to give them back the jewels they had robbed and the king fulfilled Jayadeva's wishes. Under the instructions of Jayadeva the robbers were escorted by a group of royal attendants on their way back through the jungle.

The robbers, overtaken by the greatness of Jayadeva, narrated before the royal attendants the foul-play against Jayadeva. It so happened that the robbers were struck by thunder and died in the jungle. The noble hearted Jayadeva became very much worried at the news of their death. His wife Padmāvatī nursed Jayadeva day in and day out. By the mercy of God he got back his limbs that had been chopped off by the robbers. Then he and his wife spent the rest of their life in *Śrīkṣetra* singing the *Gītagovinda.*

Legends also tell us that *Maharṣī* Vyāsa Deva had appeared as Jayadeva in the *Kali Yuga.* He had extraordinary talents in the *Vedas* and *Purāṇas.* As mentioned in the *Padma Purāṇa* he had narrated the divine and mysterious *līla* of Śrī Rādhākṛṣṇa through the lucid, soft and enchanting songs of the *Gītagovinda* for the liberation of mankind.

The saint Jayadeva used to take his daily bath in the *Trievṇī saṅgama* of the Prācī and worship the Triveṇī Mādhava who is still worshipped on the *ghāt.*

Once he fell down unconscious on the road while returning from the river. Fortunately the king saw him and took proper care. The king offered a vehicle and requested him to use it for going to the river daily. But Jayadeva politely declined the king's magnanimity and continued with his old habit.

The pious couple intensely desired to go on pilgrimage to Vṛndāvana *Dhāma* with the images of Rādhā-Kṛṣṇa which were rather heavy. As told in a dream by the Lord, the problem of carrying those images was solved by the transformation of the idols into *Sāḷagrāma,* which on arrival at Vrindāvana, assumed the original shape of stone idols. The couple worshipped the images till the end of their life.

PERFORMING ARTS

Music

Nilamadhava Panigrahi

The *Gītagovinda* surpasses all other preceding works of the great master-poets by its sheer lyricality and inspiring expressiveness, though not so much through its poetic greatness. For example, Kalidasa's *Meghadūta* is a far greater *kāvya* in terms of poetic value. But, by its three-dimensional[1] appeal of music, poetry and mystic spiritual contents, the *Gītagovinda* has earned unsurpassed popularity, tantamount to adoration. So amazing has been its popularity for the last eight hundred and odd years that it can be said to have 'charmed, enraptured, feasted and fed' the mind and soul of the people of India and abroad.

The *Gītagovinda* was regularly sung and danced in the temple of Jagannātha at Puri till recently as a part of the Lord's nocturnal liturgy, perhaps from the days of Jayadeva and undoubtedly from the days of Gajapati Pratāprudradeva who promulgated an order, perpetuated by an inscription dated AD 8.7.1500, to the effect that the singing of the *Gītagovinda* would henceforth be a compulsory daily ritual in the temple of Jagannātha. The king even appointed singers and dancers for the purpose.[2]

The inscription still survives there in the temple wall but the song and dance have since been silenced. It is difficult to believe that there was any regular and unbroken musical tradition in the Indian subcontinent, not excluding Odisha, right from the first part of the 13th century AD, when the *Gītagovinda* was supposed to have gained wide admiration and popularity. By musical tradition we mean what is commonly known as *guru śiṣya paramparā* or *sampradāya*.

The art of music being an art in 'time' and not in 'space' and there being no mechanical device to record the music prevalent in mediaeval India, it is unthinkable how any kind of music could retain, even its

Facing page: *Kṛṣṇa fluting beneath a* kadamba *tree, palmleaf painting Museum Rietberg Zurich.*

Page 125: *Kṛṣṇa pining for Rādhā and on the lower panel dancing with* sakhī*, palmleaf painting Museum Rietberg Zurich.*

---

1 K.N. Mahapatra, *Śrī Jayadeva Ó Śrī Gītagovinda* (Oriya), p.12.

2 Ibid. p. 15.

pristine 'form', not to speak of its transient 'content', that keeps on changing with time despite being cultivated by the most conservative and rigid performers, particularly of vocal music. And again, admitting that Jayadeva, the poet-musician, had himself tuned the songs of his *Gītagovinda* in the *rāga* and *tāla* which are found mentioned with each song and probably copied out without interpolation in the later texts, was it not open to and possible for other musicians to sing or tune the songs in a different form and style within the sound structure of the original *rāga* and *tāla* in a more evolved manner? Was it, again not a possibility for such other better styles to influence, alter and even efface the original and in a way supplement the original? These questions arise naturally when one has to ponder over the original *rāga* and *tāla* set by Jayadeva.

According to Rāṇā Kumbha, the *prabandha* composed by the poet Jayadeva lacks proper form as it goes without all the different *aṅga* (limbs or constituents) that characterise a *prabandha*. Therefore, he was, he says, fixing up the different limbs such as *svara*, (*tāla*, *pāṭa*, *tena*) etc and shaping them properly, putting it to practical singing and introducing it after discarding the bad commentaries thereon.[3]

Kumbha's *Saṅgītarāja* and *Rasikapriyā* were written almost simultaneously in the year 1456 AD [4]. So the 'bad commentaries' referred to by Kumbha are those that were written prior to the year 1456 AD namely, *Sāradīpikā* by Jagaddhāra (who also wrote a music treatise named *Saṅgītasarvasva*), *Sandakbhadīpikā* by Dhṛiti Kara alias Dāsa, *Sarvāṅgasundarī* by Nārāyaṇa Dāsa, *Tippanikā* by Manāṅka and last but not the least, *Bhāvavibhāvinī* by Udayana Acārya, which perhaps was the very first commentary on the *Gītagovinda*. These were not the only ones; some more, as some of these commentaries show, had also been written and some of the commentaries have tried to elucidate some of the *rāga*. By the end of the 18th century many more commentaries were added.

A study of most of the available commentaries reveals that perhaps the commentators were learned scholars in Sanskrit but were not equally proficient in the theory and practice of music. Perhaps they did not possess adequate knowledge in respect of the most vital aspect of Indian

---

3 Two copper plate inscriptions of King Narasimha Deva IV of Orissa in *J.A.S.B.* Vol. LXIV, 1895.

4 S.N. Rajaguru "The Kenduli copper plate grant of Narasimha Deva IV", in *O.H.R.J.* Vol. V, No. 1, pp. 1-100, 1956.

music namely, *rāga*. Music being the finest of the fine-arts and being different from poetry, the sentiments of *rāga* cannot be equated with the poetic or dramaturgical sentiments. It has its own language and *rāga* have to be defined, described and introduced in that language.

Most of the commentators disappoint us in our quest for the *svara* structures of the *rāga* of the *Gītagovinda* songs.

As regards the tradition, the comments of Barbara Stoller Miller, one of the most well-informed and erudite editors of the *Gītagovinda*, seem to be true. She observes:

> "Although the oldest manuscripts show striking agreement in designating a group of eleven different *rāga* for the twenty four songs, there has been no traditional transmission or notation to assure that these names designate the same melodic patterns they do in later time. The fact that many commentators are preoccupied with defining the *rāga* in terms of the Indian music theory suggests that the songs were variously interpreted throughout their history"[5].

We would not like to deal with the other musical aspects of the *Gītagovinda* with the observation that in the absence of a living tradition as old as the poet Jayadeva the only other way of forming an idea of the melodic implications of the *rāga* in question is to take the help of music treatises written either during the period to which Jayadeva belonged or during the not-too distant past. Treatises of the period posterior to the poet will, when relevant, be consulted.

The *Gītagovinda*, as its very name suggests, is a work which sings the glories of Govinda, the cowherd lord or, simply Kṛṣṇa. It may also mean 'Songs on the Art of Love of Govinda or Kṛṣṇa'.

5 H.K. Mahtab, *History of Orissa*, Vol. 1, pp.203-204.

Kṛṣṇa in the forest standing under a kadamba *tree flanked by cows and deer, palmleaf painting, Museum Rietberg Zurich.*

Songs or *gīta* are believed in India to be one of the best things that please God.[6] So poet Jayadeva has offered his devotion to Him in the form of *gīta.*

Immediately after the opening stanza, the poet says that he was composing a *prabandha* containing the amorous sports of Lord Kṛṣṇa.[7]

What is a *gīta* and what is a *prabandha?*

In common parlance any versified composition meant for singing is a *gīta.* But technically, i.e., in the sphere of musicology it has been differently conceived of and differently defined in the different periods of its history and evolution in India. Perhaps the first treatise to define *gīta* is *Mānasollāsa*, an encyclopaedia of the 12th century AD. According to it, a composition where *svara*, *pada* and *tāla* have been blended is called a *gīta.*

The compositions of the *Gītagovinda* seem to conform to the definition of *Mānasollāsa* whose author may be taken as a representative of the age to which Jayadeva, the author of the compositions, belonged. That there has been the happiest blend of *pada* and *tāla* in the compositions of Jayadeva is an unquestionable truth and the introduction of *svara* into the blend is now a job for the performer.

As regards *prabandha*, an epithet used by the poet Jayadeva for his *Gītagovinda*, it is used perhaps to signify both a literary and musical *prabandha* which is called so because it is, says *Saṅgītacuḍāmani* (12th century AD).

The *dhātū* are different parts of the melodic structure of a *prabandha.* The four *dhātū* are

(1) *udgrāha*

(2) *melapāka*

(3) *dhruva*

(4) *ābhoga.*

A *prabandha* need not always have all the four parts. It can have even two or three.[8] When it is composed of two parts the *melapāka* and the *ābhoga* part are discarded. In that case it consists of the *udgrāha* and the *dhruva.* When it is composed of three parts, either of the two parts *melapāka* and *ābhoga* is dropped.[9]

---

6 C.V. Ramachandra Rao, *Administration and Society in Medieval Andhra,* p. 231.

7 *South Indian Inscriptions,* Vol. IV. pp. 1191-94.

8 H.C. Das, *Socio cultural life during the rule of Imperial Gaṅgas,* Vol. XXVII, No. 1-4, pp.73-74.

9 Ibid.

The six *aṅga* or limbs of a *prabandha* are the different elements used in framing both its melodic, verbal and rhythmic structure.[10]

A *prabandha* can have any number of *aṅga* but always more than one. Thus it can have six, five, four, three or two. According to the number of these, it will be deemed to belong respectively to *medini, ānandinī, dīpanī, bhavāni* and *tārāvali* class.

Thus, in the medieval period of Indian music, a *prabandha* was conceived of as a living, dynamic embodiment of music the '*prabandha puruṣa*' having *svara* and *tāla* as two legs, *pāṭa* and *viruda* as two hands and *tena* and *pada* as two eyes.

It is strange that none of the music treatises of the 13th, 14th and 15th centuries have referred to or quoted any of the songs of Jayadeva's *Gītagovinda* in connection with *prabandha* despite the widespread popularity and excellence of the compositions. The only exception in this respect is the *Saṅgītarāja* of Rāṇā Kumbhakarṇa who, as we have already mentioned, wrote his *Rasikapriyā* commentary on it. The apparent attitude of indifference on the part of musicologists as well as the shallow analysis of the musical aspects of the *Gītagovinda* can only be explained historically.

Indian music was passing through a ferment during the 13th and 14th centuries particularly after the advent of Amir Khusro who, it is believed, was trying to bring about a fusion of the music of India and that of Persia which the Muslims brought with them. The ancient music system of India, based on *grāma, murchanā*, etc for expressing the theoretical aspects of the *rāga*, was gradually giving way to the new system based on *mela* which was adopted from Persian music. Introduction of new musical instruments for playing the Indian *rāga* added to the confusion resulting from the fusion referred to above. Thus the music of the *Gītagovinda* could not find proper expression theoretically and, as we have already shown earlier, its continuation in its pristine melodic form and content was not possible.

---

10 S.N. Rajaguru, *Inscriptions of Orissa*, Vol. III, pt-I, p.251.

View of a forest, with monkey, deer, mongoose and a peacock. Palmleaf painting, Orissa State Museum.

As regards the outer structure of the songs, they appear to be the earliest examples of their kind in Sanskrit literature. In the regional languages, however, composition of that kind had already gained popularity. Particularly in the languages of the north-eastern part of India (Odisha, Bihar, Assam and Bengal) quite a large number of songs had been composed by Buddhist monks of the *Sahajiyā* cult and were known as *caryāpada* which were esoteric and spiritual in content. Popular images in common language had been chosen from common social life and used in the songs so as to attract the common mass. Almost each of these songs which were first discovered for us by M.M. Haraprasad Sastri is earmarked to be sung in a particular *rāga* named above it. A few such *rāga* are *gauḍa, gurjarī, deśākhya, rāmakeri, bhairavī*, etc.

These have been recognised as *caryāprabandha* in music treatises like *Mānasollāsa, Saṅgītaratnākara* of Śārṅgadeva, etc. Both these volumes were works of the medieval period and the first one was almost contemporary to the *Gītagovinda*, while the second was written just about a century later.

On an analytical assessment, many a song of the *Gītagovinda* will be found to be *Caryāprabandha.*

The second trait of *Caryāprabandha* is *antyānuprāsa* or 'endrhyme'. This is so obvious and so perfect in each of the songs of the *Gītagovinda* except No. 2, that it need not be pointed out.

The third trait of a *Caryāprabandha* is that it should have spiritual ideas as its content. That the *Gītagovinda* is almost a religious scripture for a large number of people is too well-known to need any proof. As the *caryāpada* of the Buddhist monks have an inner, different, spiritual meaning apart from what is outwardly conveyed, so, too the songs of the *Gītagovinda* have a spiritual meaning under the apparently erotic garb. The fourth trait of a *caryāprabandha* is the employment of a *tāla* named *dvitīyādi* which, according to its definition, comes to be one of eight *mātrā* or beats. The *tāla* or time-measure can be very suitably employed in the songs scanned above and in many more songs having lines of sixteen mores. The *tāla* will have two complete cycles (*āvarta*) in each line and will present no difficulty.

Thus song No. 9 of the *Gītagovinda* conforms to all the conditions of a *caryāprabandha* of the *Saṅgītaratnākara* and is of the *viśamadhruva* variety or genre of *caryā.*

"*Nātha Hare sīdati Rādhā vasagṛhe*"

Similarly, songs numbering 14, 16 and 18 will also come under the *caryā* class.

The *caryāprabandha*, nay, most of the numerous medieval *prabandha*, lost their popularity in course of time and the *caryā* songs were lost in oblivion with the advent of new religious cults. It is, therefore, not surprising to find some later music treatises differently classifying most of the *Gītagovinda* songs. Thus, the *Gītaprakāśa*, a 16th century treatise written by Kṛṣnadāsa Baḍajenā Mahāpātra of Odisha, says that the *Gītagovinda* of *Mahākavi* Jayadeva contains a large number of songs of a hybrid class as they bear characteristics both of the *citrapada* and *citrakala* varieties.[12] The *Saṅgītakalpikā* (c. 1635 AD) written by Haladhara Mishra is also of the above opinion and has tried to justify it by concrete analysis of a song of the *Gītagovinda*.

However, we think that according to the 12th-13th century concept of Indian music, many of the *Gītagovinda* songs would perhaps be termed as *caryāprabandha* and all the songs would be classified as *taravali* as they have only *pada* and *tāla*.

Of course Rāṇā Kumbha, the author of the *Rasikapriyā* commentary on the *Gītagovinda*, in his great zeal to give a grand, medieval musical setting to Jayadeva's compositions, attempted to introduce into them almost all the parts of a *prabandha* (namely, *svara, tena, pāṭa*, etc) and even *āḷāpa*. But to project the songs of Jayadeva exclusively or even predominantly as musical compositions would perhaps be incompatible with the spirit of the *Gītagovinda* which, according to the poet himself, is intended to satisfy the three-fold objects, namely of music, poetry and spirituality. One has to remember always that the *pada*, i.e. the verbal aspect of the *Gītagovinda* should never be weighed down or subordinated to the melodic and other musical aspects.

Let us first look at the *pada* and try to understand the rhythmic side of the *Gītagovinda*.

Rhythm and *tāla* (time-measure)

Each of the compositions of the *Gītagovinda* (including even the stanzas in syllabic meters such as *śārdūlavikrīḍita, vasantatilaka, drutavilambita*, etc) can be treated as *nibaddha gīta* and can be put to singing. In fact, the *Rasikapriyā* commentary of Rāṇā Kumbha made a laudable attempt in this direction. The songs of the *Gītagovinda* being *nibaddha gīta*, they have to be set to befitting *tāla* while rendering them to actual singing. The *Sarvāṅgasundarī* commentary of *Kavirāja* Nārāyaṇa Dāsa of Odisha is silent on the *tāla*, though the names of the *rāga* have been indicated for each of the songs. Indicating *tāla* for the songs appears to have been acts of musicians and commentators later than Jayadeva and had vexing variability in this respect which is noticed in the manuscripts.

Tāla or time-measure in lyrical music

Lyrical music (by which we mean that type of music in which sweet poetry is attempted to be made sweeter still by the employment of melody) employs time-measures of a simple pattern. These time-measures are generally 'even' i.e. they consist of equal number of beats in each division and are preferred to the 'uneven' ones which demand more time-consciousness and are bolder in rhythm than the even time-measures. The melody aspect of a composition gets comparatively free scope to express itself in the even time-measure and that is what lyrical music needs most.

The tempo or *laya* in music is a big factor that determines its emotional quality and character. Lyrical music generally favours the fast and the medium, rarely the slow tempo.

As already seen, the *Gītagovinda* of Jayadeva consists of twenty-four songs of which only four are composed in metres favourable for the uneven time-measures. The rest are meant for the application of the even time-measures.

Metres in Sanskrit are broadly of two classes, known respectively as *vṛtta* and *jāti*. All the twenty-four songs of the *Gītagovinda* are composed in moric metres and the rest i.e. all the other stanzas are in syllabic metres excepting a few in *āryā* metre which is a variety of moric metre.

We have already shown earlier that most probably, Jayadeva had, before his creative vision, the *caryāprabandha* as his ideal as far as the form of the *Gītagovinda* songs was concerned. The most 'common' metre for these was the *paddhati* alias *pajjhatika* metre having sixteen mores or *mātras* in each *pada* although other metres could also be used.

This has no end-rhyme but rhyme is not the only aspect that singles out Jayadeva's compositions as lyrics of unparallel rhythmic beauty.

It is to be noticed that *Gītagovinda* commentators Rāṇā Kumbha, Lakṣmaṇa Sūri and Śamkara Miśra have indicated either *nissāra* or *rūpaka tāla* for song No. 9 which, we are afraid, do not fit in with the natural metrical pattern and, if employed will injure the spirit and beauty of the metre. Most of the Odia editions of the *Gītagovinda* have indicated the Odishan *ekatāḷi tāḷa* which, consisting of four *mātrā* according to its current as well as ancient application, can fit in very well with the metrical pattern. The *āditāḷa* of the second variety, i.e. *dvitīya tāḷa*, recommended in the *Saṅgītaratnākara* is the ideal *tāḷa* for song No. 9 which, as we have previously shown, is a *caryāprabandha*.

One should not forget that these *prabandha* of the *Gītagovinda* are not 'recitative stanzas' but 'songs' which have to be sung by the application of a suitable time-measure consisting of *āvartas* or rhythm-cycles of equal *mātrā*. So, if the *dhruva* which, as it is, consists of fifteen *mātrā*, is not equalised with the other lines, each of which consists of sixteen *mātrā* the *dhruva* of the other songs can be given necessary rhythmic setting on the considerations applied to the *dhruva* of song No. 9.

Melodic aspect of the *Gītagovinda*

We can now make a brief assessment of the melodic aspect of the *Gītagovinda*. In this connection we remind the readers of the valuable observation of Pandit V.N. Bhatkhande which we have quoted almost at the outset of our discussion.

It is well-known that almost all the medieval poetic pieces were intended either to be recited or sung. Those that were intended to be sung usually bore the name of some *rāga*. The choice of the *rāga* might have been made arbitrarily by the writer of the poetic piece without any consideration for the spirit or *bhāva* of the *rāga* and the spirit of the piece; yet, singing of the piece in that very *rāga* is looked upon as a matter of respect for the poet and a matter of pride of our own musical antiquity. Hence, most of us would like to hear the songs of the *Gītagovinda* in the *rāga* indicated for each. The following *rāga* are generally found to have been indicated for the twenty-four *prabandha* of the *Gītagovinda*:

1. *Mālwā* or *Gauḍamālava* or *Mālavagouḍa* - Song Nos. 1 and 13.
2. *Gurjari* - Song Nos. 2, 5, 7, 11, 15, and 18.
3. *Vasanta*- Nos. 3, 14 and 20
4. *Rāmakri-Rāmakeri or Rāmakiri* - Nos. 4, 23, and 24
5. *Gunḍakeri, Goṇḍakri* or *Guṇḍakriti* - Nos. 6 and 12
6. *Karnāṭa* - No. 8
7. *Desakhy* - No. 9
8. *Varādi* or *Deśavarāḍi* - Nos. 10, 16, 21 and 22
9. *Bhairava* or *Bhairavi* - No. 17.

Another *rāga* named *vibhāsa* also appears to have been indicated in some editions and manuscripts for song No. 23. It is only in the *Rasikapriyā* commentary of Rāṇā Kumbha that a marked departure has been made in the matter of indicating the *rāga*. Other commentaries reveal a sort of agreement in naming the *rāga*.

Jayadeva himself has used the name of only one *rāga*, namely, *pañcama* in the body of Song No. 4. It is evident that poet Jayadeva was fond of this great, ancient *grāmarāga*. Strangely however this *rāga* has not been indicated for any of the twenty-four songs of the *Gītagovinda*. If Jayadeva himself indicated the *rāga* that are now found on top of the songs, it remains to be explained how he could leave out *pañcama rāga*. But we need not enter into the controversy of whether the *rāga* now found in the *Gītagovinda* were at all the choice of Jayadeva himself. At least this much is certain that almost all the commentaries written on the *Gītagovinda* during the period beginning from the 14th century AD down to the 18th century AD have 'generally' used the *rāga* we have listed above and the songs were sung accordingly.

The *rāga* of the *Gītagovinda* are not uncommon ones in the sense that these *rāga* are also found to have been defined and described in the music-treatises of the age to which the *Gītagovinda* belonged. Many of the *rāga* had actually been used in compositions earlier than the *Gītagovinda* and were in vogue then.

Again, many of the said *rāga* are even now in vogue under names which have been slightly changed in the process of linguistic evolution, and due to impact of regional influence. In the northern Indian system of music (Hindustani music), we now have *vasant, rāmakeli, gunkali, kanaḍa, deosakh, varāḍi, bhairav, bhairavī, gurjarī (toḍī) mālavī,* etc. Some of these are also found in the current music system of southern India (Carnatic music). But though there is a similarity in the name, the melodic content of almost all the *rāga* have changed vitally. This has been so on account of change in the vibrational values of the notes used in the *rāga* under the *mela* or *thāṭ* system which came into being from the 15th century. Prior to this, the notes were fixed according to the *grāma-murchanā* system and had different vibrational values. For example, if we compare the notes of *rāga vasanta* as it is sung now-a-days and defined in the current music treatises with the notes given in the medieval music treatises for the same *rāga*, we can at once discover the great difference.

However, this need not vex us. *Rāga* indicated in the *Gītagovinda* may just be taken as guidelines for using certain notes in singing. After all, the *prabandha* of the medieval period were not always meant to be used as vehicles for providing free and full movement of *rāga* or for the full melodic development of the *rāga*. The songs of the *Gītagovinda* really belong to that type of music where poetry and melody are of equal importance. They are not to be sung like *dhrupad* or *khayāl* of northern Indian music or to be used as mediums for exhibiting the technical skills of the art. Rather, the songs of the *Gītagovinda* are best rendered in the style of *bhajans* wherein the feelings and emotions contained in the words and *pada* are of primary importance. It is enough if the *pada* are rendered sweetly and rhythmically, with the aid of suitable musical notes so as to intensify the poetic *bhāvas.*

Even then, our reverence for antiquity and for the great poet Jayadeva would be gratified highly if we can put the songs of the *Gītagovinda* in the *rāga* which are generally indicated for them in the texts and commentaries belonging to the period that gave birth to it.

The following books and articles by scholars specialising in music, *Gītagovinda* and Odisha were consulted in support of the theories and issues discussed above relating to music and *Gītagovinda*'s impact on music and poetry of the times:

1 N.K. Sahoo, Jayadeva the poet of the *Gītagovinda*, His date and place, in *Souvenir of Shri Jayadeva* 1968, p.16.

2 S.N. Rajaguru, *Inscriptions of Orissa*, Vol. I part-II, p.163

3 "Kurumakela Charter of Shatrubhanja, *J.B.O.R.S.* Vol. II, pp.429-35.

4. S.N. Rajaguru, "Copper plate grant of Ranaka Shatrubhanja", *O.H.R.J.* Vol. II.

5 S.N. Rajaguru, *I.O.* Vol. II, p.282.

6 *The pillar Inscriptions of Rellivalsa* Vol. III, pt-II, p.279.

7 P. Acharya, "On the worship of images of Rādhā-Kṛṣṇa", in *Souvenir on Shri Jayadeva* 1968, p.56.

8 Devangana Desai, *Erotic Sculptures of India, Socio-Cultural Study*, 1973, pp.106-107.

9 P. Acharya, *Studies in Orissa History, Archaeology and Archives*, p.76.

10 S.N. Rajaguru, *Inscriptions of Orissa*, Vol. III, pt-II, p.335.

11 C.B. Ramachandra Rao, *Administration and Society in Medieval Andhra*, pp.324.

12 Kedarnath Mahapatra, *Śrī Jayadeva Ó Gītagovinda*, p.49.

Dance

Deba Prasad Das

In ancient and medieval Odisha, the temples and the *maṭha* were centres for promotion of all kinds of arts. A temple itself was the embodiment of architecture, sculptural art and painting. It gave partonage to poets, dancers, sculptors and painters. The inner yards of the temples were the places where performances were held to entertain the gathering devotees. All the best literary creations were composed in the serene ambience of the temple. The poet at the outset invoking the grace of the presiding deity of the temple indulged in poetic creations.

The *Gītagovinda* which has created a considerable sensation in the fields of art and literature of this country is believed to be the product of the Jagannātha Temple of Puri, where it is sung and recited in important rituals since several centuries.

Jayadeva in the introductory verse of *Gītagovinda* has sung the praise of Kṛṣṇa and declared himself as *Padmāvatīcaraṇacāraṇacakravarti.*[1] This declaration proves his versatility in the art of music and dance. As per a legend, Padmāvatī was a beautiful young *devadāsī* who later on became the life partner of Jayadeva. Before his marriage to Padmāvatī, Jayadeva was well-known as a master of music, dance and drama and was taking delight in singing his *Gītagovinda* in the temple of Lord Jagannātha at Puri. After their marriage, Jayadeva and Padmāvatī made a perfect pair and they together presented the *Gītagovinda* in the presence of the Lord every evening. Jayadeva's recitals were then accompanied

---

1 Jayadeva, wandering king of bards who sings at Padmavati's lotus feet, was obsessed in his heart;
By rhythms of the goddess of speech
And he made this lyrical poem
From tales of the passionate play when Krishna loved Śrī.

Barbara Stoller Miller, *The Gitagovinda of Jayadeva, Love Song of the Dark Lord*, The first part, Joyful Krishna, p.69.

Facing page: Rasakrida, *palmleaf painting, Museum Rietberg Zurich.*

by the dancing steps of his beloved Padmāvatī. *Gītagovinda* was sung, danced and enacted at several other places throughout Odisha following the traditions in the Jagannātha Temple at Puri. Undoubtedly this poem has the potential of being sung and danced and in fact it was a Sanskritised form of the folk theatre that was prevalent in Odisha.

Dancing forms a part of the rituals in any temple. Dancing is also accompanied by singing. Dancing is common to both *Śākta* and *Śaiva* temples alike. The *Vaiṣṇava* temples imitated this tradition[2] and took it up seriously for the propagation of *Vaiṣṇava* faith and *bhakti*. It is not definitely known when the *devadāsī* (divine dancers) were introduced into the temple rituals. The Brahmeśvara Temple stone inscriptions of Koḷāvatī Devī, the builder of the temple and the mother of Udyotakeśari (1040-1065 AD) gives a clear proof to this aspect.[3] Though indirect earlier references have come to our notice from the cave inscriptions at Yogīmatha and from the *Caryāpada*, composed in 9th and 10th century AD, the Brahmeśvara is the only direct evidence. After Brahmeśvara, the mention of *devadāsī* is found in the stone inscription of Madhukeśvara Temple (1082 AD) at Mukhaliṅgam and Sobhaneśvara Temple (1190 AD) at Niāli.[4] This proves the popularity of *devadāsī* tradition in temples. *Devadāsī* were dedicated to the temples and they were the temple dancers whose services in the temple were considered as a *sevā* in the temple ritual. The *devadāsī* appointed in the temple of Jagannātha at Puri were known as *māhārī*, the first mention of which was recorded in the copper plate grant of Karṇa Deva, the grandson of the king Udyotakeśari[5] stated earlier.

Māhārī, *contemporary dancer performing.*

The *devadāsī* or *māhārī sevā* was first introduced by the Gaṅga King Narasimhadeva (1278-1307 AD) in the Jagannātha Temple, Puri, as a part of daily ritual. Long after this practice Gajapati Pratāparudradeva again in a stone inscription issued in 1500 AD declared that the song and dance recitals of the *Gītagovinda* only are to be performed as daily *sevā* before the Lord Jagannātha and nothing else.[6]

From the temple records we can establish that drama presentations were frequently held in the temple courtyard of Jagannātha Temple

2 Sunil Kothari, *Odissi: Indian Classical Dance Art*, p.41.

3 Sharmila Bishwas, "The Maharis of Orissa" in *Attendance* 2003-4, p.58.

4 *Ibid.*

5 S.N. Rajaguru, *Inscriptions of Orissa*, 4, pp. 248-52.

6 The *Mādalāpāñji* maintains records of the duties of various categories of servants in the temple.

at Puri.[7] The *Gītagovinda* recital formed an integral part of the temple ritual and temple dancers called *māhārī* were retained by the temple in its service. The tradition of *māhārī* dance slowly crossed the temple precincts and was carried on by *maṭha* and other religious establishments. The dance began to spread with Rādhākṛṣṇa *bhakti* engulfing the society of the time. Since women dancers were not available because of the social taboo, boy dancers were employed by *maṭha* to perform the *Gītagovinda* dance and other Rādhā Kṛṣṇa thematic dances before the public. Such dance performances were necessary to entertain the people and arouse their religious curiosity.[8]

This dance performance is locally known as *sakhīnāṭa* or dance of the *sakhī*. These *sakhī* danced as Rādhā, Kṛṣṇa and *gopī* in *rāsa* and the *Gītagovinda*. These boy dancers were also known as *goṭipua* and this dance substantiated the present day classical Oḍissi dance. Thus the temple dance gradually was identified as Oḍissi dance and was made popular.[9] Several modern Oḍissi dancers took up the cause and spread it far beyond the temples, *maṭha* and other religious institutions.

Gītagovinda is also performed as *gīti-nāṭya* or music-drama (popularly known as dance drama) to the accompaniment of songs as dialogues. The songs were composed with proper *rāga* and *tāla* befitting the place, time and situation. The *abhinaya* or expressional dance is the

---

7 Sunil Kothari, *Odissi: Indian Classical Dance Art*, p.44. Also see Dinanath Pathy "Sakhīnāṭa: Angarag's Passionate Project" in *Angarag*, Spring 2008, pp. 95-208.

8 Dinanath Pathy, *Rethinking Odissi*, pp.29-38.

9 Barbara Stoller Miller, "Radha: Consort of Krishna's Springtime Passion" in *The Gitagovinda of Jayadeva*, pp.26-37. Also see Lee Siegel, *Sacred and Profane Dimensions of Love in Indian Traditions as Exemplified in the Gitagovinda of Jayadeva*, pp.201-205.

Kṛṣṇa, while dancing with another maiden, is watched by Rādhā, palmleaf painting, Museum Rietberg Zurich.

Above: *Ramli Ibrahim performing Kṛṣṇa from Sutra dance Theatre.*

most important factor of the *gīti-nāṭya* which is enacted keeping in view the theme and sentiment of the song. The *gīti-nāṭya* is the earliest type of traditional Sanskrit drama in India. It is easily understood and appreciated by the common viewer.

The theme of the *Gītagovinda* is based on the *rāsalīḷā* of Rādhā-Kṛṣṇa which is enacted during the spring season.[10] It is called *Vasantarāsa* which is a yearly programme observed during the spring season in the *maṭha*, *Brāhmaṇa śāsana* of Puri, Ganjam and at religious places of the other districts of Odisha. The Kṛṣṇa theme has immense popularity in India. The dance of Kṛṣṇa, first mentioned in *Harivaṁśa*, casually refers to *rāsa* and names it as *Hallisaka*.[11] But the reference to *rāsakrīḍā* has been more explicit in the *Bhāgavata Purāṇa*.[12] The term *rāsamaṇḍaḷa* has also been noted in the *Brahmavaivarta Purāṇa*. *Gītagovinda* in its distinct theatrical form is called *rāsalīḷā*. In its artistic presentations, the theme of the *Gītagovinda* provides ample scope for the performance of solo, duet and small group dances.

The first verse of the *Gītagovinda* determines the mood of the play and sets an indicator like the *Sūtradhara* of *Pūrvaraṅga* performs in a traditional drama. Out of the twenty-four songs, the first two are composed in praise of Lord Kṛṣṇa, which can be treated as *maṅgalācaraṇa* as is

10 Ibid.

11 *Caitanya Caritamṛta*, Adi, iv. p.57. Van Buitenen comments on The concept of *līḷā* (p.192): "The important conception of God's sport is best understood by its opposite *karman*. It contains free action (an action not resulting from a preceding action in an endless retrogressive succession) performed to no purpose at all; no purpose that of necessity would result in new *phalas* for the agent to enjoy or suffer. Hence it is compared to the literary inconsequential playfulness of a child... In creating, sustaining and resorbing the world God has no cause to effectuate and no end to achieve." Lee Siegel, *Sacred and Profane Dimensions of Love in Indian Traditions as Exemplified in the Gitagovinda of Jayadeva*, p.178.

12 Bharatamuni, *The Nāṭyaśāstra*, pp.291-301.

Dance Guru Debaprasad Das in Gītagovinda abhinaya.

Gitagovinda nṛtya *from Dharaṇīdhara's* Gītagovinda, *Orissa State Museum.*

being done in a *rāsalīḷā*. The invocation to ten incarnations '*Jaya Jagadīśa Haré* -' and the prayer to Lord Kṛṣṇa '*Śritakamalākuca*.....' are befitting for the *vṛndagāna* or chorus singing. Leaving aside the last song, the remaining twenty-one songs are based on the dialogues between Kṛṣṇa, Rādhā and her *sakhī*, companion, out of which Rādhā's companion sings ten songs and Rādhā herself eight. The verse between these songs describes the place, situation, time and mood of the *Gītagovinda*.

After the *maṅgalācaraṇa* and the *vṛndagāna* the *Gītagovinda rāsa nṛtya* starts with the core theme. The time suggested is the moonlit night in a spring season. On the banks of the river Yamunā and in the midst of *tamāḷa kuñja* Kṛṣṇa dances in the company of Rādhā and other young maidens. The form of dance visualised by Jayadeva is the *Hallisaka nṛtya*. Then dance is interwoven by the dialogues between Rādhā and her companions. They exchange narrations about Kṛṣṇa and his activities.

In the old *Nāṭyaśāstra* texts there is mention of rules guiding the dance performances, time of enactment, its moods and atmosphere. For different types of dances the suitable time and situation befitting the performances have also been codified. These rules can also be applicable for the performances of the *Gītagovinda nṛtya*. The *Gītagovinda* is an episode that centres around the union and separation of Rādhā and Kṛṣṇa, the hero, (*nāyaka*) and heroine, (*nāyikā*) of the work. *Abhinaya* is the major aspect of the *Gītagovinda* dance. In *abhinaya* the dancing characters express the characteristics of eight *nāyikās*. In the codified Oḍissi dance, *abhinaya* occupies a prominent place where the dancer expresses the mood of the theme.

The hero Kṛṣṇa has been depicted as *dakṣina nāyaka* and *gopī* waiting for him have been portrayed as *utkanṭhitā nāyikā* in the first canto. Kṛṣṇa dances surrounded by the young *gopī*. The dance has a prominent role to play in the first canto.

In the second canto Rādhā is dejected by Kṛṣṇa. Kṛṣṇa does not turn up at her *kuñja*. He is in his clandestine tryst in some other *kuñja*

while *gopī* keep on waiting for him to return. Since Rādhā is gloomy, dance is not suitable in this scene. Here Rādhā is *prositabhartrikā nāyikā*.

The third canto is also set in a similar mood as that of the second. Kṛṣṇa is in the midst of *rāsamaṇḍalī* dancing but suddenly leaves the place in search of Rādhā and in the course of his wandering comes to the bank of the river Yamunā. Here he is *vidagdha nāyaka*. The dance abruptly stops and is not continued anymore in the rest of the sequences.

In the fourth canto, the companion of Rādhā comes to Kṛṣṇa and reports the pitiable condition of her friend Rādhā. As Rādhā is depicted here as *utkaṇṭhitā nāyikā* the dance cannot be performed.

As noted above, the topics narrated from the second canto to the fourth canto can only be performed through *abhinaya*, not *nṛtta*.

In the fifth canto Rādhā's companion returns back from Kṛṣṇa and describes the sad plight of Vanamālī who is pining for her on the banks of Yamunā. Kṛṣṇa's attitude and the intensity of longing can be shown through the dance to elevate the mind of Kṛṣṇa for a union with Rādhā.

According to the *Nāṭyaśāstra* only the good qualities and activities of the hero and heroine are to be performed through *abhinaya*.

The songs of the *Gītagovinda* which form the dialogues between Rādhā and her companions and Kṛṣṇa and Rādhā's friend are performed through the *abhinaya* and *nṛtta*.

In the sixth canto Rādhā is unable to move due to the burden of separation. The companion of Rādhā goes back to Kṛṣṇa to report the

Above: *Illustrated folio from the* Gītagovinda, *palmleaf painting, Orissa State Museum.*

Below: *Rādhākṛṣṇa dancing, Illustrated palmleaf* Gītagovinda *painting, Orissa State Museum.*

Kṛṣṇa appeasing Rādhā inside a kuñja, palmleaf painting, Orissa State Museum.

ailing condition of Rādhā. She again requests Kṛṣṇa to come to the *kuñja* where Rādhā is eagerly waiting for him. This much can be shown in *abhinaya* and there is no need of dance.

In the seventh canto Kṛṣṇa did not come and *vipralambhā* Rādhā told her companion that Kṛṣṇa has many other beloved women to satisfy him. So Rādhā's time passed in vain waiting for him. This cannot be performed through the dance according to the *Nāṭyaśāstra*.

As the main essence of the *Gītagovinda* is the *vipralambha śṛṅgāra* followed by *māna, heta, rati,* etc these intricate situations of *rāsa* can only be better expressed through *abhinaya* than *nṛtta* or pure dance. So also the *dhṛṣṭanāyaka* and *khanditanāyikā* of the eighth canto and *kalahantaritanāyikā* of the ninth canto which cannot be normally depicted through the form of traditional dance.

In the tenth canto Mādhava tries his best to appease Rādhā and at last bows down at her feet by way of supplication. This is best shown through *abhinaya*.

Kṛṣṇa waits to meet Rādhā who as *abhisārikā* comes to the *kuñja* on the banks of Yamunā in the eleventh canto. To represent the amorous activities of the hero and the heroine dance could be an exciting and action oriented performance. This dance is called *sukumāra nṛtya* according to the *Nāṭyaśāstra*.

In the last canto, the final union of Rādhā-Kṛṣṇa takes place. Rādhā forgets everything that had happened before. Romantic mood descends and she then requests Kṛṣṇa to decorate her.

The *Gītagovinda* is a *Rāsakāvya* and starts with *rāsa* and ends with *rāsa nṛtya*. This has been divided as *hallisaka*, *mattavali*, *sṛnkhalā*, *latābandha* and *jangadi*.

Drama

Bhagaban Panda

The *Gītagovinda*, considered from the emotional, visual, musical, dramatical and literary aspects, is a unique work in the history of Sanskrit literature. It has twelve cantos, twenty-four songs and seventy-two verses. The number of cantos corresponds to the number of chapters (*skanda*) of the *Bhāgavata* and the number of *aṣṭapadi* songs to the twenty-four alphabets of *Gāyatrī mantra*.[1] In the *Gītagovinda*, at the beginning of each song the name of the *rāga* has been indicated. Subsequently different commentaries and editions of the *Gītagovinda* have added *tāla* and *rāga* as well as additional verses to each canto of the work.

Jayadeva, at the very beginning of the work has hinted upon its nature, classifying it as a *prabandhakāvya*.[2] In actuality it has only a few semblances of a *kāvya* and it exceeds beyond the limiting factor of the *kāvya*. It has more of visual possibilities along with its lyricism. Instead of going directly into the phenomenon of dramatic elements, we intend to apprise the readers of some of the important conventions of Sanskrit dramas.

The *kāvya* is the generic name comprising all forms of poetical compositions in Sanskrit literature. It both delights and instructs. Two species of the *kāvya* such as *dṛśya*, the visual and *śravya*, the audio are recognised. The *śravya kāvya* is divided as *mahākāvya*, the great poetry, *laghu kāvya*, the minor poetry which is further subdivided as *khaṇḍa-kāvya*, *dūta-kāvya*, *gīta-kāvya*, *campu-kāvya*, etc. Of the audio-visual segment again there are two classes such as *nāṭya*, drama and *nāṭa*, *nṛtta* or *nṛtya*, meaning the pure expression with a musical support. All these fundamental denotations of the *dṛśyakāvya* could roughly be applied to the *Gītagovinda* to a great extent. Moreover, it is constructed

Facing page:
Rādhā in remorse brooding, palmleaf painting, Museum Rietberg Zurich.

---

1 M. Kṛṣṇamachariya, *History of Classical Sanskrit Literature*, 1974, p.339.

2 *Gītagovinda*, Canto I, Verse-2.

with rhythmic words, in this sense, words as sound and sound as virtual meaning. There is an orchestration of syllables, a grand play with the auditory aspects of the vocabulary.[3]

The *dṛśya kāvya* in India was first represented through *nāṭya* and *nṛtya* or *nṛtta* which means the dramatic gesticulation with language and dance without language respectively. The *nāṭya* is known as *rūpa* or show because it is finally a scene to be presented. Accordingly it is called as *rūpaka*, for, it contains the assumption of parts by the character.

As defined by the sage Bharata, the representation is an act of the actor by means of which he recreates the *rasa* or sentiments inherent in the original situation forming the theme of the drama under enactment. This representation according to Viśvanātha Kavirāja is possible in four ways *viz*: physical, verbal, decorative and emotional.

There are ten *rūpaka* or principal dramas and seven, thirteen, eighteen, twenty or twenty-seven *upa-rūpaka* or the minor plays or dramas according to the great exponents in the line. But Viśvanātha Kavirāja, a famous poet and rhetorician of Odisha has accepted ten and eighteen varieties of *rūpaka* and *upa-rūpaka* respectively. The music, dialogue, gesticulation and imitation were the precursors of the Sanskrit dramas.[4] Kohala has classified all the *rūpaka* and *upa-rūpaka* or plays into *mārga* and *deśi* basing on the principle whether song and dance predominate in each of them. The song and dance are allowed to be performed not in *mārga nāṭya* but in *deśi-nāṭa* only. The plays like *Bhanaka*, *Rāmakrīḍā*, *Rāgakāvya*, *Hallisa*, *Rasaka*, etc are called *deśi* type of *nāṭya*. The *Gītagovinda* may come under any one among the last three types.

The *rūpaka* has several recognised characteristics. They are called *lakṣaṇa* or distinctions which are stated by Bharata to embellish the *kāvya*.[5]

A herd of cows on the banks of the river Yamunā, portion of an illustrated folio from the Gītagovinda, *palmleaf manuscript, Orissa State Museum.*

3 There is a tension in Sanskrit love-poetry between what is expressed and how it is expressed (the separated lover's pain described with delight and detachment) a tension between content and form, spontaneity and conventionality, feeling and the right. Lee Siegel, *Sacred and Profane Dimensions of Love in Indian Traditions as Exemplified in the Gītagovinda of Jayadeva*, London, 1979, p.33.

4 S.N. Sastri, *The Laws and Practice of Sanskrit Drama*, Vol. I, p. 2. Aristotle says in his poetics - *Epic poetry, tragedy, comedy, music of the flute and the lyre, in most of their forms are all in their general conception modes of imitation. They differ however from one another in three aspects, the medium, the object, the manner and mode of imitation, being in each case distinct.*

5 *Nāṭyaśāstra*, SVI, p.42.

But Bharata neither defines what the *lakṣaṇa* is nor illustrates the difference. But from the definitions of various *lakṣaṇa* given by different canonists, the exact nature of the *lakṣaṇa* seems to be of beautifying character. They are thirty-six *nāṭyadharma*, thirty-three *nāṭya-alaṅkāra*, thirteen *vithyaṅga* and ten *lāsyaṅga* according to *Sāhitya Darpaṇa* by Viśvanātha Kavirāja.[6] The success of the *rūpaka* and *upa-rūpaka* or plays rests completely upon these *lakṣaṇa, alaṅkāra* and *aṅga* of the *nāṭya*. The *nāṭya-alaṅkāra* were accepted as the *lakṣaṇa* of Bharata. Among the *alaṅkāra, udyama, āśraya sphā, kṣobha, pascāttāpa, abhimāna, anuvṛtti, nivedana, ākhyāna, upadeśa*, are worth mentioning and they have been properly depicted in the songs and verses which denoted different scenes and sequences of *Gītagovinda* when produced as a play. They do not form the body of the play or *nāṭyasarīra* but act as such features that signify the glory of the dramatic execution. In fact *lakṣaṇa* are the graceful characteristics of every dramatic action and are recommended for their adept use in the development of the plot.[7]

The plot is to be any one of the *prakhyāta* or well-known, *utpādya* or devised, *miśra* or mixed, *upatta* or narrowed, *prati Sanskrit* or adopted, etc. Besides, from other points of view the plot of drama can be of four kinds such as *sucya* or the indicative, *śravya* or the audible, *unmeya* or the narrative and *dṛśya* or the visible. Many other aspects of the Sanskrit drama such as *vṛttie āmukha, arthopkeṣepaka, arthaprakṛti, sandhi*, etc are not required to be discussed here. *Gītagovinda* has all the three aspects such as a well-known plot, a new device or approach to the plot and a combination of the above two.

Gītagovinda marks the transitional stage between the pure lyric and pure drama. The work is a lyrical drama composed in the 12th century AD,

Illustrated folio from the Bidagdha Mādhava Nātaka, *palmleaf manuscript, Orissa State Museum, 19th century.*

6 Viśvanātha Kavirāja, *Sāhitya Darpaṇa*, p.430.

7 S.N. Sāstri, *op. cit.*, p.188.

and is the earliest literary specimen of a primitive type of play that still survives in Odisha and must have preceded the regular dramas.[8]

The subject matter of the work is undoubtedly a Sanskritised form of local *līḷā*, *deśi-nāṭya* or *gīti-nāṭya* on the love episode of Kṛṣṇa's life as depicted in *Brahma vaivarta Purāṇa* and *Rasapaṇcādhyāyi* or *Śrīmad Bhāgavata*.[9] The love of Kṛṣṇa for Rādhā, the estrangement of the lovers and their final reconciliation are the principal components of the topic.

In the *Gītagovinda*, we have the expression of the substance of the very old form of *līḷā-yātrā*, lyric songs to which must be added the charms of music and grace of dance. The type of *mahānāṭaka* may be compared with the *Gītagovinda* composed of songs sung by Kṛṣṇa, Rādhā and her companion, intermingled with lyric-stanzas of the prayer to Kṛṣṇa.

The *Gītagovinda* has the unique advantage of a poem and can be enjoyed simply as such. In addition it has also the capability of quasi-dramatic presentation.[10] Hence the modern critics have found in it a lyric drama (Lassen), a pastoral (Jones), an opera (Levy) a melodrama (Pischel) and a refined *yātrā* (Schroeder).[11]

The *Gītagovinda Yātrā* can convincingly be identified as *Kṛṣṇalīḷā* similar to *Rāsalīḷā, Rāmalīḷā, Bharatalīḷā*, etc that are the traditional theatre forms of Odisha. We have thus narrations, descriptions and speech finely interwoven along with recitation and song, a combination of which creates a type quite new to Sanskrit literature.

Pūraṇarāsa *(Rāsakrīḍā). A page from* Bhāgavata, *paper painting, Prof. B. D. Mohanty Collection, Bhubaneswar, 19th century.*

8 M. Kṛṣṇamachariya *op. cit.*, p.340.

9 *Bhāgavata* - Ch. 10, pp.29-33.

10 A.B. Keith, *The Sanskrit Drama*, p.272.

11 Dasgupta and S.K. De, *History of Classical Sanskrit Literature*, p.339.

The *Gītagovinda* is a dramatised incident of one day and two nights being enacted from an evening, continuing to the end of the next night and going on throughout the day. It is clearly proved that the songs and verses of the *Gītagovinda* were visually rendered through the dance performances of his beloved wife Padmāvatī. Because of this, the poet Jayadeva wanted himself to be known as "*Padmāvatī caraṇacāraṇacakravartī.*" Most probably Jayadeva used to render his voice to his poetic compositions. This unique combination was the prime mover for large and elaborate enactments. The poet sang his melodious songs in praise of his propitious Lord Jagadīśa (equated with Kṛṣṇa or Jagannātha) and his Padmāvatī danced to the tune of the songs.

The *Gītagovinda* dance could be performed or is/was being performed with proper gesticulation according to the theme and sentiments of the song. This *nṛtta, nṛtya* or dance as a combined gesticulation of body and mind can be named as *abhinaya.*[12] This is an important property of traditional Oḍissi dance form. This combined enactment is also known as *nāṭa, lāsya, lāsyaka* and *nṛtya.*[13] For a general comprehension of the work, it is visualised in the following ten sequences or dramatic events.

First Scene

The poet opens the *Gītagovinda* with a dramatic situation where Nanda, Kṛṣṇa and Rādhā appear on the stage on the bank of the river Yamunā, which is dense with thick *tamāḷa* trees. It is evening. The sky is overcast by dark clouds. Kṛṣṇa is afraid of the gloom of the night. Nanda, the head of the cowherds commands Rādhā to take him home. Rādhā and Kṛṣṇa leave the place, but instead of going home they get involved in secret love games in the *tamāḷa kuñja.*[14]

First scene of Gītagovinda, *palmleaf manuscript, Orissa State Museum.*

This is the preamble to the whole work. Here in the opening scene Nanda the *sūtradhara*[15] and the poet, the *gāyaka* (*gāhāka*) or narrator announces the beginning of the enactment and prays to Jagadīśa (Kṛṣṇa) as is generally done in most of the *gīti-nāṭya* in Odisha.[16]

---

12 *op. cit.*, p.395

13 *op. cit.*, p.395

14 *Gītagovinda*, Canto-I, Verse-1.

15 *Sahitya Darpana*-VI-26-27.

16 *Gītagovinda*, Canto-I, Verse-2-4, *Prabandha*. 1-2.

Second Scene

The scene depicts spring season. The tender *malaya* breeze gently waves the lovely creepers in the forest. The groves are filled with the fragrance of the scented flowers. The sounds of the cuckoo intermingled with the sounds of honey-making bees rend the air.

Love stricken Rādhā and her companion appear. The companion of Rādhā discloses to her friend about the amorous sports of Kṛṣṇa who had been dancing with young women happily under the arched creepers in Vṛndāvana. She, again and again describes vividly the *rāsa nṛtya* of Kṛṣṇa with many young women of Gopapura.[17]

(As Rādhā's companion describes *rāsa nṛtya*, its enactment can be performed as a supporting visual aid.)

Third Scene

Conceited Rādhā, on account of jealousy, goes in another direction but appears on the stage. She is seated hiding in a grove of creepers and looks sad and dejected. She narrates to her companion about her first love experience with Kṛṣṇa.[18]

Fourth Scene

Love-stricken Kṛṣṇa, having pursued Rādhā here and there, is seen on the stage. He is wounded, struck by the arrows of the love God Kandarpa, sitting excited in a *kuñja* on the bank of the river Yamunā. He recollects his past deeds with beloved Rādhā who left him in anger without speaking a word of love. He visibly repents for his misadventures.[19]

17 *Ibid.* Canto-I, Verses-1-4 and p.5-6.

18 *Gītagovinda*, Canto-III Verse - 1-6 and p.7.

19 *Ibid.* Canto, Verses-1-6 and pp.8-9.

A gopī convinces Rādhā and bades her to meet with Kṛṣṇa, palmleaf painting, Museum Rietberg Zurich.

Fifth Scene

The companion of Rādhā appears on the stage where Kṛṣṇa is sitting with a dejected face bowing down in grief. She narrates the pitiable condition of love stricken Rādhā who is struggling and is in pain.[20]

Sixth Scene

The friend of Rādhā is seen on the stage returning from Kṛṣṇa to console her dear companion who sits looking downcast. She narrates the condition of Kṛṣṇa before Rādhā and advises her to go to the bank of Yamunā where the lover is eagerly waiting for her.[21]

Seventh Scene

On the stage Kṛṣṇa is seen waiting for Rādhā. He looks around, breathes deeply and sighs in frustration. He is beaten by the cruelty of love. At this moment the companion of Rādhā enters the stage. She approaches Kṛṣṇa and explains Rādhā's inability to come.[22]

Eighth Scene

Rādhā is seen on the stage lying in a hut of creepers. She, being unable to move, looks passionately and waits for the arrival of her lover. But Kṛṣṇa does not come at the appointed time. She repents when her friend returns silent and depressed from Mādhava. Rādhā narrates the amorous sports of Kṛṣṇa with other young women as if she had seen it. She tells her companion in anger not to say anything about Kṛṣṇa henceforth.[23]

---

20 *Ibid.* Canto, V Verses-1-6, pp.10-11.

21 *Ibid.* Canto, VI Verses-1-3, p.12.

22 *Gītagovinda*, Canto, VII, Verses 1-9, pp.13-16.

23 *Ibid.* Canto, VIII Verses 1-2, p.17.

Kṛṣṇa admits his fault and appeals to Rādhā with folded hands, palmleaf painting, Museum Rietberg Zurich.

Ninth Scene

Night has passed away. Kṛṣṇa appears before Rādhā who is seen in the creeper house.[24] All his submissions, requests and prayers have been rejected by Rādhā. But her friend consoles Rādhā to become calm and behave in a friendly way towards Mādhava. She advises Rādhā not to weep helplessly as others may laugh at her. She asks her to place the lotus feet of Hari on her person and make her eyes worthy.

Kṛṣṇa again comes in the evening and adulates Rādhā very politely. Her companion persuades Rādhā to meet Kṛṣṇa with a clear mind and loving heart.

Tenth Scene

In the last scene Rādhā and Kṛṣṇa entreat each other before their union. Then a dance is performed on the stage where Rādhā, Kṛṣṇa and other *gopi* take part. After the dance is over Rādhā and Kṛṣṇa recede into the *kuñja* and again appear before the audience in the form of a *yugala.*[25]

The picturisation of the songs has been so successfully done in the *Gītagovinda* that each sequence is a complete dramatic event. The whole incident takes place on the banks of the river Yamunā inside the *tamāḷa kuñja* in a romantic atmosphere, surcharged with the sweet fragrance of *madhu, mādhavī, māḷatī, keśara* flowers. The characters Kṛṣṇa, Rādhā, and her companion appear on the stage in different moods. The story of the drama advances being interwoven with several melodious songs. The verses as well as the songs of the work guide the place, time, scenes and sequences with the progress of the plot.

According to convention, *Gītagovinda* could not strictly be identified with any *rūpaka* or *upa-rūpaka* as a whole. But some of the dramatic elements of *kāvya, rāsaka* and *nāṭyarāsaka*[26] type of *upa-rūpaka* are traced in *Gītagovinda* for which it may be newly named as a *nāṭya-rāsaka-kāvya.* Hence Jayadeva's *Gītagovinda* is more a drama than a *māhākavya.*

Above: *Kṛṣṇa as a true lover bows down at the feet of Rādhā, palmleaf painting, Museum Rietberg Zurich.*

Below: *A* sakhī *points to the sky with the moon and indicates to Rādhā the right time to make the tryst, palmleaf painting, Museum Rietberg Zurich.*

---

24 *Ibid.* Canto, IX Verses-I, p.18.

25 *Ibid.* Canto, X Verses-1-7, p.19;
Canto, XI Verses-1- 5, pp.20-21.

26 *Sāhitya Darpaṇa,* VI-284-285, 288-290 and 277-279.

VISUAL ARTS

Sculpture

Bijaya Kumar Rath

Daśāvatāra panel sculptures is a post-Gupta phenomenon in Indian sculptural art. Two such sculptures those of Kṛṣṇa-Baḷarāma and Vāmana could even be traced to the 1st century BC,[1] while Varāha, Nṛsiṁha and Rāma sculptures belong to the Gupta period. The colossal Varāha sculptures[2] at Eran and Udayagiri near Vidiśā in Madhya Pradesh and figures of Rāma in the Daśāvatāra Temple at Deogarh[3] are assigned to the Gupta period. The other *avatāra* sculptures such as Matsya, Kūrma, Paraśurāma and Buddha are also of post-Gupta period.

The development of *daśāvatāra* sculptures in sculptural art is further supplemented by literary and epigraphic references. Besides, the conception of *daśāvatāra* or the ten incarnations of Viṣṇu vary from region to region and *Purāṇa* to *Purāṇa*. The *Harivamśa* gives the description of Hamsa, Kūrma, Matsya, Varāha, Nṛsiṁha, Vāmana, Rāma, Kṛṣṇa, Kaḷki and Buddha.[4] It, thus, has description of Hamsa in place of Paraśurāma incarnation. The *Bhāgavata Purāṇa* included a number of *avatāra*. The list of *avatāra* found in the *Agni* and *Varāha Purāṇa* are Matsya, Kūrma, Varāha, Narasimha, Vāmana, Paraśurāma, Rāma, Kṛṣṇa, Buddha and Kaḷki, in that order.[5] The list and order of *avatāra*, as found in the *Agni* and *Varāha Purāṇa*, seems to have been adopted by Śrī Śankarācārya in his *daśāvatāra* verse.[6] The Kashmiri poet Kṣemendra[7]

1 Kalpana Desai, *Iconography of Viṣṇu*, p. 123 and 135, New Delhi, 1973.

2 *Ibid*, p.75 and 116, Fig. 64.

3 Kṛṣṇa Deva, "Northern Temples" in *Archaeological Remains, Monument and Museums*, p. 159, *ASI*, New Delhi, 1974.

4 Kedarnath Mahapatra, *Śrī Jayadeva O Śrī Gītagovinda* (Oriya), p.92, Bhubaneswar, 1973.

5 J.N. Banerjea, *The Development of Hindu Iconography*, 3rd edn., New Delhi, 1974. p.391.

6 *Śankarācārya Granthāvali*, Published by Dharmajṇāna Pracāra Mandir, pp.4-6.

7 *Kṣemendra Laghukāvya Saṁgraha*, published by the Osmania University, p.6.

Facing page: *Matsya avatāra, stucco Mādhavananda Temple, Madhab.*

Page 155: *Kṛṣṇa and Rādhā in an arbour (top and middle panels),* sakhī *and Rādhā talking, Kṛṣṇa dancing with* gopī *(bottom panel left and right).*

of the 11th century AD also follows the same list and order in describing the ten incarnations of Viṣṇu. The Ajmer Stone Inscription[8], belonging to the 12th century AD in ten verses (verses 12-21) describes *daśāvatāra* and depicts Kṛṣṇa as the eighth incarnation. All the above depict Kṛṣṇa as the eighth incarnation.

Contrary to this the Varāha Perumāl Temple inscription[9] records the names of the ten incarnations in a verse as such:

> *Matsya kūrma varahaśca narasimhaśca,*
> *Rāmorāmaśca rāmaśca buddha kalkica te daśa.*

The inscription has been dated to the 8th century AD. This is the first instance where Balarāma has been included as the eighth incarnation. This has been the case in the *Naiśadhīya Caritam* of Śrī Harṣa. In this work, twelve verses have been devoted to describe Kṛṣṇa-Balarāma and depict their oneness in a total of forty verses dedicated to the description of *daśāvatāra*. The work has been assigned to the first part of 12th century AD and it is considered to be a work of Odisha.[10]

Matsya avatāra, *Kūrma* avatāra *Maṇibhadreśvara Temple, Bhubaneswar.*

Thus we observe that in the order of the ten incarnations, the depiction of the eighth incarnation varies from region to region. As seen already, Balarāma in Odisha, is always treated as the eighth incarnation. This is further supported by sculptural evidences found in Odisha. One important aspect of the Odishan *daśāvatāra* sculptures is that these, like their counterparts elsewhere in India, are post-Gupta in origin. Surprisingly enough, we do not come across many *daśāvatāra* sculptures in Odisha and the few that are found cannot be dated earlier than the 10th century AD. Inside the Nīlamādhava Temple at Gandharāḍi are found two small sculptures representing Matsya and Kūrma incarnations in their zoomorphic status. These two, no doubt, are part of a set of ten sculptures and can be placed in the 10th century AD as per the stylistic and iconographic considerations. It is difficult to ascertain the figure of the eighth incarnation here as it is missing now.

The *daśāvatāra* sculptures, as a group, are first noticed on the Manibhadreśvara Temple at Bhubaneswar, which is assigned to circa

---

8 *E.I.*, Vol. XXIX, p.179.

9 H. Krishna Sastri, "Two statues of Pallava kings and Five Pallava Inscriptions in a rock-cut temple at Mahabalipuram", in *Memoirs of the Archaeological Survey of India*, No.26.

10 K.N. Mahapatra, *op.cit.*, pp.96-97.

Varāha avatāra,
Nṛsiṁha avatāra
Prācī valley.

Left: *Varāha* avatāra, *Maṇibhadreśvara Temple, Bhubaneswar.*

Right: *Vāmana* avatāra, *Maṇibhadreśvara Temple, Bhubaneswar.*

11th century AD[11] on the basis of its architectural peculiarities. This temple is situated close to the Vaitāla Temple to the north-east direction. Even in its dilapidated structure, it depicts a *pañcaratha* style with parts of its *gaṇḍi* and *mastaka* having already fallen down. The *bāḍa* portion of the temple had the ten incarnations placed inside niches. But at present we find only eight of them. They are Matsya, Kūrma, Varāha, Nṛsiṁha, Vāmana, Rāma, Baḷarāma and Kaḷki. The Paraśurāma idol is lost while the Buddha one is mutilated and only its lower portion, showing a *dharmacakra* flanked by deer, is visible. It is significant that the first two incarnations of fish and tortoise are depicted in their zoomorphic forms on lotus pedestals.

The next group of *daśāvatāra* sculptures in chronological order would be the figures of Paraśurāma, Rāma and Baḷarāma, found along with a host of other sculptures at Tīrthamaṭha, preserved inside a monastery. It is possible that the other missing *avatāra* sculptures might be lying buried inside the mounds found nearby. The sculptures found here indicate the presence of an earlier Viṣṇu shrine. These images are found carved in relief on oblong stones and stylistically can be assigned to the 10th-11th century AD.

A *daśāvatāra* panel is noticed on the *bāḍa* of the 12th century Jagannātha Temple at Puri, at its upper *jaṅghā* portion. Here too, the first two incarnations are depicted in their zoomorphic forms. These sculptures are also contemporary to the temple. Similar representation

11 B.K. Rath, *Cultural History of Orissa,* (AD 1885-1110), p.179.

of *daśāvatāra* sculptures are found on the *bāḍa* portion of the Mādhavānanda Temple at Mādhava, of Cuttack district, which can be assigned to the 13th century AD, during the Gaṅga rule in Odisha. Here, too, the first two incarnations are found in their zoomorphic representation. In the *daśāvatāra* sculptures of this temple, which are depicted in the lower and upper *jaṅghā* portions of the *bāḍa*, Paraśurāma has been shown seated on a reclining seat carrying in his right hand the *paraśu*, which is placed over the shoulder. Besides, the order of the *avatāra* is not properly followed here.

The outer walls of the Gauri Temple at Bhubaneswar contain some of the *daśāvatāra* sculptures. But these are probably placed in the temple at a very later date.

Daśāvatāra sculptures also adorn the lion's gate of the Jagannātha Temple at Puri. For the first time, the ninth incarnation in this panel is depicted as Jagannātha seated in the lotus posture replacing the conventional Buddha. This lion's gate as well as the outer wall surrounding the temple have been constructed much later than the main temple in the 17th century.

We find a reference to the image of *Patitapāvana*, inside the lion's gate, in the *Jagannātha Caritāmṛta* of Dibākara Dāsa.[12] As a departure the later incarnation figures of fish and tortoise are depicted in their anthropomorphic forms where Viṣṇu is shown emerging out of a fish and a tortoise. These later sculptures do provide a stylistic contrast and help us to study the evolution.

From the illustrated *Gītagovinda* palmleaf manuscript,[13] collected from Cuttack and preserved in the Orissa State Museum, bearing catalogue No. Ext. 166, which has a commentary called *Sarvāṅgasundarī Tīka* by Dhanaṇjaya Dharaṇideva, we come across the

Nṛsiṁha, avatāra *Tirthamaṭha.*

Above: *Parasurāma,* avatāra *Tirthamaṭha.*

12 G.N. Dash, "Jagannātha and Oriya Nationalism", *in The Cult of Jagannātha and the Regional Tradition of Orissa,* ed., A. Eschmann and Others, p.362, New Delhi, 1978.

13 Dīnanath Pathy, *History of Orissan Painting,*.

daśāvatāra illustration wherein the ninth incarnation has been depicted as Buddha. This manuscript is dated in the 17th century AD as per its colophon[14].

From this it can be inferred that Jagannātha was never included in the *daśāvatāra* as the ninth incarnation in place of Buddha, at least up to the early 17th century in Odishan tradition.

Another important aspect regarding these group of *daśāvatāra* sculptures is that in case of the Vāmana *avatāra* only a dwarf is depicted, which is completely different from the conventional Trivikrama form of Viṣṇu, generally found as a *pārśvadevatā* of Viṣṇu shrines, along with Varāha and Nṛsiṁha figures.

We find these three of Varāha, Nṛsiṁha and Trivikrama in large numbers either as *pārśvadevatās* or loose sculptures in many places and shrines. The occurrence of these three as loose sculptures would indicate the existence of an earlier Viṣṇu shrine in the nearby area of their find spot or the popularity of the particular sculpture as a cult deity.

Daśāvatāra sculptures are found as a group in another form. They are depicted around a centrally placed sculpture, generally of Viṣṇu. One such example is the Kṛṣṇa-Viṣṇu sculpture exhibited in the Orissa State Museum. Here the ten incarnations are depicted around the main sculpture on its pedestal and *prabhāvaḷī* portions in clock-wise manner. Starting with Matsya *avatāra* in the left proper of the pedestal, it has Kūrma in the centre of the pedestal, Varāha in the right proper of the pedestal, Nṛsiṁha on the right jamb of the *prabhāvaḷī*, Vāmana, Paraśurāma on top right corner of the *prabhāvaḷī*, Rāma, Baḷarāma and Buddha on the left top corner of the *prabhāvali* and Kaḷki on the left jamb. The find spot of the sculpture is Dharmaśāḷā police station, of the Cuttack district and notwithstanding the earlier views it can be assigned to circa 13th century AD on its stylistic consideration.

Nṛsiṁha avatāra, *Maṇibhadreśvara Temple, Bhubaneswar.*

14 *O.H.R.J.* Vol. XI, No. 4 pp. 255-59, 1963, Vol. X, No. 4, p.73.

Another such sculpture is found near the Śiva Temple at Dadapur, about 15 kms from Bhawanipatna. Here the central sculpture is a four-armed Viṣṇu image. This sculpture is probably earlier than the Kṛṣṇa-Viṣṇu images of the Orissa State Museum from its iconographical point of view.

Two other similar sculptures are reported[15] from Saintalā in the Bolangīr district. From the earlier reports, it would seem that these two sculptures belong to an earlier date. But from the sculptural style these two should be contemporaneous to the image found at Dadapur as

Above: *Nṛsiṁha* avatāra, *Mādhavananda Temple.*

Below: *Rāma* avatāra, *Mādhavananda Temple.*

15 P.C. Rath, "Saintalā" *JOHRS*, Vol. II, No. 2. pp. 123-33, 1947; *Bolangir District Gazetter*, ed. N. Senapati, p.35 and 493; *OHRJ*, Vol. X No. 4, p.73.

these two sculptures reveal late features such as *prabhāvaḷī* and three dimensional carving. A few more of such sculptures are reported from the Prācī valley.[16] Another Viṣṇu sculpture with *daśāvatāra* figures also known as the Ballabha Nārāyaṇa image of the same temple is in the compound of the Bhagavatī Temple at Jeypore. Here the *daśāvatāra* figures are found around the outer perimeter of the halo behind the main deity, which can be, on stylistic grounds, placed in the 13th or 14th century AD.

Besides these two categories, we have individual *daśāvatāra* sculptures found at a few places in Odisha. The Varāha image having two arms and found inside a medallion on the Narasimhanāthasvami at Bargāon of Ganjam district can be included in this group. Similarly the figure of Rāma on the Dakṣya-Prajāpati Temple at Bāṇapur is also included in this group.

Thus we find full *daśāvatāra* sculptures only after the 10th-11th century AD. Besides, from the above discussion it would appear

Both above: Daśāvatāra *wood carving on door of Jagannātha Temple, Righagada.*

16 P.K. Ray (ed.) *Archaeological Survey Report, Praci Valley*, p.69, Bhubaneswar, 1975.

Left: *Rāma* avatāra *(close up view), Mādhavananda Temple.*

Right: *Vāmana* avatāra, *Stone Sculpture, Mādhavananda Temple, Mādhab.*

Below: *Nṛsiṁha* (Pārśvadevatā), *Mādhavananda Temple, Madhab.*

that the Viṣṇu sculptures bearing *daśāvatāra* panel on them were influenced by the *Gītagovinda* of Śrī Jayadeva, assigned to the 12th century AD. In the *daśāvatāra* verses, Jayadeva depicts Kṛṣṇa as *daśakrtikṛte* or one who had assumed the ten *avatāra*. This feature seems to be the only influence of *Gītagovinda* in Odishan *daśāvatāra* sculptures.

Painting

Dinanath Pathy

The *Gītagovinda* has influenced the art, music and literature of India to such an enormous extent that it is almost impossible to believe a school of thought in the field of literary, visual and performing arts without the magic touch of the *Gītagovinda.* In particular, the impact of the *Gītagovinda* on painting is so profound that the *Gītagovinda* paintings are available in hundreds and thousands in India in several regional schools. The pictorial traditions of the *Gītagovinda* extend from East to West touching Odisha, Nepal, Bengal, Himachal Pradesh, Rajasthan and Gujarat. It is however surprising that no *Gītagovinda* illustrations are known from Andhra Pradesh, Tamilnadu, Kerala and Manipur where *Gītagovinda* singing has a long tradition.[1]

In Odisha, so far we have collected more than thirty illustrated *Gītagovinda* palmleaf manuscripts which are in the collection of the Orissa State Museum at Bhubaneswar. This number includes complete *Gītagovinda* manuscripts, *daśāvatāra* paintings and stray leaves with illustrations. Several leaves of the *Gītagovinda* are scattered in the collection of different museums in India and abroad. *Gītagovinda* illustrated palmleaf manuscripts of Odisha are in the collections of L.D. Institute, Ahmedabad, Chandigarh Museum (one or two folios), Salarjung Museum and Kamal and Jagdish Mittal Museum of Indian Art at Hyderabad, Asutosh Museum of Indian Art, Kolkata, Indian Museum, Kolkata, Museum Rietberg Zurich, Switzerland, British Museum, London and India Office Library, London. Each of the *Gītagovinda* palmleaf manuscripts contains more than fifty illustrations on an average. All these illustrations on palmleaf, taken together, will number to more than a few thousands even though our calculations

Navanāri kuñja, *New elephant composed of damsels, Puri, contemporary.*

Above: Kandarparatha, *chariot of Cupid composed of damsels, Puri, contemporary.*

1 Kapila Vatsyayan "*Gītagovinda* and its Influences on Indian Art," in *Chavi, Rai Krishnadāsa Felicitation Volume.*

would remain vague. Besides palmleaf, *Gītagovinda* paintings on paper are in the collections of Bharat Kala Bhawan in Varanasi, British Museum in London and National Museum in New Delhi. These paper paintings including the paintings on palmleaf cover a period of four hundred years from the 16th to the 19th centuries. But the period from the 17th to the 19th centuries is the most prolific time during which the *Gītagovinda* paintings have been executed in Odisha and elsewhere.

Jayadeva composed the *Gītagovinda* in the 12th century. It is doubtful but not impossible to believe that the first *Gītagovinda* manuscript was illustrated.[2] In absence of evidence it is difficult to conclude that Jayadeva composed the *Gītagovinda* and also illustrated it. With the now available illustrated palmleaf manuscripts, there is a wide gap of 400 years between the first composition and the first available illustrated palmleaf manuscript. Because of non-availability of evidence this gap is apparently wide. Therefore there is scope for assumptions. Since it is a tradition in Odisha to copy and re-copy old palmleaf manuscripts for better preservation, the illustrated palmleaf manuscripts of the 16th century and after, now available, might have been the copies of the earlier manuscripts with illustrations. The earliest *Gītagovinda* painting in India belongs to the 15th century[3] and comes from Gujarat and no available painting is dated to the 12th century, the time of the creation of the *Gītagovinda.* Because of this, it is natural to think that at a certain point of time the *Gītagovinda* as a theme had caught the imagination of painters and scribes who had poured in their creative renderings into paintings. The popularity of the *Gītagovinda* had spread to different parts of India and the process of assimilation into different regional cultures took two to three hundred years. Then several commentaries were written and a number of imitations were also attempted. The most notable one was the *Abhinava-Gītagovinda* by Gajapati Puruṣottamadeva in the 15th century. The royal author who even attempted to replace Jayadeva's *Gītagovinda* with his own composition in the rituals of the Jagannātha Temple at Puri never thought of illustrating it. The *Abhinava-Gītagovinda* palmleaf

Page 166: *Srimati Rādhā and Sri Kṛṣṇa painting on wooden board, Digapahandi workshop, 19th century.*

2 According to a popular tradition Jayadeva had scribed the *Gītagovinda* on palmleaf. Once while he was composing the verses, he stumbled upon a couplet which did not satisfy his creative genius. He put down the folios and went to the river (or to the sea) to have a bath. During his absence Lord Kṛṣṇa came in the guise of Jayadeva and scribed the last line of the couplet - *dehi padapallava mudāraṁ.* But astonishingly it was not mentioned that Kṛṣṇa ever illustrated his poems.

3 *Journal of the University of Bombay,* 6, pt 7(1973) in Barbara Stoller Miller, 1977. Also see Kapila Vatsyayan, *op.cit.*, p.254.

manuscript in the collection of the Orissa State Museum belonging to the 15th century[4] does not have illustrations. So it adds a further credential to our thinking that provision of illustrations to the *Gītagovinda* palmleaf manuscripts is a later development and is partly due to the impact of the *Gītagovinda* theme on Odishan painting and partly for the general creative psychic temper heightened by the waves of *bhakti* movement.

A thematic analysis of the Odishan paintings reveals that more than half portray Kṛṣṇa themes and the rest of the paintings could be divided between Jagannātha, Rāmāyaṇa, Śākta and other secular and erotic subjects. The *Gītagovinda* paintings will then form a very minor portion (would be less than ten per cent) of the total paintings on Kṛṣṇa theme. Apart from major *Gītagovinda* paintings that are on palmleaf and paper, the other Kṛṣṇa paintings depict the *gopalīḷā* of Kṛṣṇa. In these paintings Kṛṣṇa figures out as a God-hero who displays all super human powers either while vanquishing the Nāga Kāliya or tearing open the beak of Vakāṣura. The essence of the *Gītagovinda* which manifests mostly in the outpouring of *ādi-rasa* or the sensuous love play of Rādhā and Kṛṣṇa in *tamāḷa kuñja* on the banks of the river Yamunā is absent in general paintings on Kṛṣṇa.

The Kṛṣṇa (*Bhāgavata*) paintings in Odisha are the outcome of *bhakti* movement that reached a climax in the 15th and the 16th centuries. A large number of literary creations were undertaken. *Bhāgavata* was translated into Odia and its daily reading was made popular through a new institution called the *Bhāgavata ghara* or *ṭungi*. The idea of monastic order and the preaching of *Bhāgavata doctrines* came to stay permanently. A sense of educating the people or making the people alive to the needs of the Rādhā-Kṛṣṇa faith developed and resulted in the establishment of *maṭha*. Therefore it is very significant that all the available paintings in Odisha belong to a period from the 16th to the 19th centuries coinciding with the period of the emergence of Rādhā-Kṛṣṇa *bhakti*.

The walls of the medieval *maṭha* and later temples of Odisha are painted mostly with *Kṛṣṇalīḷā* murals based on the *Bhāgavata* narrations. The sensuous and highly erotic *Gītagovinda* paintings could not get the benefit of an inclusion in the thematic narrations of the wall paintings because of the fear of outraging public modesty. It is also pertinent here to mention that inside the main shrine of Jagannātha, as well as in other

4 *Abhinava-Gītagovinda* has a colophon dated to the 15th century but it is difficult to ascertain whether this particular manuscript belongs to the 15th century or is a copy of some other earlier manuscript along with its 15th century colophon which is not available now.

minor temples inside the Puri Jagannātha Temple complex, not a single painting of the *Gītagovinda* was ever painted whereas *Kṛṣṇalīḷā* paintings dominate the inner chambers. Even the outer walls of the sanctorum are embellished with stone panels on *Kṛṣṇalīḷā*.

The only thematic essence of the *Gītagovinda* murals accepted by the traditions and also included in the *paṭa* painting repertoire is the *daśāvatāra* panel. But even this has been accepted with modifications. Although Jayadeva has personified Buddha as the ninth incarnation, the identification of Jagannātha with Viṣṇu or Kṛṣṇa in Odishan paintings was only successful within the format of *Daśāvatāra* paintings. Because even today in the traditional painting practices prevalent in Odisha, the figure of Jagannātha is painted for the ninth incarnation replacing Buddha. The *Daśāvatāra* prayers of the *Gītagovinda* though do not form the core theme of the *kāvya*, yet, it is a very popular identifiable aspect, the common people generally know of the *Gītagovinda*. The *daśāvatāra* paintings which ultimately were regarded as the incarnation paintings of Jagannātha (*Jaya Jagdīśa Harê*) were painted along with *Kṛṣṇalīḷā* paintings in *maṭha* and temples. The earliest *daśāvatāra* wall paintings belong to the 18th and 19th centuries in the Vāsudeva Temple, Jayantigada, Viraṇcinārāyaṇa Temple, Buguda, Jagannātha Temple, Dharakote, and Emāra Maṭha, Puri. *Daśāvatāra* paintings of the 20th century are found on the walls of several maṭha and temples all over Odisha. The main entrance (*Simhadvāra*) to the temple of Jagannātha at Puri has painted *Daśāvatāra* stucco works on the top frame. Kedarnath Mahapatra ascribes the date of the construction of this temple entrance to the 12th century.[5] But the painted stucco works are definitely of a later period.

In the areas of *paṭa* paintings, the *daśāvatāra* paintings (ten figures in a group) have appreciable representations though individual *daśāvatāra* paintings are very rare. The intention, gamut, style and techniques of *paṭa* paintings are totally identified with Jagannātha paintings and the *daśāvatāra* paintings form a part of Jagannātha paintings. A large variety of Jagannātha paintings are executed by the *citrakāra* that are meant for sale to the pilgrims who visit the Jagannātha Temple at Puri. In these paintings Jagannātha, Baḷabhadra and Subhadrā are shown inside a temple and the *daśāvatāra* paintings occupy an arch like space over and above the temple, just below the top decorated border. The

5 Kedarnath Mahapatra, *Śri Jayadeva O Śrī Gītagovinda* (Oriya) p.109.

Daśāvatara *painted wooden cover for* Gītagovinda, *palmleaf manuscript, Orissa State Museum, 20th century.*

daśāvatāra paintings are very conspicuous on *ṭhiābaḍhiā* paintings. In these paintings Jagannātha is painted for the ninth incarnation instead of Buddha. We have several *daśāvatāra* paintings on painted wooden manuscript covers. A few covers are in the collection of Orissa State Museum.[6] Some of these were the covers of the paper manuscripts which could be determined from the large width of the covers while the narrow formats were of palmleaf ones. Since these are now detached from the manuscripts they once belonged to, it is difficult to ascertain whether those manuscripts were the *Gītagovinda* ones. But because of the strong thematic links, one could easily proclaim that they once belonged to the *Gītagovinda* palmleaf and paper manuscripts. *Daśāvatāra* paintings are also done on *gaṇjapā*, a circular traditional playing card. *Gaṇjapā, gaṇjifā* or *ganjef* has been introduced in India by Babur, the first of the Mughals, in the 15th century.[7] This *gaṇjapā* is an eight coloured one (*āṭharaṅgi*). Evidences show that the *daśāvatāra gaṇjapā* was in vogue in India much before the introduction of *āṭharaṅgi gaṇjapā* during the

---

6 **(a) *Daśāvatāra***: (from Matsya to Vāmana)
Size 40 x 17 cm. (including border), colours — red (background), terreverde, chrome yellow and black, figures have been done inside the arches, painted directly on board, on use of cloth, lacquered, findspot not known, used as cover to paper manuscript not known, date - not known.

(b) *Daśāvatāra*: (from Paraśurāma to Kalki)
Size - 40 x 17 cm. colours — red (background) terreverde, light green, indigo, chrome yellow and black (three shades of green have been used), findspot - not known, date - not known, used as cover to paper manuscript not known.

(c) *Daśāvatāra*:
Size - 43.5 x 3.5 cm. directly painted on wooden board, not lacquered, colours - red (background), chrome yellow ultramarine, terreverde and black, no border, perforated, fine spot - not known, date - not known, used as cover to palmleaf manuscripts - not known.

(d) *Daśāvatāra*:
Size - 43 x 3.8 cm. painted directly on board, colours dull red, (background), indigo blue, light yellow, black, perforated in middle, find spot - not known, date - not known, used as cover to palmleaf manuscript not-known.

(e) *Daśāvatāra*:
Size - 50 x 3.5 cm. colours - red, green chrome yellow and black painted directly on board, not lacquered but perforated. In place of Buddha, Nārāyaṇa is painted, but not Jagannātha, find spot - not known, used as cover to palmleaf manuscripts-not known.

7 R.N. von Layden, "Ganjifa, the playing cards of India" in *Marg*, Vol. III, No. 4, 1979, pp.36-55.

Pharuā, *painted wooden casket with* daśāvatara *motifs, 20th century.*

time of Mughals. The Malla king of Viṣṇupur, as popular tradition goes, had introduced *gaṇjapā* in the 8th century much before the composition of the *Gītagovinda* in the 12th century[8]. It also referred to the unorthodox position of Buddha as the fifth incarnation in the *daśāvatāra* cards which is again indicative of the existence of the game before the 11th and 12th centuries, when the codification of the orthodox list as a sequence was laid down in the scriptures. The popularity of *daśāvatāra gaṇjapā* in Odisha was due to the wide acceptance of the *Gītagovinda*'s *daśāvatāra* concept by the elite group. This was being played like the *āṭharaṅgi gaṇjapā* more commonly in *Brāhmaṇa-śāsana* and inside the palaces of the king and by the people associated with the king's court. Although in proper terms no court existed in Odisha, it was a favourite pasttime of the aristracracy and the rich in *gaḍajāta* and *zamindāri* areas which were once the seat of royal power. While it may be improper to attribute the influences of the *Gītagovinda* to the prevalence of *daśāvatāra gaṇjapā* in Odisha, it is definitely a fact that the *daśāvatāra gaṇjapā* underwent an orientation with the introduction of Jagannātha for the ninth incarnation and was made recurrent as an artistic indoor play material for the higher order of people in the society. Although we do not get individual *daśāvatāra* paintings of earlier date, one could imagine that these paintings were in existence in Odisha. The *citrakāra* of Odisha now paint *daśāvatāra paṭas* in large numbers. These *paṭas* sometimes depict *daśāvatāra* paintings along with Jagannātha or in other cases are painted along with Rādhā-Kṛṣṇa *yugala*.

Daśāvatāra pictures are also painted on dowry boxes, *pharuā*, vermillion containers, and other wooden caskets used for storing jewellery. This tradition seems quite old and these served as gift items and souvenirs. Kedarnath Mahapatra has mentioned the tradition of offering these items as gifts to the kings, ministers, courtiers and other respectable personalities on the *Vijayā-daśami*.[9] Even though he has not

Parśurāma hāṇdi *with* daśāvatara *paintings. These pots are carried by* Janughaṇṭa *Parśurāma who parades in the middle of the village street to collect voluntary alms. In addition to a pot he also carries an axe in imitation of the Parśurāma incarnation of Viṣṇu.*

8 Haraprasad Sastri, "Notes on Vishnupur Circular Cards" in *Asiatic Society of Bengal*, Vol. LXIV, 1895, Calcutta, p. 284.

9 Kedarnath Mahapatra, *Śrī Jayadeva* 'O' *Śrī Gītagovinda*, Oriya, p.181.
As long as clouds can be
As gracious as the rain tinsel cloud
Kissing the shining sky.
Shame, which had lingered in her downcast eyes
Departed ashamed and like the mighty deep
Which sees the moon and rises, all his life
Uprose to drink her beams., Sir Arnold, *The Indian Song of Songs*, London, 1875, p.203.

quoted any historical evidence to support his statement, we are led to believe in such a tradition because of the availability of these souvenir materials with *daśāvatāra* paintings in Odisha.

Daśāvatāra palmleaf manuscripts with illustrations were such other items for gifts. These manuscripts were used for the recital of the *Gītagovinda* in temples, and house shrines and were also used as objects for veneration. The leaves in these *daśāvatāra* manuscripts were joined by strings to provide a wider format. As the manuscript is unfolded, incarnation pictures appear one after another to make a vertical panel. A number of such manuscripts are in the collection of the Orissa State Museum and Raghunandan Library, Puri. The modern version of the *daśāvatāra* folded folios use stencil methods to project the *daśāvatāra* pictures in medallions at the centre of the leaf. Glazed paper is contrasted from the back side to heighten the projection effect in these stencils and each medallion is provided with folding doors resembling miniature home shrines.

In a few of these palmleaf *daśāvatāra* hangings, the scribe also makes an attempt to depict *kāma bandha*

Above: *Jagannātha* Jātripata *with* daśāvatara *panel at the top, Museum Rietberg Zurich 20th century.*

Dowry box with daśāvatara *paintings, contemporary.*

(erotic postures). The *kāma bandhas* are hidden beneath the half open medallions. An improvised half circular palmleaf door separates the *avatāra* from the *bandhas*. Probably the *bandhas* earlier depicted Rādhā-Kṛṣṇa in sexual coition, and were meant to be concealed underneath the *daśāvatāra* paintings in the apprehension of losing the devotional value of the hangings, but later changed to the sexual union of the mortals to please some sensuous courtiers or may be even the commoners. The idea of *daśāvatāra* and the *kāma bandha* taken together in a single hanging has far-reaching consequences in the area of popularising the *Gītagovinda*. In Odisha, while assessing the impact of the *Gītagovinda* on paintings one has to read it along with Jagannātha which emerged as a state deity almost at the same time. Like the Gresham's Law in Economics, Jagannātha has pushed back everything into a lesser position after imbibing the best out of it. The idea of Jagannātha or the cult of Jagannātha, was the most popular concept which was opposed to the classical poetic creativity of the *Gītagovinda*. *Gītagovinda* is a pure poetic creation saturated with high erotic symbolism, impregnated with deep feelings of *ādi-rasa*. Although Kedarnath Mahapatra and several other authors and historians, young and old, have emphasised the religiocity of the *Gītagovinda*, the pictorial renderings and also the poetic frankness in depiction of sensuous love have exposed its erotic character beyond doubt. As far as the paintings are concerned, the leanings are more to eroticism than to religiocity. Because the visual registrations of the *Gītagovinda* cannot but be erotic to a greater extent Jayadeva has spoken in clear terms that he is depicting the *Vāsudeva ratikeli kathā* and *vilasakalā* which is a clear indication that the *Gītagovinda* is more of a love poem and its religious tone is superimposed and mostly undermined. Jayadeva has further mentioned that he has composed the poem for the delight of his most beloved Padmāvatī.[10] Despite such direct and clear statements by Jayadeva, several attempts have been made by the Sanskrit pandits and the elite group, to give a thick coat of religious fervour to the work and super-human powers to the poet, so that he could be able to display miracles. All these stories or legends have been woven around with an intention to make the *Gītagovinda* popular and acceptable in the society. Such moves have been done in connivance with the ruling authorities. The engagement of four *Vaiṣṇava* singers in the Jagannātha Temple at Puri, to sing the *Gītagovinda* to the illiterate people for their education is an indication to popularise the *Gītagovinda*.

10 *Padmāvatī caraṇācaraṇa cakravarti*.

The sculptural art of Odisha does not include *Gītagovinda* themes except the *daśāvatāra* sculptures. Although the temple of Koṇārka was constructed after the *Gītagovinda* was composed, and there was a gap of a hundred years, we do not find sculptures on the *Gītagovinda* theme. This shows, that in all probability, the earlier manuscript including the one scribed by Jayadeva had no illustrations, or it was not popular and understood properly by the artisan community, and had probably no royal or religious sanction for its visual depiction. On the other hand, it would be tempting to relate the erotic amorous couples in the Koṇārka Temple to the prevailing mood of the time, which might have provided the incentive material to the artists, artisans and poets for such aesthetic creations, and perhaps due to this, both the *Gītagovinda*, and the temple of Koṇārka following it in the next century have displayed erotic frankness. Probably, Rādhā and Kṛṣṇa, the main characters in the *Gītagovinda* because of their association with religiocity did not appear directly on the stone but went through a process of impersonification before they could be translated into sculptural motifs.

Paramananda Acharya, Kedarnath Mahapatra and others have deliberated at length the idea of Rādhā Kṛṣṇa *yugala*, Mādhava, Gopīnātha, Kṛṣṇa, Viṣṇu and *daśāvatāra* sculptures to show the influences of the *Gītagovinda* on the sculptural art, or at least, to show its link. Not a single sculpture with the depiction of Rādhā Kṛṣṇa *ratikrīḍā* exists anywhere in Odisha, as portrayed boldly in the palmleaf illustrations. The palmleaf manuscript which is intended for personal reading (*Svādhyāya*) and not for public display like the sculptures, had no inhibition in depicting the frank love play of the divine couple. The visual erotic frankness went hand in hand with subtle poetic deliberations. A number of visual sequences in these palmleaf illustrations justify the spirit of the poem. The frank and sensuous copulating poses of Rādhā and Kṛṣṇa inside the *tamāḷa kuñja* repeated on several folios, and the depiction of *viparīta ratī* in the manner of the erotic sculptural representations of seductive *mithunas* on temple facades are the most direct expositions of *ratikrīḍā*. There are hundreds of such sequences in the palmleaf illustrations. We have explained the pictorial sequences of

Kṛṣṇa putting a mark of kumkum *on Rādhā's forehead.*

Top and Middle: *Kṛṣṇa performing* sringāra *to Rādhā on the banks of river Yamunā.*

Facing page: Daśāvatara *cutout medallions on palmleaf. Each medallion houses an incarnation at the front and on the reverse an erotic couple, Orissa State Museum, 20th century.*

a sample *Gītagovinda* manuscript from the collection of the Orissa State Museum bearing catalogue No. Ext. 166, which is (given as Appendix A). Although this manuscript is comparatively later, it has the maximum number of pictorial possibilities with a *ṭīkā* by Dhananjaya Dharaṇideva along with a dated colophon.

Above: *Kṛṣṇa and Rādhā in erotic dalliance, inside a* kuñja.

Below: *Kṛṣṇa fixes Rādhā's ear ornament, palmleaf painting, Orissa State Museum.*

From an overview of the palmleaf illustrations, one notices the preference of the scribe for erotic exuberance. The sequences with a little bit of hidden sensuous appeal are the ones where Kṛṣṇa undresses Rādhā, and Rādhā, as if making a mild protest, bites the end of her sari to cover her breasts, or where Kṛṣṇa dresses up Rādhā obviously after *ratikeli* and fixes a flower in her chignon or where either Kṛṣṇa or Rādhā wait with all eagerness for the arrival of their loves to quench sexual desire. There are several sequences where Rādhā has been painted in much sex infatuated moods reclining on her back with breasts bare and projected, sequences with copulating ducks and monkeys to heighten

the sensuous moods, sequences where ordinary couples (maybe man and his wife or lover and beloved) engaged in sex acts to emphasise the erotic nuances of art work. The scribe illustrators understood the spirit of the poem and in consonance with the poetic intent have illustrated it to bring out the real significance of the *Gītagovinda*. It seems more probable that the scribe is also a pandit, knowledgeable in Sanskrit and the art of poetics and who is not merely a copyist but as a creative person has exhibited the free play of his imagination much beyond the prescribed limits of earlier manuscripts which he has followed for copying the text. The manuscript cited at Appendix A is one such volume that runs into ninety folios whereas the other manuscripts are limited to thirty or forty folios. One who sees and enjoys leisurely the pictorial depictions will undoubtedly fail to be influenced by the hidden religious temper unless he is a devout of the highest order with the least botheration for the worldly activities around. Paintings of the *Gītagovinda* with similar depiction of love, but with finer sensibility of colour-harmony have been achieved in Kāngrā, Basholi and other Pahāri schools, where the pictorial compositions of the *Gītagovinda* reached the emotional perfection amidst the blue hills, green valleys, winding rivulets, and decorative trees laden with flowers and foliages.

The slim *Pahāri* Rādhā with a narrow waist, a pair of sweet golden hued breasts half hidden under the embroidered *choli*, clad in swinging *ghāgrā* marks the pleasant contrast in the bosom of a dark indigo hued boyish Kṛṣṇa with a pair of bewitching eyes and pink lips. But in spite of such lovely pictorial possibilities, there is hardly any frank eroticism like that of Odishan varieties except for a very few paintings.

On the contrary Rādhā[11] in the Odishan palmleaf manuscript is a sensuous pastoral woman with heavy prominent breasts, bulging out with

11 She is her beauty dark shall look
As long as can be
As gracious as the rain tinsel cloud
Kissing the shining sky.
Shame, which had lingered in her downcast eyes
Departed ashamed and like the mighty deep
Which sees the moon and rises, all his life
Uprose to drink her beams., Sir Arnold, *The Indian Song of Songs*, London, 1875, p.203.

Kṛṣṇa adorning the breasts of Rādhā at the end of love making, palmleaf painting, Orissa State Museum.

dark nipples, fleshy thighs and mischievous smiles, and Kṛṣṇa a seemingly effeminate character, sporting a long plait at the back, wearing a nose pendant (*daṇḍi*), with a broad forehead, and a pair of bewitching eyes appears as a well groomed young man, displaying all his exuberance, pranks and dalliance mostly depicted in *rāsalīḷā* or *ratilīḷā*. Even devoid of colours the figures of Rādhā and Kṛṣṇa make the best of their appeals and do not leave any room for thoughts of religiocity and devotional pride.

The description of landscape that Jayadeva has picturised in his *Gītagovinda* fully conforms to the landscape of the Odishan variety. The rural Odisha has plenty of *keśara, vakula, mandāra, kadamba, madhuka, aśoka, mādhavī, atimuktā* and *palāśa* trees and creepers, which the scribes have best depicted in the illustrations. The river Yamunā of the *Gītagovinda* with palm groves on the bank and the mango arbours with *tamāḷa* and *mālatī kuñja* is the most common scene in Odisha. The sandy sea beach bathed in silvery moonlight and high surging waves is typical of the Puri sea coast. The description of Malayagiri, and the fragrance laden mild breeze carrying the scent of cloves is a great inspirer for poetic creativity which has influenced Jayadeva for a transcendental poetic experience. The whole land of Odisha he traversed in his poetic imagination to compose his songs stood as a great picture.

In the later years the scribes and illustrators have tried to capture the poetic imagination and ambience of the *Gītagovinda* in pictures and have been successful to a much greater extent, in illustrating themes of the *Gītagovinda*. This pictorial exercise was later transferred to the depiction of other illustrations.

For example in *Uṣāharaṇa* or *Uṣāharaṇa Citrāvali*, the love play between Uṣā, the daughter of Bāṇā and Aniruddha, the grandson of Kṛṣṇa has been depicted in identical pictorial sequences as in the

Folios from Uṣābhilāsa *palmleaf, Orissa State Museum.*

Facing page: *Folios from* Uṣābhilāsa *palmleaf, Orissa State Museum. These have been influenced by the drawings from the* Gītagovinda.

Gītagovinda. Similarly the illustrations in *Bidagdha Mādhava Nāṭaka* where Kṛṣṇa and *gopī* are in sexual dalliance resembles exactly Rādhā and Kṛṣṇa of the *Gītagovinda* painted in erotic postures.

Considering the *Gītagovinda* manuscripts, the commentaries and work on *Gītagovinda*, available in different parts of India, Kapila Vatsyayan has classified these into six categories such as (1) theological works (works of *Goswāmin*), (2) literary commentaries (*alaṅkāra* text, *nāyaka nāyikā bheda, Rasikapriyā, Rasamaṇjarī*), (3) works of erotics (*Kāmasūtra, Kokaśāstra*), (4) point of view of music (*Rājaraṅgiṇi, Saṅgītarāja, Saṅgīta Kalpalatā*) (5) prose dramatised works (*Saṅgītanāṭaka, Goṣṭhi Pīyūṣalaharī*) and (6) imitation in verse (Kṛṣṇa is substituted for Rāma etc). Out of these categories mentioned above, the literary commentaries and the works of erotics only contain illustrations.[12] The tradition of the *Gītagovinda* paintings in several regional styles are in the miniature format all over India. Since no *Gītagovinda* paintings are available in South India, the general styles that constitute the *Gītagovinda* miniature paintings are western, northern and eastern paintings traditions. The scholars have identified a group of miniature paintings of similar love themes belonging to the early 16th century in pre-Mughal styles. The miniatures are *Caurapaṇcāsika* (fifty verses of the love thief), a Sanskrit love poem by the 12th century Kashmiri poet Bilhaṇa, *Gītagovinda* by Jayadeva or *Candāyan*, a version of a popular North Indian ballad in eastern Hindi (*Avadhī*) composed by Maulana Da'ud earlier in the 14th century. These miniatures taken as a whole have been ascribed to the painting style of the Mewar court before it was captured by Akbar. Somewhat similar group of manuscripts of course executed in several periods beginning with the 15th/16th centuries in Odisha are *Amaruśataka, Gītagovinda, Uṣāharaṇa, Bidagdha Mādhava Nāṭaka, Daśa-poi* and *Causaṭhi Ratibandha* paintings. These groups of miniature paintings, though they depict eastern (Odishan) traditions, are

Rādhā and Kṛṣṇa enjoying in an arbour Gītagovinda, *palmleaf manuscript, Orissa State Museum.*

12 The *Kokaśāstra* manuscripts from the Kastur-bhai Lalbhai collection, Ahmedabad dated to 17th/18th centuries, (quoted by R.D. Dasgupta in *Eastern Indian Manuscript painting*, p. 92.).

Abhinava Candrikā of Mahesvara Mahapatra and the *Abhinaya Darpaṇa* of Raja Jadunath Singh belonging to the 18th/19th centuries (we do not agree with the date, it would probably be of the 20th century considering the styles of the illustrations published in *Marg*) quoted by Sadāsiva Ratha Sharmā in *Marg*, Vol. XIII, No. 2, p. 20.

not free from the influences of the Mewar group and the late Vijayanagar style as apparent in costumes and the treatment of body features and stances.

Gītagovinda of Jayadeva undoubtedly had an unusual musical appeal to the people in the society but since it was a Sanskrit composition it remained more with the court, temple and the elite groups like the *Brāhmaṇa* groups. The introduction of the singing of the *Gītagovinda* in the Jagannātha Temple at Puri while highlighting its popularity also exposes its high classical order because there had been several attempts to replace Jayadeva's *Gītagovinda* with *Abhinava-Gītagovinda*, its discontinuance and reintroduction in the temple. This has a corollary with the attempts that had been made to identify Jagannātha with Kṛṣṇa in painting, the idea being to make Jagannātha more popular through visual arts which could not be successful and was given up in later paintings. But in literature it continued unabated. The cult of Jagannātha has always accepted the popular ideas, in preference to classical ones. The intention was to accept the best from the popular thoughts, arts and religion and try to assimilate those in the system. In the sphere of painting, it was Rādhā and Kṛṣṇa of the *bhakti* movement which dominated the entire scene from the 16th and the 17th centuries onwards, and the theme of Jagannātha had to compromise with this (or accept Kṛṣṇa theme for Jagannātha in many cases). In such a background the paintings of the *Gītagovinda* which had the tinge of eroticism could not gain currency. But on the other hand such a sensuous poem with such erotic pictorial sequences would have to elicit the greatest admiration and love of the people but would have restricted the growth of popular Jagannātha idea. Perhaps for this reason the pictures were not allowed to cross the limits of the palmleaf folios on to the *paṭa* or walls normally dealt by the professional *citrakāra* attached to temple service. The superfluous dimension of the *Gītagovinda*, the prayers to *daśāvatāra* were only given adequate

Rādhā and Kṛṣṇa enjoying love in reverse Gītagovinda, *palmleaf manuscript, Orissa State Museum.*

T. 287

exposure. The "mythology of the incarnations of Viṣṇu, the *avatāra* scheme which by the 12th century had become a conventional subject for *kāvya* is utilised by Jayadeva to make sacred the profane erotic" and ironically used by the vested groups to popularise the *Gītagovinda*. The *Brāhmaṇa* or the scribe illustrators of the higher caste-order were not adept in *paṭa* and murals and the *citrakāra* were only patronised to paint *daśāvatāra* and *Kṛṣṇalīḷā* scenes of the *Bhāgavata* and not the erotic pictures of the *Gītagovinda*. The *Brāhmaṇa* who wanted to exploit this situation in their favour, patronised Jagannāthism and remained satisfied with the promulgation of the *Gītagovinda* recitals inside the Jagannātha Temple which were Greek and Latin to the common illiterate people and several stories were created that Jagannātha was fond of listening to the *Gītagovinda*.

Two folios from the Gītagovinda, *painted on paper, National Museum, New Delhi, 19th century.*

Facing page: Gopī *on the bank of river Yamunā, pages from a Raṇapur* citrakara, *19th century, Sketch Books, Ashutosh Museum, Kolkata.*

Textiles

Eberhard Fischer and Dinanath Pathy

The *Gītagovinda bāndha* are made of pure local silk, decorated by the interesting *ikat* (or *bāndha*) technique. These show sacred texts as the main pattern and are ritualistically used at the time of *baḍasiṁhāra veśa*[1] of Jagannātha, Baḷabhadra and Subhadrā in the Jagannātha Temple of Puri, the most important religious centre of Eastern India. *Gītagovinda* textiles form a part of the *Gītagovindasevā* in the temple. These textiles need more investigation and scholarly attention. Here we present some samples from the public collection[2] and give what random information we could gather.

Until recently the only publication—as far as we know—mentioning these *Gītagovinda bāndha*-textiles was *Ikat Fabrics of Orissa and Andhra Pradesh.*[3] We added some comments and some bits of new information in our entry "Ceremonial Textiles" in the book, *Orissa Kunst und Kultur in Nordost Indien.*[4] In that chapter we dealt at length with the historical questions concerning *ikat* in Odisha and its connections with Andhra Pradesh. We do not want to take up the discussion again, but repeat the basic assumptions shared by all authors: The *ikat* technique of tie-dying threads before weaving to produce multicoloured designs in the warp, or in the weft, or in the combined warp and weft and as 'double *ikat*' which has a single pattern in warp and weft, was practised by Odisha weavers since several centuries in simple forms, especially in the region of Nuapāṭaṇā and Tigiriā where silk was used as raw

1 "Record of Rights", Part II, *Orissa Gazette*, Cuttack, 1956, pp.26-27; Calico Museum of Textiles (Ahmedabad).

2 Ethnographic Museum, Basle (Switzerland); Seattle Museum of Art (United States of America).

3 BC Mohanty and Kalyan Krishna, *Ikat Fabrics of Orissa and Andhra Pradesh*, Ahmedabad, 1974, pp. 20-21 and Plates 19 and 19a.

4 Eberhard Fischer, Sitakant Mahapatra and Dinanath Pathy, *Orissa Kunst und Kultur in Nordost Indien, Zurich*, 1980, pp. 290-92 and plates 690 and 691.

Facing page:
Śādhi *with* Gītagovinda śloka, *Museum Rietberg Zurich.*

material. For cotton textiles, but most probably for silken ones too, the various design possibilities offered by this technique were explored by the Odisha weavers only during the last hundred years when a very large variety of pictorial motifs were incorporated and all technical possibilities developed. All known *Gītagovinda bāndha* textiles are from this period, but it is likely that older samples will be discovered in the Puri Temple in the future. The earliest historical document, which unfortunately we could neither see nor verify seems to be a court-order by King Rāmacandradeva II, dated 1641 *Śaka* (*i.e.* 1719 AD) and kept as a *Madalāpāñji* or diary of Puri Temple activities in the archives of the Jagannātha Temple.[5] It informs us that the *bāndha Gītagovinda* set of cloths previously being woven by Kenduli weavers could not be done there, and therefore the order was to be placed with the eight weaver brothers of Nuapāṭaṇā, (Tigiriā) and they were to be remunerated for their labour by *Śrīkṣetra* by way of *bhoga-prasāda* and other gifts.[6] During the 18th century Tigiriā/Nuapāṭaṇā flourished as a textile centre and in those decades weavers from other regions (like Dhenkānāl and Badambā) settled there. Proof is the report of Thomas Motte in 1766.[7] But there is no information available on the *ikat* technique or on the *Gītagovinda bāndha* textiles being manufactured there.

We know four legends describing how these textiles were introduced into the worship of Lord Jagannātha in the Puri Temple. The first one is told by Pandit Sadāsiva Rath Sharmā.[8] According to Pandit Sharmā, originally there were twelve pieces of cloth used in the temple of Lord Jagannātha inscribed with verses of the *Gītagovinda*. These textiles were made by the poet himself. But the pandits of Puri did not want to accept these textiles as garments for the image of Lord Jagannātha and started a discussion as to whether the *Gītagovinda* is

---

5 **(a)** As corollary evidences we may cite the following incidents which have bearing on the use of *Gītagovinda* textiles in the *Gītagovindasevā*. The introduction of *Gītagovindasevā* in the Jagannātha Temple of Puri in the 13th-14th century as mentioned in *Madalāpāñji*. The translation of the extracts is as follows. After this the poet King Narasimhadeva became the king. He introduced *Gītagovinda* (*Mādalāpāñji*, Prācī edition, p.36).
(b) Pratāparudradeva in the 16th century had introduced the singing and dancing of *Gītagovinda* in the Jagannātha Temple at Puri by a royal proclamation inscribed on a stone slab fixed on the Jaya Vijaya entrance to the temple (K.N. Mahapatra, *Śrī Jayadeva* O *Śrī Gītagovinda*, (Oriya), pp.89-90.

6 BC Mohanty and Kalyan Krishna, *op. cit.*, p.20.

7 *Ibid.*

8 Lee Siegel, *Sacred and Profane Dimensions of Love in Indian Traditions as exemplified in the Gītagovinda of Jayadeva*, 1978, p.23.

Facing page:
Śādhi *woven with* Gītagovinda *ślokas Yamunatiravanira etc. Museum Rietberg Zurich.*

a sacred or profane text; "*Pandita* Nīlādri Miśra insisted that devotees should be concerned with ritual functions and prayers, and that a song which tempted them with desire and pleasure was bad. But Jayadeva answered him politely, *kāma* is the basis of human nature. It is the *ādi-rasa* of the world. Without *kāma*, the mind cannot be attracted to anything, the devotee cannot love the Lord. This is supported by the *Veda*. This is especially true in the *Kaḷi Yuga*. *Puruṣa* enjoys *Māyā*, Śiva enjoys Pārvatī, Viṣṇu enjoys Lakṣmī. It is universal. Then the *Rājā* declared, "If the Lord wants the cloth, he will tell us. Let Jayadeva throw the cloth into the Mārkaṇḍeya tank and if it does not sink we shall know that Lord Jagannātha does want the *Gītagovinda* cloth in his temple." Everyone gathered to watch the test. Jayadeva sang the first *sarga* of the *Gītagovinda* with love and then in tears, he threw the cloth into the tank. Through the mercy of Lord Jagannātha the cloth did not sink. All the people of Puri declared that Jayadeva was no ordinary poet but a great *sādhu* and an excellent *bhakta* of the Lord. He was known from then as *Sādhu-pradhāna Jayadeva-Gosvāmi*. Although the cloth was admitted into the temple, the songs of the *Gītagovinda* were not allowed to be sung there during Jayadeva's lifetime. The poet was very disappointed so he left Puri and went to Bengal where he was engaged for sometime as the court pandit of *Rājā* Lakṣmaṇa Sena". This legend however, is not popular in Odisha.

Another legend[9] is retold again by Sadāsiva Rath Sharmā of Puri. "Jayadeva, the great poet ... desired to offer his *Gītagovinda* to Lord Jagannātha. He could not think of any other medium except a fabric which could be in contact with the Lord similar to other fabrics offered to him (the Lord) by the devotees. He decided to get the fabrics with the lyrics of the *Gītagovinda* woven in them. He got them woven in Kenduli village which was his birthplace and offered them to the deities, Jagannātha Baḷabhadra and Subhadrā...."

Another version—perhaps of the same legend in its original form—is taken from the *Bhaktamālā* and was translated (perhaps for the first time) by the German Indologist Ernst Trumpp.[10] It reads: "Once the *rājā* of Nīlāchal also composed a *Gītagovinda* and then called together

---

9 BC Mohanty and Kalyan Krishna, *op. cit.*, p.20.

10 Ernst Trumpp, "Die aeltesten Jindui-Gedichte", *Sitzungs berichte der philosophischen- philologischen and historischen class der K.B. Akademie der wissenschaften zu*, Munchen, Vol. I, Munich, 1879, p.6.

all the *Brāhmaṇa* to show them his book. They refused to take notice of his manuscript saying they already possessed one. They decided thereupon to bring both books to the temple of Lord Jagannātha to give him the liberty to do as he pleased. It is reported that Lord Jagannātha decorated his own neck with the book of Jayadeva, using it as a shawl, but threw the book of the *rājā* out of his temple. Since the *Bhaktamālā/ Bhagatmāl* texts were composed by Nebhaji/Nabhadās at the end of the 16th century, these two legends indicate that textiles with the *Gītagovinda* inscriptions have centuries old tradition in Puri".[11]

The fourth story is again by Pandit Sadāsiva Rath Sharmā as quoted by Lee Siegel[12] and will be reproduced in full length on a later page of this article, because it points out why a specific verse has become common on these *Gītagovinda bāndha*-textiles.

However all these legends do not state in which technique these texts were patterned on the textiles, *i.e.* whether they were brocaded, embroidered, block printed, painted or tie-dyed—all techniques used for inscribing ritualistic cloths in India.[13] In fact, we know from George Watt in his book *Indian Art at Delhi* that in the Bengal provinces (which included at his time parts of Odisha) and possibly in Berhampore "printed silks in the form of *nāmāvaḷī* handkerchiefs or *chādars* were formerly produced but have been discontinued. They contain religious symbols or texts printed in brick-red over a yellow or golden coloured soft *korah* silk". Since George Watt very well knew the difference of *ikat* and block-printed textiles, it is very easily possible that tie-dyed textiles are a late local replacement of block printed and mordant dyed ones (possibly done as well in Tigiriā/Nuapāṭaṇā).

Printing as well as dying of multicoloured *Kalamkār* cloths seem to be techniques given up in Odisha in the 19th century. The decline of these dying techniques and the development of *ikat* may have gone hand in hand.[14]

The term used in Puri for the *Gītagovinda* textiles is *pheṭā*, i.e. small turban cloth. This denotes the main use of the small rectangular textile pieces. In fact, on several of our photographs these silken cloths are used

---

11 *Ibid* and M. Winternitz, *Geschichte der Indischen Literatur*, Vol. III, 1920, pp.127-32.

12 Lee Siegel, *op. cit.*, p.230.

13 A Buhler, E. Fischer, M.L. Nabholz "Indian Tie-dyed Fabrics", in *Historic Textiles of India*, Vol. IV, p.145.

14 George Watt, *Indian Art at Delhi*, 1903, p. 305.

as turbans or as shoulder cloths. Three functions can be distinguished. The *Gītagovinda bāndha*-textiles are used (1) as garments for the images of the three deities of Puri, (2) as crown turban by the *Rājā* of Khurdā as Gajapati, and (3) as shoulder cloths or turbans by the *daitā*, servant-priest of the Jagannātha Temple in Puri.

Eight sets or *saja* of *Gītagovinda* textiles are needed for the deities during a year in the Jagannātha Temple of Puri. Each *saja* consists of the following:

(a) *Śāḍhi* - three pieces (size 12 hands x one and half hand)
(b) *Khaṇḍuā* - three pieces (size 6 hands x 3 hands).
(c) *Pheṭā* - four pieces (size 12 hands x 2.5 hands).
(e) *Phuṭā or phunṭā* - two pieces (size 24 hands x 1.5 hands).

The functions of the above textiles inside the temple are: *Śāḍhi* to be worn by the deities, *Khaṇḍuā* to be used as the front decorative piece hanging from the waist, *Pheṭā* as shoulder cloth and *Phuṭā* to be tied around the arms and hands of the deities. We have seen the use of the textiles inside the temple.

Since photographing is prohibited in the Jagannātha Temple of Puri, we have no proof that the *Gītagovinda* textiles are worn as shoulder cloths by the deities of Puri. But according to Pandit Sadāsiva Rath

Daitā *wearing the* Gītagovinda *textiles as shoulder cloth and shawl in front of the sacred tree while singing in praise of the Lord.*

Sharmā[15] these textiles are prepared in three colours: yellow, green and red, each being reserved for one of the deities. Yellow symbolises salvation and is used for Jagannātha; red signifies *śaktī* or energy and is used for goddess Subhadrā; green standing for life is the colour of Baḷabhadra.

But as recorded in the temple *Record of Rights*[16] the *cāṅgaḍā mekāpa* supplies *bāralāgi śāḍhi* with *Gītagovinda* inscribed on it for the *badasiṁhāra veśa* of the deities. *Bāralāgi śāḍhi* consists of seven varieties of coloured saris.

There is a specific colour for a specific weekday and the colour of the sari is finally determined by the colour significance of the presiding deity of each weekday. For example on Sunday, the day of the Sun God the deities are dressed in red coloured clothing and the *Gītagovinda* textile specified for Sunday is of red colour. Appended below is a table which explains in detail the colour of the textiles depending on the weekdays:

Day	**Deity**	**Colour**	**Textile**		
Sunday	Sūrya	Red	*Nāli nāhakā*	-	Sari with a red piece
Monday	Candra	White	*Buṭā śukla* nāhakā	-	White centre piece with *buṭā*
Tuesday	Maṅgaḷa	Colour of sparkling star	*Paṭā paṭā nāhakā* or *citravicitra nāhakā*	-	Centre piece with stripes of white, yellow, green, red etc
Wednesday	Budha	Blue	*Nīḷa nāhakā*	-	Blue centre piece
Thursday	Bṛhaspati	Yellow	*Haladīā nāhakā*	-	Yellow centre piece
Friday	Śukra	White	*Dhaḷā nāhakā*	-	White centre piece
Saturday	Śani	Black	*Kaḷā nāhakā*	-	Violet centre piece

From the above, it will be clear that the total colour of the sari is not of one shade of colour. On either ends of the sari there are inscriptions of the *Gītagovinda* with red and yellow colour and the middle portion has a distinguished colour depending on which the colour of the sari is known. The centre piece is known as *nāhakā*. It is very interesting to know that the colour of the presiding deities are determined by their respective *dhyāna* and each colour has a particular influence on the human being,

15 BC Mohanty and Kalyan Krishna, *op. cit.*, p. 21.

16 *Record of Rights*, *op. cit.*, pp. 26-27

inanimate and animate world. The *dhyāna*[16a] of the Sun god *javā kusuma saṁkāśam* like the red colour of the China rose flowers, of moon is *dadhi samkha tuṣārābham* like that of divine conch and like the glamour of the snow, of Maṅgaḷa is *vidyut puñja samaprabhā*, like the sparkling of the stars, of Budha is *priyaṅgu kalikā śyāma*, like that of a blue creeper, of Bṛhaspati is *kanaka sannibham*, like that of gold, of Śukra is *hima kunda mṛṇālābha* like that of ice, of kunda flower and stem of a lily flower, Śani is *nīlāñjanacayā*, like that of black collyrium. We have verified the *Gītagovinda* textiles in the *cāṅgaḍā ghara* or textile store room of the deities inside the Jagannātha Temple at Puri.[17]

Until now we have only come across the red variety of *Gītagovinda bāndha* textiles. It is likely that red garments are offered more often to the goddess than the yellow or green ones which are offered to the gods. Therefore red ones exist more often than the other colours because it is a widespread custom to make the offering of a red silk-cloth to a goddess in India. The only visual proof that these textiles are used for Lord Jagannātha and his image ritualistically is a photograph showing the newly cut log called *dāru* out of which the image of Lord Jagannātha will be carved, covered with a large *Gītagovinda bāndha*-textile. The Puri *Rājā* who is considered the first servant of Lord Jagannātha, receives *Gītagovinda bāndha*-textiles, probably of red colour which he wears on his coronation. It was Hermann Kulke who reproduced for the first time a photograph supplied by the Government of Odisha, of the Puri *Rājā* Divyasiṃhadeva IV wearing the Gajapati-turban on the day of his coronation. The turban, which contains the verse of the *Gītagovinda*, had been worn before by Jagannātha. "The photograph is dated 30.1.71.[18] Two saris with the *Gītagovinda* inscriptions are used by the king during the coronation. Each sari measures 12 hands in length. These are called *Prasāda Śāḍhi* because the colour is red and yellow. One sari is tied as turban and the other put on the shoulder as *uttarīya*. For the coronation of the king *Śāḍhi bandhāṇa* is done inside the temple but each year on the day of *Suniā* the king is also presented

16a It is also argued that each day has a specific colour as well as *svara*. See Itishree Sahoo, *Odisi Music*, p.119.

17 We are thankful to Bhagirathi Chāngadā Mekāpa aged 81 of Gudiasahi (Balisahi) in the Puri town for the information on *Bāralāgi Śāḍhi* and to Rabinarayan Mishra Assistant Administrator of Jagannātha Temple, Puri who allowed us to see the *Gītagovinda* textiles in the temple store.

18 Hermann Kulke, "Jagannātha - Kult and Gajapati Koenigtum" *Suedasien Institute der Universtaet Heidelberg*. Vol. 23, 1979, Plate 20.

with such *Gītagovinda* saris which he uses in the palace. Besides this, on two other occasions, *daśaharā* and *puṣyābhiṣeka,* the king is presented with such *Gītagovinda* saris from the temple. Nowadays in the absence of *Gītagovinda* textiles only *pāṭapatini* or even *lugāpatini* are presented.[19]

It is not uncommon in India that the *Rājā* wears a red silk textile which was first offered to the goddess or deity of whom he is a devotee or servant. It would be important to ascertain the colour of the turban cloth and to discover whether the textile is traditionally connected with Lord Jagannātha or with the deity Subhadrā (who is Bhubaneśvarī) who is wearing a red *sari* on the *anavasara paṭi.*

It seems that this turban is considered a sari turban and we know through *Mādalāpāñji* temple records that already *Rājā* Rāmacandra was crowned with such a cloth in 1568 as the new Gajapati.[20] For shoulder cloths as well as turbans *Gītagovinda bāndha*-textiles are common as ritualistic garments of the *daitā*-priest-servants of the Puri Temple.[21] It seems that these cloths are worn as status symbols at important events like the cutting and transportation of the wooden logs for carving the new images of the deities, but not at the daily or festival rituals inside the temple. A photograph of the dāru-log of Lord Jagannātha surrounded by several *daitā* priests shows that at least four of them wear such textiles as shoulder cloth.

Even today these textiles are called according to their usage; *pheṭā*, turban, are the original sari-turbans which the authorities of the Jagannātha Temple in Puri invest on their servants. About these we are

19 Information given by Krishna Chandra Rajguru, aged 73 of Balisahi (the royal priest of the Puri rājā's family). He is now the visiting professor in the Sanskrit University at Puri.

20 H. Kulke, *op. cit.*, p.129.

21 E. Fischer, D. Pathy and S. Mohapatra, *op. cit.*, plate 690.

Gītagovinda *textile with* śloka *woven in it. Museum Rietberg Zurich.*

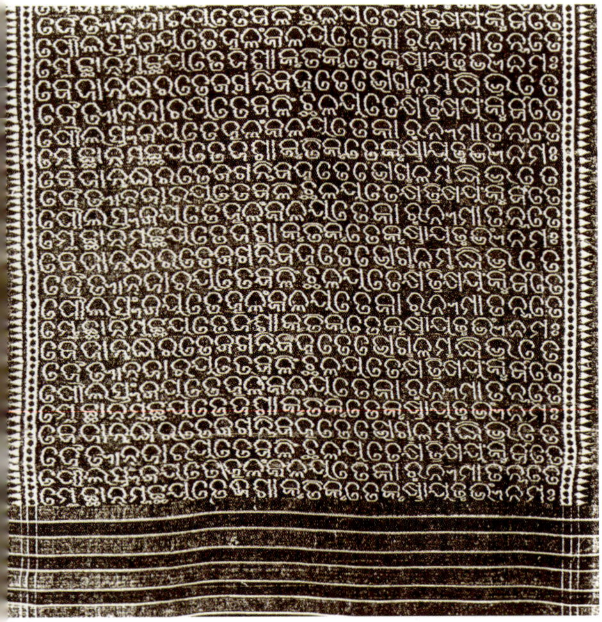

informed by J.P. Das.[22] "The ceremony of *śāḍhi bandhā* consists of tying round the head a piece of cloth in recognition of the appointment of the particular person in the service of the temple. On the appointed day, the young man has to take vegetarian food, dress himself in new clothes, and after the ceremony must invite his kin and neighbours to a feast. In the old days he would go to the palace of the *Rājā*, where the *Pāṭajoshi Mahāpātra* would tie on his head a silk sari and give him a handful of *nirmālya* (sundried) rice and some *guā* (betelnuts). He would then proceed to the temple where he would leave half the rice and take the other half to his house to be placed on the *tulasi* shrine there. On his way to his house, he would be accompanied by temple servants carrying *ghanṭā* (gong), *chati* (umbrella) and *kāhāḷi* (pipe) and would be given an appropriate welcome by the womenfolk before entering the house ... Today ... (this *sāḍhi* ... is not really a sari but an ordinary piece of inexpensive cloth".

It is also a tradition in Puri to use a strip of red cloth over the neck like a garland. The cloth is known as *Śrīkapaḍā* (auspicious cloth) and is worn by the deities. Traditionally this should be a silken cloth but now cotton cloths are also used in lieu of silk.

The same author quotes (and reproduces) a very interesting old *cāmu ciṭāu* or *Rājā*'s order for the *sāḍhi bandhā* or sari *bandhā* appointment which is translated by J.P. Das as follows: "Puri *Rājā* Dewan's office. For the information of *Deuḷa Karaṇa, Tadau* and others. *Citrakāra* Jagannātha Mahārāṇā's son Dīnabandhu and nephews Gaṅgādhara and Vāmana. Do the *śāḍhi bandhā* of these three and see that they perform *citrakāra sevā* etc. Let there be no negligence. November 14, 1885." It is very likely that for centuries the *Gītagovinda* inscribed textiles were used for sari *bandhā* to document the person's affiliation to the Puri Temple. Astonishingly *bāndha*-textiles can be inscribed with a variety of *Gītagovinda* verses. Right now we know of only a very limited number of such textiles in public museums. The following list cannot claim to be complete. The most common text ikated on silk fabrics from Odisha is

A ritual sāri with the verse of the Gītagovinda *woven into it. Length 149" width 55" from the collection of Mr and Mrs Jeremeja Singh Hundal, West Hollywood, California.*

Facing page: *A* sāḍhi *woven with* śloka–*kansārirapi samsāram vāsanabādha śṛnkalā etc. Museum Rietberg Zurich.*

22 J.P. Das, *Pata paintings of Orissa*, unpublished thesis, Sambalpur University, 1981, p. 35.

verse one of canto three of the *Gītagovinda*. It appears on two specimens of the Calico Museum of Textiles in Ahmedabad and on three of the Basle Ethnographic Museum in Switzerland.

Example 1

Ethnographic Museum, Basle (Switzerland), No. IIa 6429, purchased in Nuapāṭaṇā, woven by weavers of the *pāṭarā*-caste "for the Jagannātha Temple in Puri", acquired 1975 by M.L. Nabholz and E. Eschler-Krechl. The textile measures length 109cm. and width 138cm. Warp and weft are silk, only at the side-borders black cotton yarn; plain weave; the main warp is dyed red, at the borders black, the central stripe yellow like six more narrow stripes between the side borders and the ornamental side borders containing twelve petalled-flowers in weft—*ikat* in the colours white, yellow, red and green. The text is in Odia characters, tie-dyed in the weft, the white reserved in the red, and is repeated five times between one main adjusting hand and the other, marking the height of the textile. The warp *ikat* consists of sets of four threads, tie-dyed together.

The text reads:

Kaṃsārirapi saṃsāra-vāsanā bandha śṛmkhaḷa
Rādhāmādhavaya hṛdayey tatyāja braja sundariḥ

This corresponds entirely with the version printed in the book of Lee Siegel[23] except that *bandha śṛmkhaḷa* should be spelled *baddha*

23 Lee Siegel, *op. cit.*, p.293.

The first verse of the third canto of the Gītagovinda *woven on a scarf* (Pheṭā).

śṛmkhaḷa and *hṛdayam* should be *hṛdaye*. A rhythmic translation of the verse is given by Barbara Stoller Miller.[24]

"Kṛṣṇa, demon Kamsa's foe,
Feeling Rādhā bind his heart with chains
Of memories buried in other worldly lives
Abandoned the beautiful cowherd girls".

Lee Siegel[25] has translated the verses in prose:

"Moreover, the enemy of Kamsa, having placed Rādhā in his heart as the chain binding him with desire for the world, abandoned the beauties of Vraja". According to Siegel[26] the canto 3 describes that Kṛṣṇa begins to long for Rādhā, to suffer over his separation to her. He is called here "enemy of Kamsa", the demon-like king of Mathura, who tried in vain to destroy young Kṛṣṇa to prevent the prophecy of his own death through the hands of Kṛṣṇa.

We do not know why exactly this verse was selected to be inscribed on *bāndha*-textiles. But there are at least two interesting suggestions, one in the form of a legend, the other more historic. Pandit Sadāsiva Rath Sharmā of Puri has told a poetic story to Siegel.[27] According to him, originally twelve cloths existed as there are twelve cantos of the *Gītagovinda*. It was the poet Jayadeva himself, who asked the weavers of his home village Kenduli to weave the *Gītagovinda* in cloths. They consented on the condition that he would sing his song while they were working. "One day while they were on the seventh *sarga* Jayadeva became overwhelmed with emotion and went into a state of *taṭastha* (a spontaneous loss of consciousness, an ecstasy induced by his poem). The weavers stopped their work but at that time a cheerful *sādhu* came along playing the coconut *karatāla* (cymbals) and he said to the weavers, "Do not stop your work. I am Jayadeva's younger brother and I know the *Gītagovinda* by heart. I'll sing it so you can finish your sacred work". The *sādhu* left before the poet woke up. When he finally regained consciousness the weavers told him what had happened. Jayadeva said to them, "I have no brother. Only Padmāvatī and I know

The first verse of the third canto of the Gītagovinda *woven on a scarf* (Pheṭā) *by the weavers of Nuapāṭaṇā in Cuttack district.*

24 Stoller Miller, *Jayadeva's Gītagovinda*, 1977, p.82.

25 Lee Siegel, *op. cit.*, p.253.

26 *Ibid.*, p. 28.

27 Lee Siegel, *op. cit.*, p.230.

the *Gītagovinda*". The weavers showed Jayadeva the line the sādhu was singing for they had woven it into the cloth:

> *kamsārīrapi samsāra-vāsanā bandha sṛmkhalāṃ*
> *rādhāmādhavaya hṛdaye tatyāja vraja sundariḥ.*

[Moreover, the enemy of Kamsa, having placed Rādhā in his heart as the chain binding him with desire for the world, abandoned the beauties of Vraja) (III. 1).]

Jayadeva said to the weavers: "Only Lord Jagannātha could have sung this to you. I salute you, true *bhakta*". But it was the Caitanya movement[28] which realised the power and meaning of the *Gītagovinda* and especially of the lines quoted on the textiles (canto 3, verses 1-2). It was Śrī Rāmānanda who told Caitanya about the "inner sense" of the poem and comments: "And these two verses, O Lord, are full of meaning. And the more we look at the inner sense, the sweeter will be the meaning that they will reveal." According to Siegel, "the verses quoted present the crucial mystery of the Kṛṣṇa-cult. The highest Lord becomes truly human; he who is 'liberated from phenomenal-existence' (I. 21) enters into phenomenal existence, becomes bound and subject to pain like a man, as a man." And according to Caitanya, "Kṛṣṇa is the *Bhāgavat*, the Lord and Rādhā is the *mahābhāva*, the incarnation of the highest loving sentiment; Kṛṣṇa is the *śaktimat* and Rādhā is the *hlādini śakti*[28] The same text appears on a fragment of the same textiles (or at least from the same workshop) in the Basle Ethnographic Museum (No. IIa 6430) and on two pieces from the Calico Museum of Textiles in Ahmedabad (No. 2274 and 2418) collected and published by BC Mohanty and K. Krishna.[28a] All the details seem to be similar to our first example.

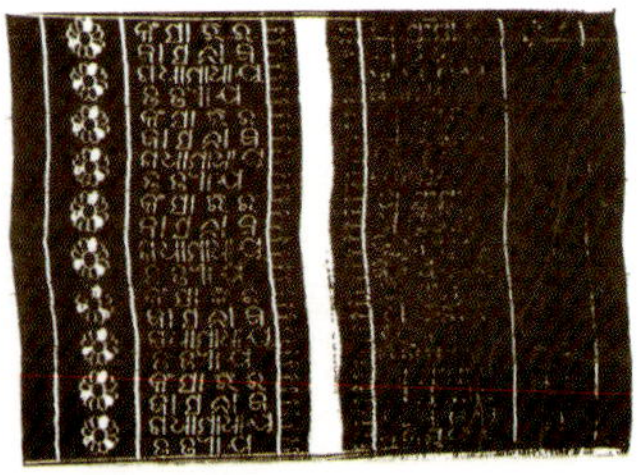

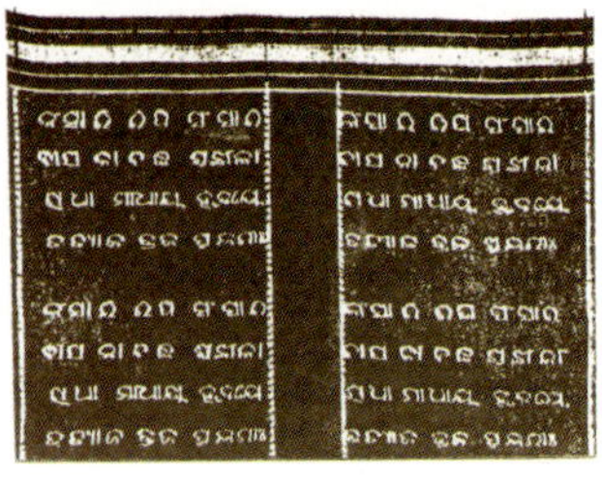

Gītagovinda *woven tie and dye textile, used as a ritual textile.*

A portion of the Gītagovinda *woven tie and dye sari.*

Example 2

Ethnographic Museum, Basle (Switzerland), No. IIa/5999, purchased by late Prof. Alfred Buhler in Muktanagar, Cuttack district in 1974. The silk textile may be old and could have been in use for quite sometime. It measures 133cm. width and 38cm. length. The colours are red with white reservations in the weft, with yellow, white and green stripes. The text is in Odia script of four lines which are repeated once up-side down. It is only tie-dyed in the weft. The text reads:

28 Lee Siegel, *op. cit.*, p.185.
28a Lee Siegel, *op. cit.*, p.30.

Vedānuddharate jaganti bahate bhūgolamudvibhrate
daityaṃ dāryate balim
chalayate kṣatra kṣayam kurvate.
Paulstyam yayate halam kalayate kārunyamtanvate
Mlechānmūrchayate dasākṛtikṛte
Kṛṣṇāya tubhyam namaḥ
Kamsārḥrapi samsāra vāsanābhadhya sṛimkhala
Rādhā mādhavā hṛdaye tatyaja vraja sundari

The first three lines belong to canto one, verse 16, the last line is again the beginning of canto 3, verse one of the *Gītagovinda.* In Lee Siegel's edition[29] the text of canto one verse 16 is the same except some minor variations and the lines of the ikated version are notes of verse but to fill the entire space available equally. The text is translated by Siegel[30] "Lifting the Vedas, supporting the world, raising-up the globe, tearing the demon (Hiraṇyakaśipu) to pieces, outwitting Bali, destroying the Kṣatriyas, conquering Paulastya (Rāvaṇa), bearing the plough, extending compassion, deranging the barbarians, creator of ten forms, homage to you Kṛṣṇa. This verse summarises the first song of the *Gītagovinda* which beautifully describes the *daśāvatāra* or ten incarnations of Viṣṇu, *i.e.* Matsya the fish, Kūrma, the tortoise, Varāha, the boar, Nṛsimha, the man-lion, Vāmana, the dwarf, Paraśurāma, Rāma, Baḷarāma, Buddha and Kaḷki. It is interesting to see that in this textile, the very traditional, rather orthodox verse of the ten reincarnations of God Viṣṇu (leaving out Kṛṣṇa or Jagannātha) are connected with the Rādhā Kṛṣṇa verse of the third canto, so much liked by the *bhakti*-movement of Caitanya, as if a kind of compromise was made. The same four lines of canto one, verse 16 (but without the addition of other verses) appear as well on a large *ikat*-cloth (length 149, width 55) in a private collection in the United States (West-Hollywood), of which unfortunately, we only could see a Xerox copy of a photograph without additional information, but kindly supplied by Mrs K. Hacker of Seattle Museum of Art (United States of America).

Example 3

Ethnographic Museum, Basle (Switzerland), No. IIa 2452, purchased from a Dutch dealer in 1963 without additional information. Two text columns

29 *Ibid.*, p.186.

30 *op.cit.*, p.243.

flanked by rows of squares and arrow-head motifs, divided by a broad, plain yellow central field. The script is, along with these motifs, tie-dyed in the weft, white reserved on dark red ground. There are a few warp stripes in green. The end pieces are multi-coloured. The textile measures 370 cm (length) and 133 cm. (width). The text is inscribed in *Devanāgari* script and is composed of verse one of canto four and verse one of canto three. On the textile, the ikated inscription starts with the fifth line, the actual beginning is a repetition of the last four lines of the same verse. With line 12 the well-known third canto starts.

> *Jamayamunā tīravanira nikuṇje mandamasthitam*
> *Praha premabhāro bharaitam mādhave rādhikāsakhiḥ*
> *Kamsārirapi samsāravāsanā badha śṛmkhalā*
> *Rādhāmādhava hṛdaye ta.....*

This inscription again, is very near to the printed version[31] except that the beginning *Yamunā tīra vanira* has changed to *jamayamunā tīra vānira* and *Mādhavam* is *Mādhave.* The translation provided by Siegel[32] is "Rādhikā's friend spoke to Mādhava, who was distracted by the burden of love, who was welling languidly in a grove of reeds on the bank of the Yamunā". Why exactly these lines were chosen for a ritualistic textile is difficult to imagine. The dimensions of this large cloth may be interpreted as those of a sari (possibly of a devotee or a lady employed in the services of Lord Jagannātha like a *māhārī* or dancer) or of a shoulder cloth for the monumental images of the three deities of Puri.

31 Lee Siegel, *op. cit.*, p.288

32 *Ibid.*, p.243.

LITERATURE

Style

Bhagaban Panda

The *Gītagovinda* is a short Sanskrit poem of unique character based on the love of Rādhā and Kṛṣṇa in Vṛndāvana. The poem is divided into twelve cantos and is endowed with most of the characteristics of a traditional *kāvya*. But it is not a stereotyped *kāvya* according to the rhetoricians. Though it is not strictly a drama, its literary form prompts dramatic sequences. The dialogues in the poem create an atmosphere of theatrical enactment. The modern scholars like Jones, Lassen, Pischel and Levi for this reason label it as a drama[1]. The poet Jayadeva, himself categorises it as a *prabandha* which can be sung and can also be performed with the accompanying music and dance. So strictly defining, the *Gītagovinda* is neither a *kāvya* nor a drama in its logical sense but a combination of both, which has given it a novel touch as a unique literary piece in the whole of Sanskrit literature. It has a form of its own and therefore rightly defies a conventional classification as prescribed by the rhetoricians.

The *Gītagovinda* probably bears a mixed phenomenon of old *līlā* or *yātrā* which was prevalent during the time of the poet. He was inspired by this local *yātrā* and wrote such a popular poem for his Lord Kṛṣṇa.

According to Keith[2], to conceive writing such a poem, *Gītagovinda*, was a remarkable feat with originality, for it is an immense step away from the popular songs of *yātrā* to be produced so remarkably as a beautiful work. It is a combination of narration, description and speech which form a unique form in Sanskrit literature. As noted by the scholars, Jayadeva's *Gītagovinda* appears to be a noteworthy example of an attempt to remodel older forms of composition by absorbing the newer characteristics of the vernacular literature.[3]

Facing page: *Rādhā and* sakhī *conversing inside a leafy arbour, palmleaf painting, Orissa State Museum.*

Page 201: *Lakṣmī seated on a lotus, palmleaf painting, Museum Rietberg Zurich. A* sakhī *pulls Rādhā to her side to part with some confidential talk. Palmleaf painting, Orissa State Museum (below).*

---

1 Śrī Kṛṣṇa Caitanya, *A New History of Sanskrit Literature*, p.413.

2 A.B. Keith, *A History of Sanskrit Literature, London*, 1966, p.192.

3 Dasgupta, *History of Sanskrit Literature*, Vol.I, 1962, p.395.

The poem has been divided into 12 cantos, 24 *prabhandha* or songs and 77 verses. According to the tradition, the *Gītagovinda* contains 72 verses only, which has been attested by the poets of Odisha beginning from the 17th century.[4] The first and the tenth *prabandha* contain eleven and five stanzas respectively, but the rest twenty-two *prabandha* contain eight stanzas each for which the songs are called *Aṣṭapadi.* The poet has noted the names of ten *rāga* such as Mālava, Gujjari or Gurjari, Vasanta, Varāḍi, Deśi or Deśi-varāḍi, Deṣākśya, Karnāṭa, Bhairava for twenty-four songs. They are divided as follows according to the *Bālabodhini ṭīkā* by Caitanya Dāsa. One *prabandha* each in Deśi, Deśvarāḍi, Deśākṣya, Karnāṭa and Bhairavi, three each in Rāmakeri, Varāḍi and Vasanta, two each in Mālava and Guṇḍakeri and six in Gujjari. According to the *Śrutiranjanī ṭīkā* by Lakṣmaṇa Sūrī the *prabandha* should be sung eight each in male, female and neutral *rāga* and each one alternatively.[5] But variations are found not in directions of *rāga* but also in the use of the *tāla* which were not found mentioned in older manuscripts of *Gītagovinda* available so far in India. But in different editions of the *Gītagovinda* the number of *rāga* vary from 11 to 13 and number of verses from 72 to 113.

The first canto begins with introductory verses (v. 1-4) and two invocations to Viṣṇu in his ten incarnations (v. 5-6, p. 1-2). The poet through a companion of Rādhā describes the beauty of spring season in the Vṛndāvana where Kṛṣṇa plays with the *gopī* (v. 6-12, p. 3-4). The canto is named *Sāmodadāmodara* or Dāmodara who is full of delight. In the second canto Rādhā's sorrow and her complaints and happy moments with Kṛṣṇa are described (v-14, p. 5-6). This is named as *Akleśakeśava* or Keśava without sorrow. In the third canto the lamentation of Kṛṣṇa within himself for Rādhā is expressed beautifully (v. 1-7. p.7). This is called as *Mugdhamadhusūdana* or the enamoured Kṛṣṇa. In the fourth canto a companion of Rādhā meets Kṛṣṇa and tells him about Rādhā's suffering and her longing for union with Him (v. 1-6, p. 8-9). This canto is named *Snigdhamadhusūdana* or Kṛṣṇa who was feeling happy and at peace.

In the fifth canto Kṛṣṇa requests the companion to bring Rādhā to the bower where he will wait for her (v. 1-6, p. 10-11). This is named as *Sākāṅkṣa Puṇḍarīkākṣa* or lotus eyed Kṛṣṇa who was full of desire. The sixth canto describes Rādhā's weakness due to separation from Kṛṣṇa for which the lady messenger comes to Kṛṣṇa and requests him to come to Rādhā who

4 K. N. Mahapatra, *Śrī Jayadeva O' Śrī Gītagovinda*, pp.341-352.

5 B.Panda, ed. *Gītagovinda,* Directorate of Culture, Orissa.

is waiting for him (v. 1-3, p.12). This is named *Sotkaṇṭa Vaikuṇṭha* or Kṛṣṇa who is eagerly waiting for Rādhā. In the seventh canto it is described that Kṛṣṇa was not able to come to meet Rādhā. Rādhā apprehends something negative and her apprehension grows stronger when she sees her companion returning alone. Rādhā scolds the breeze, God of love and Yamunā who enhance her pangs of separation (v. 1-9, p. 13-16). This canto is named *Nāgaranārāyaṇa* or Nārāyaṇa as the lover of Rādhā.

In canto eight Kṛṣṇa comes to meet Rādhā in the morning. He places himself at her feet. But Rādhā rebukes and asks him to leave (v. 1-2, p. 17). It is named as *Vilakṣya Lakṣmīpatī* or the lord of Lakṣmī who is surprised. The title of the ninth canto is *Mugdha-Mukunda* or Mukunda who was enchanted while Rādhā was thinking, and her friend in a consoling voice asks her to be kind to Kṛṣṇa (v. 1-2, p. 18). The tenth canto narrates the scenes of evening and Kṛṣṇa praises Rādhā and supplicates her to put her feet on his head to remove the poison of passion (v. 1-7, p. 19). This is named as *Caturacaturbhuja* or Viṣṇu, the cleaver with four arms.

In the eleventh canto Kṛṣṇa was able to solace Rādhā and the companion helped them to unite and they both went into the bridal chamber (v. 1-9, p.20-22). This is named *Sānandadāmodara* or Dāmodara who is full of joy. The last canto describes the frank sport of love of Rādhā and Kṛṣṇa. At last Rādhā requests her lover *Pitāmvara* to decorate her as before (v.1-7 p.23-24). The poet then concludes the work saying about his own knowledge of music, his devotion to Viṣṇu, his delicate discrimination of sentiments and his poetic charm and grace and mentions the names of his parents and friends (v.8-10). The twelfth canto is named as *Suprīta Pitāmvara* or Pitāmvara who is wholly pleased.

The *Gītagovinda* is a beautiful work endowed with sweet, simple and melodious words and remains unparalleled in the whole of Sanskrit literature. As the scholars say the exclusive reliance on the beauty of form or outward expression in a piece of literary creation is certainly a drawback or handicap since, perhaps much more than the form, the subject matter or the contents is important. And herein, in the appreciation of the *Gītagovinda,* the approach of the reader, his subjective attitude is the determining factor.[6]

The *Śṛṅgāra*, which is variously described as physical love, is the main *rasa* or sentiment of the *Gītagovinda.* The description of the scene of nature with trees, creepers, flowers, hills, streams, singing birds and bees and the seasons, mainly the spring, serves as the background of the work.

---

6 S.K.Chatterji, *Jayadeva*, Sahitya Akademi, New Delhi, 1981, p.48.

Imitation

Banamali Rath

In appreciation of the qualities of the *Gītagovinda*, a host of Indian writers, highly inspired by its universal appeal, have attempted at different times, to compose poems in imitation of this masterpiece. The scholars from all parts of India in general and the poets of Odisha[1] in particular born and brought up in that glorious tradition[2] of Sanskrit culture, have composed, in Sanskrit, more than one hundred and thirty imitative works giving vent to their poetic ingenuity and erotico-devotional ecstasy.

Apart from a few works of this type available in print, a bulk of such imitative works continues, to be discovered in manuscripts and a number of them have been lost in the course of time. But many interesting stray verses and fragmentary songs and, in some cases, the names only of such *gītakāvya* have been preserved in the later commentaries, rhetorical works, anthologies and works on musicology. For our discussion here, we have taken into consideration the whole bulk of imitative works of the *Gītagovinda*. These present a critical estimate of the works which have been either published or preserved in manuscript form in different Oriental Manuscript Libraries, or appear as references in different catalogues of Sanskrit manuscripts prepared by Indological institutions in India and abroad. The limited space here does not permit us to go into it at length but elsewhere,[3] a list of such works has been annexed to this article for ready reference.

Much has been said and discussed elsewhere on the literary beauty and devotional fervour of the *Gītagovinda* and its imitations; but two vital points

Facing page: *Rādhā conversing with a* sakhī *in a forest with a resting tiger, palmleaf painting, Orissa State Museum.*

---

1 Banamali Rath, "Contribution of Orissa to Indian Lyrics" in the *Proceedings of the International Sanskrit Conference*, Vol. I, Part I, 1975, pp.382-400.

2 Banamali Rath, "A family of poet-cum-rhetoricians in Orissa" in *Jhankar*, (Oriya) Feb. 1958, Vol. IX, No. 12, pp.1048-90.

3 Banamali Rath, *A Study on the Srikṛṣṇalīlāmṛtam*, Ch. VIII.

regarding their form and sentiments need clarification which would solve the problems posed by the accepted canons of literary evaluation in India.

Literary form of the *Gītagovinda* and the tradition

The literary style of the *Gītagovinda* and its imitations, which is a mixed feature of traditional verses and newly improvised songs, has been introduced for the first time[4] by the celebrated poet Jayadeva. But, about the form of the *Gītagovinda* there is diversity of opinion amongst scholars. Lassen has classed it as a lyric drama, Jones as a pastoral drama, Levy as an opera, Pischel as a melodrama and Von Schroeder as a refined folk-play or *yātrā*.[5] But the poets of these *gītakāvya* have termed their works as *mahākāvya*,[6] though they do not conform to the conventional pattern of the *mahākāvya*.

The divergent views of the scholars are in no way helpful for an exact assessment of the subject. It will not be out of place, here, to trace the history of this new development in the field of Sanskrit *mahākāvya*. In the whole field of Sanskrit literature, we have a few standard *mahākāvya* complete in all respects in comparison with shorter *kāvya* (*khandakāvya*) and dramas. The art of writing *mahākāvya*, in its proper sense, was fully and assiduously cultivated by the vaunted court-poets, patronised by the cultured kings of the past. By the 9th century AD, with the rare exceptions of the works of the versatile scholars like Śriharṣa and Rājaśekhara, the production of the *mahākāvya* and dramas of unnecessary verbosity and bombast, artificial ornateness, etc have petered out, perhaps, due to the severe stricture[7] passed by the great critics like Ānandavardhana and others. As a result of this, hundreds of shorter *kāvya* less ambitious in verbal tropes and rigidity in texture, came into being. The more formal compliance with the formalities advocated by earlier theorists were gradually disapproved by the writers as well as readers. The later poeticists like Vidyādhara and Viśvanātha[8] came to the rescue of these

---

4 S.K. De, *Aspects of Sanskrit Literature*, 1959, p.138; Also see A.R. Dasgupta, *Indian Lyrics*, 1962, pp.21-24.

5 *Śrī Kṛṣṇa Caitanya, A New History of Sanskrit Literature*, p.413.

6 The colophons at the end of the *Gītagovinda*, *Śrikṛṣṇalīlāmṛtam* by Nityananda, and *Mukunda vilāsa* by Jatindra Raghuttama, Tirtha, etc. Manuscripts preserved in the Orissa State Museum, Bhubaneswar.

7 *Dhvanyāloka*, II.19-20, and *Vṛtti* thereon: *Vivakṣa tatparatvena*, etc and III. 14 and *Vṛtti: Dṛṣyante ca kavayo lamkāraniban dhanaikarasa anapekṣitarasa prabandheṣu.*

8 *Sāhitya Darpaṇa*, Ch. VI.p.328.

shorter creations and practically a place of honour was given to them. So the tradition of writing *mahākāvya* continued without a stop, but the popular *kāvya* too were compiled with the definitions of *mahākāvya* in their own way.

Kṣemendra (11th century) and the early medieval poets like Dāmodaragupta and Kavirāja introduced a new style for the short *kāvya*. Poets as well as readers attached much importance to the *yamaka-kāvya* and *śleṣa-kāvya*.[9] Thus the *kāvya* of the day tried to exhibit the power of displaying the poet's mastery in wordy jugglery and pedantry in *śabdāḷankāra*. Less talented poets began to write hundreds of *kāvya* by mere elaboration of the episodes, taken from the great epics and *Purāṇa*. Some have used this form in writing mere summaries, whereas a band of poets utilised this to write biographies and historical *kāvya*. All these writings, though named as *mahākāvya*, were far away from the compactness, textural rigidity, artificial ornateness and the pedantic bombast of the earlier classical ones, yet all these later varieties of works were called *mahākāvya* in a general sense. Jayadeva, the author of the *Gītagovinda* and a host of other writers of *gītakāvya* also used this form of *sargabandha* and introduced a new genre. Jayadeva could keep up the standard and even exceeded the early masters of classical epics in enriching the external texture of the *kāvya*. But, often he lags behind, so far as the inner essence is concerned. Of the type of *kāvya* under the name of *mahākāvya* discussed above, a few exceptions are always there. Though the counterfeits of the *Gītagovinda* have declared themselves as *mahākāvya*, yet with equal footing they can match neither the older classics nor the *Gītagovinda* in certain respects. Nevertheless, they have their own brilliant features which can never be underestimated.

The main sentiment of the *Gītakāvya* and the canonical deliberations

It is well-known that the poets of the *gītakāvya* (termed as *mahākāvya*) also intended their works to be appreciated by the readers from the standpoint of a purely literary work.[10] Now to go deep into it, it should be

---

9 S.P. Bhattacharya, "The Vṛndavana Yamaka and its author", in *V.R. Society Bulletin*, 1931.

10 *Srikṛṣṇalīlāmṛtam*, the last verse, No. 181. *cetas cet kavitā sudhā jalanidhavaplavamasamsati*. (the manuscript of the *Śrikṛṣṇalīlāmṛtam* is preserved in the Manuscript Library of the Orissa State Museum, Bhubaneswar).

made clear that the early and later poeticists have framed the rules[11] for the guidance of the poets to study and to create standard *mahākāvya* in the field. At least a few of the most important features of the technicalities became imperative and binding on the medieval writers of this literary type. Amongst the notable features, prescribed by the critics in the canons of literary judgement, specially the recipes for the plot (*vastu*), the hero (*netā*) and the sentiment (*rasa*), dominant and accessory, were invariably adhered to by the poets.

It is stated that the poet must be aware of the fact that all his descriptive and narrative analysis of the plot, the creative ingenuity, poetic device and the ideational subtlety which are generally employed to beautify the theme, should be made subordinate to the supersensuous transcendental delectation of the poem. Ānandavardhana, the master critic, prescribes that *rasatātparya*,[12] quite distinct from *vastutātparya*, should be the main aim of the *mahākāvya* and proper emphasis should be laid thereon, which has been accepted, elaborated and sincerely adumbrated by the host of later theorists of the Dhvani school.[13] Perhaps, critics like Ānandavardhana and Abhinavagupta, prescribed this restriction keeping the whole early medieval literary works in view, which marked a great diversion from suggestive beauty and were striving to be mere narrative ones, dilating upon much hackneyed *Purāṇic* themes. Especially the *kāvya*, dealing with the Kṛṣṇa legend, advanced too much, in this respect, without caring for the recipes of the canons of poetic judgement or the views of the master critics in the field. The problem is, whether the description of love between Kṛṣṇa and the *gopī* in the manner of the well-known *Purāṇic rāsalīlā*, is to be accepted as proper or improper, legal or illegal.[14] If it is legal, then there is no problem. It goes without saying that the work dealing with such a highly erotic legal theme will be accepted as a standard work suggestive of *Śṛṅgāra-rasa* in consonance with the accepted maxims. If it is construed as illegal[15] according to the

11 *Kāvyādarśa*, I. p. 18-19; *Dhvanyāloka*, III. pp. 10-14; *Sāhitya Darpaṇa*, VI. pp.315-324.

12 *Dhvanyāloka*, III. p. 7 and *Vṛtti thereon: Sargabandhe tu rasatātparyeṇa yathārasamauchityam anyathā tu kāmāchāraḥ.*

13 *Kāvyamīmāmsā*, pp. 44-45; *Kāvyanuṣāsana*, VIII; *Kāvyādarśa*, I.pp.16-17.

14 The illegality of love referred to here is *parakiyā prīti* (the love between man and woman wedded to another person). In *rāslīlā* we find this type of love as the main theme of the *Kṛṣṇite kāvya*.

15 This question of legality or illegality of love has been raised in the *Śrimad-bhāgavatam* itself. *Śrimad-bhāgavata*, 10.33 pp.227-29.

code of Indian life, the work dealing with such an episode should be regarded as suggestive of *sṛṅgārarasabhāsa*; and, thereby the principle of maintaining the *rasatātparya,* which is the criterion of a work, is shattered. As a result of which a great bulk of our literature would be branded as second-rate creations.

It is a noteworthy fact that propriety in thought and expression has played a great role in the analysis of human sentiments and feelings in literature. In the ancient literature of India we find that much importance has been attached to and much emphasis laid on the idealism and proper conduct of life. The Indian critics, who have been born and brought up in such traditions, had to declare their measured deliberations in connection with poetic judgement as what is a decent, decorous and agreeable picture in the ideational treatment of a sentimental theme. But on the other hand, it is quite natural on the part of a man to have lapses and incongruity in his action, thinking and feeling and literature being a true picture of the human life is also to record all these. In the context of such deliberations the critic had to pass his remark as to what should be and what should not be recorded in literature. When it is admitted and realised on all hands that only by suggestion of sentiment and feeling the ultimate goal of poetry is achieved, it was the main job of the critic to treat the sentiment and feelings from the stand-point of propriety (*aucitya*) in relation with the standard code of conduct as sanctioned by the sacred lore and popular usage. Thus we find much controversial deliberations on the subject under the name of *rasa* and *rasābhāsa*[16] in Indian poetics.

So according to the Indian poeticists, in general, the love between a man and a woman, who is not a wedded wife, is improper and the suggestion of impropriety in love is called *śṛṅgāra-rasābhāsa.*[17]

From the standpoint of this poetic judgement all the *kāvya*, dealing with the love-episode between Kṛṣṇa and the *gopī*, turn into *kāvya* suggestive of *rasābhāsa*. Practically most of the poets in their *gītakāvya* deal with the *rāsalīlā*, the *Purāṇic* love-episode between Kṛṣṇa and

---

16 *Kāvyaprakāśa* ed. *Jhallkikar*, p. 121, *Sūtra* 49 and *Vṛtti* thereon: *Tadābhāsah anaucitya-pravarititah.*

17 *Sāhitya Darpaṇa*, ch. III. 262-263 and the example there of: *anaucitya-pravṛttatve ābhāso rasa-bhāvayoḥ and Upanāyaka-samsthāyām.....*
Example:
"*Raterupanayakanisthasya yatha-*
Svami mugdhataro vanam ghanamidam balaha
mekakim/tanme sundara munca krsna ....

the *gopī*. Kṛṣṇa is depicted here as a paramour[18] and the *gopī* as others' housewives in the manner of other *kāvya* of the same theme. Viśvanātha Kavirāja, the later poeticist, unlike others, though counts it as *rasābhāsa*, finds no difference between *rasa* and *rasābhāsa*, in delectation, and regards it on a par with *rasa*.[19] Viśvanātha in his masterly work *Sāhitya Darpaṇa* deals with the poetic sentiment exhaustively and declares with cogent arguments that *rasa* is the only criterion in judging a work as a piece of literature. According to him, a creative work quite suggestive of beautiful experiences of human feelings, irrespective of social propriety or impropriety can be accepted as a first rate literature on the basis of sound *rasa* theory. This has been established by him with hair-splitting analysis of the subject. Thus the Sanskrit *gītakāvya*, dealing with the amorous dalliances of Rādhā and Kṛṣṇa are regarded as the best type of works even if there is a sense of impropriety according to the code and conduct of Indian social life. A later theorist, while dilating on propriety (*aucitya*) of the hero, makes a significant concession in the case of Lord Kṛṣṇa[20] who according to him cannot be judged by the ordinary principle of *rasa* theory. Later on, the famous *Goswāmin*, the master of *Rasa-śāstra* of Bengal *Vaiṣṇavava* doctrines, developed the theories of their own to appreciate devotional *Vaiṣṇava* works. Practically in that spirit the readers will have to appreciate the works under reference. It should be borne in mind that the movement of *bhakti* in medieval India created such an impetus and environment that life and thought were bound to assume newer significance. The aim of the poets was to glorify the deeds[21] of Kṛṣṇa and attain emancipation thereby. Moreover, their attempts were aimed at sublimating the activities of Kṛṣṇa, the Supreme Being[22] who

---

18 *Srikṛṣṇalīlāmṛtam*, verse Nos. 85,92,95; song No. 17:
Upapatiratimanditatapada....
songs No. 24:
patisutabandhavama-
pahaya.

19 *Sāhitya Darpaṇa*, III. 259.
Rasabhāvau tadabhāsau bhāvasya prasamodayau/
Santih sabalata ceti sarve 'pi rasanad rasah //

20 Introduction to *Hari-caritam*, ed. S.P. Bhattacharya, p. 5, fn. 25; the pre-Caitanya *alaṅkāra* writer Sudeva Mishra in his *Rasavilāsa*.
Nesta yadangini rase kavibhih parodha-
stad gokulāmbujadṛśam kulamantareṇa /
aśamsayarasavidheravatari-tānām
kamāriṇa rasikamaṇḍala sekhareṇa //

21 *Srikṛṣṇalīlāmṛtam*, verse Nos. 1-9 *Gopalalīlā*, 1.5.

22 *Śrimadbhāgavatam*, 10.33. 30-40, This point has been discussed at length.

descended on earth to impart godly grace through the manifestation of his *līlā*.[23] It may be pointed out here that the poet Jayadeva and a host of his followers were aware of all these viewpoints and framed their works accordingly where the critic meets neither with the rigid sectarian doctrinalism nor the stereotyped ways of mere formal compliance with the conventionalities of *kāvya* making, as was expected of Jayadeva and other poets who had proper training and balanced grounding in *kāvya* and *Purāṇic* literature which contributed substantially to their skilful literary compositions.

From a careful perusal of the bulk of the *gītakāvya* referred to in the Annexure, it can be generally remarked that though most of them have their elegance and sentimental subtleties, yet they cannot be estimated at par with the superb *Gītagovinda*. Though all the works have been written in imitation of the *Gītagovinda*, they vary in the choice of themes. While most of the works have been written in praise of Rādhā-Kṛṣṇa-līlā, after the manner of the *Gītagovinda*, yet some of them depict the Siva-līlā, Rāma-līlā, Kātyāyanī-līlā, Viṣṇu-līlā and so on. All these works are of devotional character and they present different aspects of the *līlā* with a background of highly sensuous charm. At times the erotico-religious compositions of the devoted poets are considered to be the products of spontaneous inspiration, while some of them appear to be mere meretricious display of artificial and erudite fancy. Nevertheless, in the treatment of their highly luscious and erotico-devotional theme, the poets have invested their mystic poems with the whole gamut of erotic motif, imagery and expression, along with the exquisite verbal melody and pictorial fancy which have substantially contributed towards their popularity in the field. In spite of the applause they receive for their vivid exuberance of erotic fancy and emotional inflatus in the depiction of the much hackneyed romantic theme where the emotional and rhetorical contrivances have been sufficiently displayed, one would scarcely come across a genuine poetic talent of an independent and original character in these imitative *gītakāvya*.

But in the history of devotional literature in Sanskrit, these *gītakāvya* are, to some extent, responsible for bringing out a new development. Perhaps for the first time, the advent of the *Gītagovinda* created a new genre and a forceful impetus for the creation of religious poems, essentially devotional and emotionally religious, based on transfigured

23 *Srikṛṣṇalīlāmṛtam*, verse No. 179.

sex-passion. The blending of eroticism in the speculative religious thought sufficiently enlivened the medieval religious movement of bhakti and its literature. The poets of the *gītakāvya*, following the footprints of the celebrated poet. Jayadeva, lifted one of the most powerful impulses of human mind into a means of glorious exaltation. In the field of religion and literature, it attracted the masses through its emotional and aesthetic appeal against the high intellectuality of dry dogmas and doctrines. Thus the new application of the apparatus and inventory of *rasaniṣpatti* along with the technicalities of the *Kāmaśāstra* in the making of the religio-literary *gītakāvya* became novel, intimate and inspiring; as a result of which the erotic sensibility, in its devotional ecstasy often rose above the rhetorical formalities that provided the scope for the depiction of intimate personal feeling with the touch of empirical investigations of the gifted poets. But on the other hand, one must accept that a few poets of this age carried the erotic sentiment to such a lamentable extreme that the descriptions of the dubious acts and jests, which are frank expressions of physical passion, undoubtedly appear unpalatable to the cultured mind. However esoteric the sense may be, they are presented as literal facts, for which sex and sex alone supplies the incentive.

In spite of this solecism the poems bear the stamp of poetic merits that are responsible in savouring the suavity of the romantic subject and sentiment. The passion in these poems is genuine. The pictures possess delicacy of feeling and gratefulness of poetic touch. The reality and richness of the emotion often attained the appreciable standard. But the works being fashioned after the standard pattern of the *Gītagovinda*, have become too much alike, the subjects lack variety and strikingness of inventive thought; the treatment is somewhat similar and the style and diction employed more or less the same series of decorative devices and conceits; yet it cannot be gainsaid that we often find in them a rare and pleasing charm, the succulent possibilities of a highly erotic subject, the luscious exuberance of picturesqueness and mellifluousness, produced by the harmonious adjustment of sound and sense, though the employment of befitting method, manner, form and diction are often remarkable and convincing. Though the *gītakāvya* along with their mighty sex-impulse have been viewed from different standpoints of human values, yet it is accepted on all hands that undoubtedly it was a positive literary gain of immense importance which could successfully inspire the people in their religious and literary pursuits for the last few centuries.

Facing page: Kandarparatha, *pata painting, Puri.*

Annexure

A list of the Imitations of the Gītagovinda

SI. No.	Name of the work	Name of the Author	Date. AD
1	Abhinava-Gītagovinda	Gajapati Puruṣottamadeva	1480
2	Ānandalatikā-nāṭikā	Rāmakṛṣṇa	
3	An unknown work of King	Puruṣottama (Bhānudeva-II)	1328
4	An unknown work of Kṛṣṇadāsa		1570
5	An unknown work of RājāRaghunātha Haricandana		1620
6	An unknown work of Govindadāsa		1577
7	An unknown work of Rādhāmohana Thākura		1698
8	An unknown work of Harihara Miśra		18th cent.
9	Balabhadra-vijaya	Nārāyaṇa Miśra	
10	Bahubalisvāmin Aṣṭāpadi (Gīta vitarāga)		
11	Bālarāmāyaṇa	Puruṣottama Miśra	
12	Bhāgavata-gītāvallī		
13	Bhonsale-vaṃśāvali-campū	Naidhruva Kāśyapa	
14	Brajayuva-vilāsa	Kamalalocana Khadgarāya	1790
15	Candikā-carita-candrikā	Kṛṣṇadatta	1646
16	Cārugita-kāvya	Nañjarāja	
17	Chandomakhānta [Chandomakaranda]	Puruṣottamabhatta	1550
18	Citrayajña-nāṭikā	Rāmakṛṣṇa	
19	Dārukavana-viįāsa	Ratnaradhya	17th Cent.
20	Gaṅgavamśānucarita-campu	Vāsudeva Rath	
21	Gītagaurīśa (Gītagaurīpati)	Bhānudatta	1320
22	Gītamukunda	Kamalalocana Khadagarāya	1790

23	Gītagiriśa	Rāma Bhatta	1513
24	Gītasaṃkara	Bhiṣma Miśra	
25	Gītaśaṃkara	Hira	
26	Gītagopīpati	Kṛṣṇadatta	1646
27	Gītarāghava	Hariśankara	
28	Gītapītavasana	Syāmarāma Kavi	
29	Gītasītāvallabhaṃ	Sītikanṭha	
30	Gītāvalī	Rūpagosvāmi	1470-1554
31	Gītadigāmbara	Haṃsamani	1655
32	Gītagopāla	Caturbhuja	
33	Gītasankariyam	Jayanārāyaṇa Ghosal	
34	Gītagangādhara	Kalyāṇa	
35	Gītarāghava	Prabhākara	1674
36	Gītagaurīvara(Gītagari)	Tirumalla	
37	Gītabhāgavatam	Rayadurga Nṛpati	
38	Gītavītarāga	Abhinava Cārukirti	
39	Gītagaṅgādhara	Rājaśekhara	
40	Gītagaṅgādhara	Chandraśekhara	
41	Gītapradīpa	Jagaddhara	
42	Gītāvalī (Bhāgavata-gītāvali)		
43	Gītasītāpati	Acyutarāya Modaka	
44	Gītavītarga (Bahubali-swami Aṣṭapadi)		
45	Gītagaṅgādhara	Ga¿gādhara	
46	Gītagirīśa	Śrīharṣa	
47	Gītagirīśa (Śivāṣṭapadi)	Mahākavi Ramabhaṭṭa	
48	Gītarāghava-kāvyam	Rāmakavi	
49	Gītaśankara	Anantanārāyaṇa	
50	Gītasundara (Sangīta-sundara)	Sadādśiva	
51	Gītagopāla	Caturbhuja	
52	Gītadāmodara	Śaṃbhurāma	
53	Gītamādhava	Revārāma	
54	Gītarasa	Lakṣmaṇasoma Yati	
55	Gītamaheśvara	Lakṣmaṇasoma Yati	
56	Gītāṣtaka	Sundarācārya	
57	Gītagaurīpati	Śankara Miśra	
58	Gītamakaranda		
59	Gītagaurīśa	Rāmabhadra	

60	Gītamahanāṭa	Vamśamaṇi	
61	Gītagovindāṣtaka		
62	Gopagovinda		1625
63	Gopālakeli-candrikā	Rāmakṛṣṇa	
64	Gopāla-campu	Jīvagoswāmi	1511-1566
65	Harismṛti-sudhānkura	Raghunandana	
66	Jagannāthavallabha-nātaka	Rayarāmānada	1500
67	Jānakīgīta	Hariharācārya	
68	Kāśīgīta	Chandradatta	
69	Kṛṣṇagīti	Somanātha	16th Cent.
70	Kṛṣṇavijaya		
71	Kṛṣṇagīti	Mānadeva	1652
72	Kṛṣṇavilāsa	Kaviratna Nārāyana Miśra	1644
73	Kṛṣṇalīlā-taranginī	Bellamkondā Ramāramaṇa Śāstri	1857
74	Kṛṣṇalīlā-taranginī	Rāmasāyaka Kavi	
75	Kṣamadadgīta-cintāmaṇi	Viśvanātha Cakravarti	1664
76	Mādhavagīta-sudhā	Rāghava Apakhandekara	
77	Mudita-mādhava	Śatañjiva Miśra	1650
78	Mukundavilāsa-mahākāvya	Yatīndr Raghūttama Tīrtha	1667
79	Mukundānanda	Kāśikapati	
80	Nandighoṣavijaya-nātika	Rāmakṛṣṇa	
81	Nañjarājadasamollāsa-campu	Nīlakanṭha	
82	Nañjarāja-campu	Srinivasacārya	
83	Patavilāsa(Sahaji-vilsa)	Dhundivyāsa	
84	Rāghava-Prabandhaṃ		
85	Rāghavāṣtapadi		
86	Rāmagītagovinda	Jayadeva	
87	Ramoda-harana-gitakāvya	Venkatapā Nāyaka	
88	Ramagītakāvya	Vṛttamani Sriṇivāsacārya	
89	Rāmagīta	Kṛṣṇabhatta	
90	Ramoda-harana-gitikāvyam	Nārāyaṇa Svāmi	
91	Rāmachandrodaya	Puruṣottama Miśra	

92	Rāmābhyudaya	Puruṣottama Miśra	
93	Rāmakathā-sudhodaya	Saiva Śrīnivāsa Sūri	
94	Rasavihara	Mādhava	
95	Rukmiṇipariṇaya	Nārāyaṇa Bhañja	
96	Rukmiṇyastapadi		
97	Sahaji-vilāsa(Patavilāsa)	Dhundi vyāsa	
98	Sahaji-rājāṣtapadī	Śrī Śrīnivāsa	
99	Samṛddha-mādhava-nātaka	Govinda Sāmantarāya	1594
100	Sangīta-cintāmaṇi	Kamalalocana Khadgarāya	1790
101	Sangīta-rāghava	Gangādhara	186
102	Sangīta-raghunandana	Priyādāsa	1832
103	Sangīta-gangādhara	Nañjarāja	1750
104	Sangīta-mādhava	Prabodhānanda Sarasvatī	
105	Sangīta-mādhava	Govinda Dāsa	1537
106	Sangīta-rāghava	Cinnābommā Bhupāla	
107	Sangīta-sundara	Sadaśiva	
108	Sangīta-Govinda	Madhusūdana	
109	Śankara-vihāra	Nārāyaṇa Miśra	
110	Sankari-sangītaṃ (Gītasamkariyam)	Jayanārāyaṇa Ghosal	
111	Sankarī-gīti		
112	Śāntasudhārasa	Muni Vinayavijaya	
113	Sarabhoji-rajacarita	Ananta Nārāyaṇa	
114	Śivalīlāmṛta-mahkākāvyam	Nityānanda	1700
115	Śivamohinī-vilāsa	Bhāskara	
116	Śivāstapadī	Venkatāpā Nāyaka	
117	Śivagīti-mālikā	Candrasekharānanda Sarasvati	
118	Śivagīti-mālikā	Candasikhamani	
119	Śivagīta	Rāma	
120	Śivāṣtapadī		
121	Śivāṣtapadī	Ratnaguru	
122	Śrikṛṣṇalīlāmṛta	Nityānanda	1700
123	Śrīkṛṣṇalīlāmṛtam	Nārāyaṇa Miśra	1675
124	Śrikṛṣṇalīlmātam	Iśvarapuri	
125	Śrīkṛṣṇa-stava	Dinabandhu Misra	
126	Śrī-Rāmāṣtapadī-vivaraṇa	Upanisad Brahmendra	

127	Śṛngāra-rasa mandana	Vitthallesvara	1530
128	Tripurasundarīstuti-kāvya	Kālidāsa	1751
129	Uṣābhilāsa	Nārāyana Miśra	
130	Vairāgya-cintāmaṇi	Mānavikrama Kavirāja	
131	Vīraviruda	Candradatta	
132	Viṣṇupadāvali		

TEXT

Gītagovinda in Translation

Mahamedhanandanatha Saraswati

First Canto: *Sāmoda-dāmodara*

[Rādhā, the lady-love in her search of eternal lover Kṛṣṇa finds him in the forest of Vṛndāvana, where a group meet under pretext and protection.

Her trusted maid, from a hideout, points out at Kṛṣṇa delightfully won over by *gopī* women who fasten him with their love-rope. The Lord also is extremely pleased with them.

Hence, the name of the Canto-I is 'Sāmoda-Dāmodara'. Dāmodara who is fastened with the garland of sweet flowers of love at the waist is revelling in happiness in the Spring season.]

The sky is overcast with clouds.The forest is getting dark with the *tamāḷa*-trees. Kṛṣṇa the child fears darkness.

O Rādhā! take him home.

Rādhā and Mādhava, at the command of Nanda, on their way back proceeded to every *kuñja* (a bower laden with flowers) for their secret love-play on the bank of the river Yamunā. Let that secret love be victorious. [Verse-1]

The poet Jayadeva, whose mind has the imprint of the movements of 'Sarasvatī', the Goddess of Learning composes this *prabandha* (the well knitted musical *Gītagovinda*) about the love play of Śrī (Rādhā) and Vāsudeva (Kṛṣṇa), the God as another one to take the credit of serving at the feet of 'Padmāvatī (Rādhā)', the Goddess on Lotus. [V-2]

If your mind is flavoured with remembering the names of Hari and is curious about the pleasurable arts, then listen to the poetry of Jayadeva, composed in sweet, tender and lovely words. [V-3]

The poet Umāpatidhara exaggerates the words, Śaraṇa is praiseworthy for the quick and complex composition, Govardhana Ācārya is unrivalled in erotic poems, Śrutidhara is a famous poet and Dhoyī is a king of poets. But only Jayadeva, and none else, is famous for regular coherence of words. [V-4]

Facing page: Sakhī *departing with assurance from Kṛṣṇa, palmleaf painting, Orissa State Museum.*

Page 221: *Inscribed folios of the* Gītagovinda, *palmleaf manuscript, Orissa State Museum.*

***Daśāvatāra Gīta (Aṣṭapadī)*-I:**

O' Hari! You preserve the Vedas without being fatigued. You, like a boat, uphold it in the sea waters at deluge. O' Keśava! You bear the form of the Fish. O' Lord of the World! Be victory unto you. [*pada*-1]

O' Hari! The (vast) earth rests on your broad back, which bears the rings of sores on it. O' Keśava! You bear the form of the Tortoise. O' Lord of the world! Be Victory unto you. [2]

O' Hari! The (green) earth rests on the point of your (white) tusk, like a dark spot on the body of the moon. O' Keśava! You bear the form of the Boar. O' Lord of the World! Be victory unto you. [3]

O' Hari! On your lotus hand you have wonderful pointed nails, which tear open the black-bee-like body of Hiraṇyakaśipu. (It is a wonder because it is seen in common that the black-bee with its elongated proboscis pierces through the tender body of the lotus, but here it is a reverse act that the elongated nails of the lotus hand of the God, tear asunder the black-bee like hard body of the demon.) O' Keśava! You bear the form of the Man-lion. O' Lord of the World! Be victory unto you. [4]

O' Hari! You out-witted Bali (by begging him for a small piece of land measuring only three steps of yours in length and breadth, but when granted, you expanded yourself to such an extent that you covered the whole of the sky with one foot and the whole of vast earth with your other foot and then produced another foot from the navel to press the demon down to the nether world). You purified the earth with the water, that flows down from your toenail. O' Keśava! You bear the form of the Dwarf. O' Lord of the World! Be victory unto you. [5]

O' Hari! You cleanse the sins of the world with the blood of the *kṣatriya* clans (the warring class) and calm down its burning pain. O' Keśava! You bear the form of Bhṛgu Paraśu-Rāma-pati, the chieftain of the Bhṛgus. O' Lord of the world! Be victory unto you. [6]

O' Hari! You killed Rāvaṇa in the battle and offered the ten severed crowned-heads to the presiding deities of the ten quarters. O' Keśava! You bear the form of Rāma. O' Lord of the world! Be victory unto you. [7]

O' Hari! You wear the cloud-blue-coloured garment resembling Yamunā, which comes to you with the fear of being struck by the plough. O' Keśava! You bear the form of Haḷadhara (the bearer of a plough as an insignia i.e.Baḷa-Rāma). O' Lord of the World! Be victory unto you. [8]

O' Hari! You condemn the precept of sacrifice laid down in the Vedas for the slaughter of animals. O' Keśava! You bear the form of Buddha (the wise). O' Lord of the World! Be victory unto you. [9]

O' Hari! You carry the sword like a terrible comet to kill the barbarians on the earth. O' Keśava! You bear the form of Kaḷki. O' Lord of the World! Be victory unto you. [10]

The speech of the poet Śrī-Jayadeva is the epitome of the world and gives happiness and prosperity to its listeners. O' Keśava! You bear the ten Divine-forms. O' Lord of the World! Be victory unto you. [11]

O' Kṛṣṇa! Homage to you, who rescue the Vedas (incarnating as a Fish); support the world (incarnating as a Tortoise), raise up the globe (incarnating as a Boar), tear asunder the demon (incarnating as a Man-Lion), out-wit Bali (incarnating as a Dwarf), destroy *kṣatriya* clans (incarnating as Paraśu-Rāma to use an axe as a weapon), conquer Paulastya Rāvaṇa (incarnating as Rāma, a bow-man), bear the plough (incarnating as Baḷa-Rāma, a plough-man), extend compassion (incarnating as Buddha, the wise), kill the barbarians (incarnating as Kaḷki, riding on a horse with a sword in hand) as manifesting Yourself in ten-incarnations. [V-5]

śrita-kamaḷā-kucamaṇḍaḷa gīta (Aṣṭapadī)- II:

O' Hari! You lay upon the rounded breasts of Kamaḷā, wore *kuṇḍaḷa* (earrings) on the ears and a garland of wild flowers (well sprout in all the seasons with a huge *kadamba* flower knit in the middle hanging upto the knees or upto the feet according to Kaḷinga-style). O' God! Be victory and victory to you. [1]

O' Hari! You adorn the halo round the Sun. You are the destroyer of the cycle of births, the (playful) Swan in the mental lake of holy men. O' God! Be victory and victory to you. [2]

O' Hari! You are the conqueror of Kāḷiya (the dreadful venomous serpent), gratifier of people, the Sun to the lotus like family of the Yadu. O' God! Be victory and victory to you. [3]

O' Hari! You are the destroyer of the demons like Madhu, Mura and Naraka; the master to have Garuḍa as a vehicle and the prime-cause of the sportive acts of the Gods. O' God! Be victory and victory to you. [4]

O' Hari! Your eyes are the spotless lotus-petals. You are liberator of the (sorrows of the) world and the preserver of the three worlds. O' God! Be victory and victory to you. [5]

O' Hari! You are the ornament of Sītā, the daughter of Janaka; the conqueror of Dūṣaṇa, and the destroyer of the ten-necked Rāvaṇa in the battle. O' God! Be victory and victory to you. [6]

O' Hari! You look as charming as a new cloud. You held aloft mountain Mandara (at the time of churning the ocean). You are like a *cakora* bird to the moon-like face of Śrī(-Rādhā). O' God! Victory to you. [7]

O' Hari! Know that we bow at your feet. Do good to those who are humble. O' God! Be victory and victory to you. [8]

O' Hari! This good and splendid (love) song of Śrī-Jayadeva bestows upon all the joy and happiness. O' God! Be victory and victory to you. [9]

The chest of the killer of Madhu (Madhusūdana), marked with saffron, mixed with fragrances resulting from the embraces of *kumkum* smeared breasts of Padmā, that is flooded with the sweat of sexual fatigue may fulfil your desire. [V-6]

[The Sting of Love and The Pinch of Rejection: In the spring Rādhā having delicate limbs as tender as the flowers of vernal spring season, vexed with grief and anxiety generated by the strong sting of love's feverishness, confusedly searching for Kṛṣṇa wanders in the dense and dreary forest [*kāntāra* with the derivative meaning *kāṁ* (to which lady) *tārayati* (it rescues) or *kāntaṁ* (to the lover) *ṛcchati iyarti* (where, one meets) *vā iti*]. A maid with delicate sense of humour says as follows [V-7]

'laḷita-lavaṅgalatā-pariśīḷana' gīta (*Aṣṭapadī*)-III:

O' my dear friend Rādhā! Now in this sweet season of spring the soft breeze is blowing from the Maḷaya-mountain and embracing the *lavaṅgalatā* (the clove-creeper), the *kuñja* (bower) is filled with the song of cuckoo mingled with the humming sounds of honey-bees; in spring when the feeling of love is found even in the insentient objects, then the sensuous beloved, finding the enchanting eternal lover Hari now in dalliance with young ladies, is indeed an endless misery on the part of lovers in separation. [*pada*-1]

The brides of the travellers are out of their minds with the intensity of love and the *vakuḷa* trees are laden with the flowers on which swarm of bees hum. (Both, one indicating separation and the other union, are intolerable). Now, Hari in dalliance with young ladies, is indeed an endless misery on the part of lovers in separation. [*pada*-2]

The *tamāḷa* trees full of fresh (black) leaves emitting (as if) the fragrance of (black) musk and the *kiṁśuka* (*Butea frondosa,* having odour-less blossoms of red) flowers act as the nails of the Love God to tear apart the hearts of young people. [*pada*-3]

The blooming of *keśara* (*Mesua Roxburghii*) flowers appears like the golden parasol of (the king of) the Love God and the *pāṭaḷa* (pale-red *Bignonia Suaveolens*) flowers with black bees appear like quivers. (This indicates the influence of the Cupid in the aforesaid forest) [*pada*-4]

The *karuṇa* (*Citrus Decumana=ṭabhā* in Oḍiā) trees laugh at the sight of the young people who have lost their modesty and the *ketaka*

(*Pandanus Odoratssimus,=kiā* in Oḍiā) leaves appear like the spear piercing the hearts of the deserted lovers. [*pada*-5]

This spring is lovely with the sweet smell of the bunches of *mādhavikā (Gaertnera Racemosa=niāḷi* in Odia) with white fragrant flowers and infatuates even the minds of the sages. It is a natural friend of the young folk. [*pada*-6]

The mango buds bristle with delight due to the embraces of the *atimukta* creeper (*mādhavī-latā*) and the garden of Vṛndāvana is purified with the water of Yamunā which flows around it. [*pada*-7]

The song of Śrī-Jayadeva, describing the symptoms of love and the beauty of the forest during the amorous spring season, inspires one to think of the feet of Hari at best. [*pada*-8]

The wind fills the forest with the fragrance of pollen flying from the slightly opened jasmine flowers and as a friend of *ketakī*, it is advancing to inflame the mind. [V-8]

The travellers' ears become feverish with the sweet murmurs of the cuckoo, who are playing in the mango-blossoms already shaken by the bees that are attracted by the fragrance of emerging honey. They pass through these days with great difficulty and take delight only in meditation, when they write themselves with their lady companions. [V-9]

The maid (of honour) again from a little distance showed Rādhikā how Kṛṣṇa (the enemy of Mura), fond of other women's embrace, looks captivated by their love play. She thus reproves [V-10]:

candana-carccita-nīakaḷevara gīta (*Aṣṭapadī*)-IV:

O' Lady-love, expert in amorous sports [Rādhā! See how in the forest of Vṛndāvanaī] Hari is in dalliance with a group of playful pretty young women. He around his sandal-paste smeared blue-body, is wearing yellow robes, a fresh garland [made up of *tuḷasī* (basil), *kunda* (*Jasminum Multiflorum*), *mandāra* (*Erythrina Indica*), *pārijāta* (flower of paradise) and *saroruha* (lotus) woven together] that touches his knees. His cheeks shine with the glow of his gem-studded earrings bobbing in playful movements and are gladdened with his enchanting smile. [*pada*-1]

Wife of a herdsman passionately embraces Hari pressing her plump breasts (against his chest) and then giving full vent to her amorous longing while singing gracefully in *pañcamarāga*, a musical mode of the cuckoo. [*pada*-2]

Another woman concentrates more on Madhusūdana's lotus-like face which looks lovely for the fickle eyes with sidelong glances giving rise to tender feelings of love. [*pada*-3]

And another with heavy buttocks, on the pretext of whispering something in his ears, reaches near his cheeks and kisses lovingly the lover (Kṛṣṇa) filling him with pleasurable horripilation. [*pada*-4]

The other woman, to enjoy love-play, in eagerness bades him to a beautiful bower of canes on the banks of Yamunā and longingly pulls his fine garments. [*pada*-5]

Hari in a circular sportive *rāsa*-dance of exuberance, praises a young lady dancing in rhythm by clapping her hands in tune with a mixed sound produced by the jingling of bracelets, girdles, anklets and the sweet attractive melody of the flute. [*pada*-6]

He embraces one, kisses another, gladdens the other, rejoices in the revelry of romance with someone, lovingly glances at one who smiles at a distance and chases another beauty. [*pada*-7]

Śrī-Jayadeva's song depicting the wonderful secret love-play of Keśava in the forest of Vṛndāvana may extend glory and prosperity to all who listen to it. [*pada*-8]

Oh dear! Love incarnated Hari fascinated in this season of spring sports at His will with the beautiful women of Vraja embracing them from all sides and causing amorous merriment while gratifying all (the *gopī* in accordance with their desires) by his dark (like Kandarpa, the God of Love) and tender persona resembling a bunch of blue lotuses. [V-11]

(To add insult to the injury of women pining for love) The wind blows in from the sandal mountain in the south and proceeds towards the Kailāsa mountain ranges (the abode of Śiva in the north) with a desire to bathe in the snow to cool down its discomfort on account of bites of the serpents dwelling in the sandal woods. The sweet voice of the cuckoo, out of joy becomes sharp and reverberates on seeing the advent of tender buds at the top of mango-trees. [V-12]

Thus ends the First Canto, called *Sāmoda-dāmodara*, of Jayadeva's *Gītagovinda*.

Then begins the Second Canto: *Akḷeśakeśava*

[On listening to her friend, Rādhā, finding Keśava (Kṛṣṇa) in Akḷeśa (without trouble) and at ease in the bower with other women, pines very much for His love. Hence, the name of this canto is 'Akḷeśakeśava'. The word 'Keśava' means 'one having fine luxuriant (black curly) hair' to be in comity of passionate ladies. It also means one who killed mercilessly a demon called 'Keśī', having too much growth of hair. This indicates the cruelty of the person towards people having a natural love for the growth of hair i.e. women. Either ways Kṛṣṇa justifies his name being in company with women in general and thus cruel towards Rādhā in particular.] As Hari roams in the forest with loving women in general, Rādhā, realising her importance at stake, becomes jealous and goes in another direction to hide in an arbour afloat with a swarm of honey-bees humming atop. She confides in distress her anguish to the trusted friend. [V-13]

saṁcardadharasudhāmadhuradhvani gīta (*Aṣṭapadī*)-V:

My mind recollects—this is the place, where Hari sported in *rāsa*-dance and cut jokes. It was resonating with the sound of His fascinating flute as well as the flow of the sweet nectar from His lower lips. He was turning His glance in every direction and when His head moved right and left, the (shine from the) earrings glowed on His cheeks. [*pada*-1]

His hair was adorned with the plume of a peacock and was looking like a thick cloud festooned with a magnificent rainbow. [*pada*-2]

His face was glowing with the sweet smile displayed on the lips looking as radiant as the leaves of *Bandhujīva* (*Pentapetes Phoenicea*, with a red flower which opens at midday and withers away the next morning) and was eager to kiss the faces of the cowherd-women with heavy buttocks. [*pada*-3]

Taking a thousand young cowherd women into the fold of his long extending arms thrilled with joy, He was able to dispel the darkness by the rays of ornaments that adorned His hands, feet and chest. [*pada*-4]

A mark of sandal-paste on His forehead was reviling the moon moving through a multitude of clouds. He was cruel at heart at the time of pressing and massaging the large breasts and their sides. [*pada*-5]

His lovely cheeks were adorned with the earrings studded with jewels in the shape of a *makara* (crocodile as an emblem of Cupid). He was wearing yellow garments. All the great sages, gods, demons and men obey Him. [*pada*-6]

He was standing under a pellucid *kadamba* (*Nauclea Cadamba*, with orange-coloured fragrant blossoms) tree, dispelling the fear of dross in this iron age of *Kali*. He also used to gratify me mentally somehow by His surging wave of loving looks. [*pada*-7]

Śrī-Jayadeva depicted the most handsome figure of Madhu-ripu (the enemy of demon Madhu, Śrī-Kṛṣṇa). Let it now be suitable for the pious people to have the remembrance of the holy feet of Śrī-Hari. [*pada*-8]

My mind takes into account only his virtues and never intends to get angry by mistake. It gets satisfaction by laying aside his faults. What shall I do, when my mind pines most for him, who desires strongly in playing with other young women and not me! [V-14]

'nibhṛtanikuñjagṛhaṁ' gīta (Astapadī)-VI:

At night I went secretly to the lonely arbour (*nikuñjagṛha*), where he lay hiding and when I looked around with apprehension, discovered him bursting out into laughter with ardent desire for love. O' my friend! get Keśimathana (Kṛṣṇa, with power to destroy a demon or a demonic attack of the Cupid) to be united with me. I pine ardently for His love. [*pada*-1]

I was shy at our first union. By flattering in a hundred ways, He made me agreeable to speak smilingly a few sweet words and then loosened the fine garment around my waist. [*pada*-2]

Laying me on a bed of tender leaves, he laid on my breast. I embraced and kissed Him. He too hugged me tight and drank ambrosia from my lips by kissing me too. [*pada*-3]

My eyes were closed. His cheeks were delighted. My entire body started sweating. He was restless with passion. [*pada*-4]

I cooh-coohed like a cuckoo. He was victorious in all the techniques of love-making. The flowers fell scattered from my braid. He scratched my heavy breasts with His nails. [*pada*-5]

With anklets tinkling on my feet, He extended the amorous act to His satisfaction. The girdle with jingling sound unfastened, He went on issuing kisses pulling my braid (to keep me under control). [*pada*-6]

I was tired of deriving pleasure in love, He looked (mischievously in satisfaction) with his lotus-like eyes half-opened. When satisfied, my creeper-like body fell flat and limpid, the desire (for love) again crept up in the mind of Madhu-sūdana (the honey-bee, who is an expert in obtaining the juice by pressing and crushing). [*pada*-7]

The song of Śrī-Jayadeva conveys a happy expression of an anxious cowherd-maiden about the erotic disposition of Madhu-ripu (who has finished the demon called Madhu or the honey-juice from the flower-like tender maidens of cowherds' gopa village), may accomplish pleasure. [*pada*-8]

Looking at me with sidelong glance that drove the flock of cowherd women's eyebrows to rise, whose flute of luxury got dropped down from the hands, cheeks perspired and lovely face lit with smile ambrosia seemed embarassed; I behold Govinda in the forest sorrounded by the beauties of Vraja and rejoice. [V-15]

O' friend! it is difficult to look at the blooming clusters of fresh *aśoka*. Even the breeze that blows from the grove by the lake pains me much. The blossoming of mangoes, which look charming with hovering of humming bees, also are not pleasant to me. Please tell me, what shall I do now in such a situation (*śikhariṇī*, the metre in which it is described)? [V-16]

Thus ends the Second Canto, called Akḷeśakeśava, of Jayadeva's *Gītagovinda*.

Then begins the Third Canto: *Mugdha-madhusūdana*

[Madhu-sūdana, who could kill the demons born out of the filth of the ears of Brahmā called Kaiṭabha (speaking secretly against others to keep them away) and Madhu (speaking pleasantly honeyed words to win over), is now found stupefied with and spellbound by the love of Rādhā. Hence the canto is named 'Mugdha-madhusūdana', describing the reciprocal feelings of sorrow and repentence of both Rādhā and Kṛṣṇa, the eternal lovers.]

Kṛṣṇa, (the enemy of Kaṃsa) having placed Rādhā, as a binding force of worldly desires in his heart, abandoned all the beauties of Vraja. [V-17]

With repentance he pursued Rādhikā here and there wounded by the arrows of the Love God. He entered a bower on the banks of the river Yamunā, that flows from the mount Kalinda. Mādhava was struck with grief. [V-18]

'māmiyaṁ caḷitā' gīta (astapadī)-VII:

Seeing me surrounded by women, she left. I was at fault. Afraid (of her ire), I could not also stop her. O' God! She perhaps left in anger because of the indignity towards her. [*pada*-1]

I wonder, what will she do now and say if she were to live in separation for ever ? What is there in my wealth, in my kinsmen and even with my life (without her)? [*pada*-2]

I recall her face looking like a red lotus agitated by a hovering bee and her eyebrows knitted in anger. [*pada*-3]

She is within my heart. In the heart, I shall love her. Why then, do I search for her in the forest and lament in vain ? [*pada*-4]

O' slender lady! I know, your heart is distressed with jealousy, but I cannot supplicate, as I do not know where you have gone! [*pada*-5]

It appears to me as if you move in my presence. Why then do you not hurry to hug me as before? [*pada*-6]

Forgive me. I shall not ever do such things to you. I am burning with passion. O' Beautiful lady, favour me showing your face. [*pada*-7]

With devotion to Hari, this is narrated by Jayadeva, the moon born from the ocean of Kendubilva. [*pada*-8]

This is a garland of lotus stalks on my chest, but not the lord of serpents (of Great-God Śiva).

This is a row of blue lotus-petals on my neck, but not the glow of poison (to be mistaken as Śrīkaṇṭha or Śiva). This is sandal powder (that besmears my body) but not the ashes (as in case of Śiva). O' incorporeal God of Love! do not strike me (to take my life) mistaking me to be Hara (or Śiva, who took your life and thus is your enemy). Why do you rush at me with anger! [V-19]

O' Love-God! Do not carry the mango-arrows in your hand and put the string on the bow (to charge). You have playfully conquered the whole world at ease. How is killing a swooning man an act of bravery? My mind which is torn asunder by the arrow like sidelong glances of the doe-eyed, has not even slightly recovered. [V-20]

O' slender lady! The arrow like sidelong glances placed on the bow of your brow cause me pain. Your braid of dark curly hair (*kuṭiḷa*, meaning curled and crooked) may also imitate to act as Māra (the God of Love, who tempts living beings to indulge in passion leading to emaciation and finally death) and attempt to kill me. Your red lower lip resembling the *bimba* (*momordica monadelpha*, locally called *kunduri* in North Odisha and *toraḍā* in South Odisha) fruit may spread infatuation (because it is natural for an arrow to pierce the vulnerable points, for the crooked to kill and for one inspired with love to cause affliction), but how is it that your well rounded breasts (*sad-vṛtta*, also meaning 'good conduct/manner') play with my life ? [V-21]

The pleasure of her touch, tender and wavering eyes, the mouth of lotus fragrance, indirect speech with a flow of nectar, the graceful *bimba*-like lower lip are though attachments of sense objects, my mind is fixed in meditation upon her, but alas! How then the disease with mental agony of separation does increase ? [V-22]

The brow is her bow, her sidelong glances are the arrows and the tip of her ear is the bowstring. Are these weapons transferred by the God of Love to her, the living Goddess, to conquer the world ?! [V-23]

Thus ends the Third Canto, called *Mugdha-Madhusūdana,* of Jayadeva's *Gītagovinda.*

Then begins the Fourth Canto: *Susnigdha-mādhava*:

['*Snigdha*' means tender, smooth and affectionate. In this canto Kṛṣṇa, who is not (mā) the husband (dhava) but the lover becomes exceedingly affectionate towards Rādhā, having come to know of her miserable condition from her friend that she has dried out like a flower with the scorching rays of the Sun.Thus justifies the name Susnigdha-mādhava.]

A companion loyal to Rādhā spoke to Mādhava, who was roaming about in love perplexity and was staying in a grove on the banks of Yamunā. [V-24]

nindati candanamindukiraṇamanu gīta (*Aṣṭapadī*)-VIII:

She finds fault with the sandal-paste (as of no relief) and feels no good at the (cooling) moon beams (as of causing more pain) and then gets depressed and perplexed.

She considers the (southern) breeze blowing from the Maḷaya-mountain to be an admixture of poison because of the snakes that live on the sandal trees.

O' Mādhava! She, in melancholy under separation being afraid of the arrows of the God of Love, (absorbed in your thought) thinks of you alone. [*pada*-1]

You are in her heart. To protect you from the arrows incessantly shot by the God of Love, she wears a mass of wet lotus-leaves upon her bosom like an armour. [*pada*-2]

She has prepared a beautiful bed of flowers for practising the art of love (as imagined) to have a happy blending with you, but though it (in separation from you) turns to be a bed of flowershafts of the God of Love for her (happy ending), she eagerly waits for you as if, in fulfilment of a religious vow. [*pada*-3]

Her lotus like face has been moistened with welled up tears rolling down from the eyes as good as the moon from which the nectar trickles down on account of its being torn asunder by the large teeth of Rāhu, the trouble-monger to the moon. [*pada*-4]

She, with musk, has secretly drawn your picture as the God of Love, placing underneath a *makara* (crocodile) and an arrow of new mango-buds in your hand and bows down. [*pada*-5]

She also repeats, O' Mādhava! I fall at your feet. If you once turn your face away, even the moon, a store-house of nectar, continues to burn up my body. [*pada*-6]

She looks at you straight. Since it is very difficult to attain you even with deep concentration, she moans, laughs, grieves, weeps, wanders and forgets her grief. [*pada*-7]

This song of Śrī-Jayadeva, if in exuberance allowed to dance in the mind, then recite the speech of the friend of the young cowherd woman, overcome by remorse due to separation from Hari. [*pada*-8]

She feels her abode to be a forest, dear friends as snares, the heated breath to be a zone of flames of forest-fire due to your separation and herself like a helpless doe amidst the burning forest surrounded by the hunters, chased by the God of Love to be the God of Death performing the tiger's play (known as *Śārddūḷavolrīḍitam*). [V-25]

stanavinihitamapi hāramudāram **gīta (Aṣṭpadī)-IX:**

O' Keśava! In your absence Rādhikā feels her slender body and the fine necklace placed upon her breasts as a heavy burden. [*pada*-1]

She also looks with apprehension at the smooth sandal paste on her body seeing it as if it be poison. [*pada*-2]

She is heaving high and long as if spreading the morbid heat of the burning fire of love. [*pada*-3]

She casts her tearful eyes in every direction like a lotus without its stalk. [*pada*-4]

She considers the bed of new leaves before her as one of fire. [*pada*-5]

She, by not taking off her hands from the cheeks, gives rise to an unmoving newly risen evening moon. [*pada*-6]

She, as if ordained to die of separation, repeats your name Hari Hari with a desire (to get you in the next life). [*pada*-7]

May this song sung (with the word Keśava) by Śrī-Jayadeva lead all near the feet of Keśava and rejoice all. [*pada*-8]

O' Upendra (Kṛṣṇa is so called as he subdued Indra, known to be powerful and cruel for his 'thunderbolt')! You are heartily accepted to be greater than the Divine Physician. If you do not get rid of the sickness of love-smitten Rādhā to be cured only by your ambrosia of coition, then you will prove yourself to be more cruel than even the thunderbolt. [V-26, in the metre called *upendravajrā*]. Though her body suffers from the heat due to fever of love caused by *Kandarpa* (with pride in hell of enjoyment), it is surprising that her mind gets distressed when comes the thought of the sandal, the moon, the lotus (all having cooling effect). But it is more surprising that she however lives alone waiting for the moment with the thought of you, the more cold dearest one. [V-27]

In the past she, who was not able to endure your separation even for a moment and was pained at the (natural) dropping of the eyelids (barring her vision of you), how can she breathe now on seeing the flowering tips of mango-branches (in the charged atmosphere of spring-season, when there is a feast of flowering, waiting eagerly to bear fruit). [V-28, in the metre called '*puṣpitāgrā*']

Thus ends the Fourth Canto, called Susnigdha-Mādhava, of Jayadeva's *Gītagovinda*.

Then begins the Fifth Canto: *Sākāṅkṣa-Puṇḍarīkākṣa*

['*Sākāṅkṣa*' is a state of intense desire coupled with anxiety. '*Puṇḍarīka*' signifies human-heart. Puṇḍarīkākṣa is another name of Kṛṣṇa, whose eyes are as fresh as white lotus.

He now sees the clear picture and realises his own fault, but does not dare to go to Rādhā. He in his heart of hearts, intensely desires to meet Rādhā and expresses this to the loyal maiden, who also advises him to cherish the dictates of His desire. Hence follows the name *Sākāṅkṣa-Puṇḍarikāṣa*.]

Let me stay here. You go to Rādhā and request her on my behalf as I briefed you and get her here.

Thus appointed by Madhuripu, the loyal friend went to Rādhā and communicated as follows. [V-29]

vahati maṭayasamīre madanamupanidhāya gīta (Aṣṭapadī)-X:

The gentle breeze blows along with the passion of Love God from the Malaya mountain.

Blossoms split open to crush the hearts of lovers in separation.

O' friend! Vanamāḷī sinks into despondency in your absence. [*pada*-1]

When the cooling rays of the moon started burning, he felt like dying. When the arrows of the God of Love fell on him, helplessly he lamented. [*pada*-2]

When the honey-bees hummed, he covered his ears. When the pangs of separation intensely increased, he became sick night after night. [*pada*-3]

He lives in the forest renouncing his beautiful dwelling place. He rolls on the ground repeatedly recalling your name. [*pada*-4]

The poet Jayadeva sings this dwelling in the the charm of love, in separation. Let Hari appear in the minds intensely rich with noble deeds. [*pada*-5]

He has already attained perfection in the art of love-making with you. Now again, Mādhava, meditating on you in the same arbour of love-making, chants your name as a *mantra* with an ardent desire to embrace you and drink the nectar from your pitcher-like breasts. [V-30]

'ratisukhasāre gatamabhisāre madanamanoharaveśam' gīta (Aṣṭapadī)-XI:

O' my dear friend with heavy buttocks! Don't delay departing. Follow the lord of your heart, who is well dressed to surpass the beauty of the God of Love, and who is on a rendezvous to derive the best of pleasures through intercourse.

Vanamāḷī (with a garland of fragrant flowers of all the seasons hanging down), whose hands are active in squeezing the heavy breasts, rests now on the banks of Yamunā served by gentle breeze. [*pada*-1]

He gently plays on the flute calling your name. He indeed reveres even the smallest particle that has the contact of your body and carried off by the gentle breeze. [*pada*-2]

If a bird perches or a leaf trembles, in anticipation of your arrival he prepares a bed and anxiously looks forward to hear your tread. [*pada*-3]

Please remove the anklets that sound disagreeably, like a fickle foe, during amorous acts.

O' my friend! Get into a blue cloak and get inside the dense dark arbour. [*pada*-4]

You will appear like a waving crane against a patch of dark cloud resembling Murāri's chest who wears a necklace which will play like a lightning at the time of sexual act in reverse order. Be eminent in getting the results of well done acts. [*pada*-5]

O' my lotus-eyed friend reclining on a bed of tender leaves! Get your clothes loosened, girdle dropped and loins uncovered and make it a treasure house of joy (for Hari). [*pada*-6]

Hari has a good sense of respect. The night now is also coming to a close. Be quick in obeying my words. Fulfil the desires of Madhu-ripu (Śrī-Kṛṣṇa). [Pada-7]

On hearing this most charming song by Śrī-Jayadeva, a devotee of Hari; bow down with a delightful heart devoted to Hari, who is graceful to one for noble deeds. [*pada*-8]

O' Beautiful Rādhā! Your lover is now tired of the maddenning effects of the Love God. He breathes heavily (being disappointed at your not-coming), looks forward again and again in all directions (in expectation of your arrival), enters into the bower off and on (expecting you to have entered from the other side), and with an indistinct articulation (for some untoward happening in your coming) becomes upset (in anxiety), (disappointed at your not-coming and again with a hope of your coming and sleeping) he prepares a bed and often glances (to find you somewhere hidden) bewildered (in not finding you). [V-31]

Look, the hot-rayed Sun is now set (with your perverseness as there is no sharp heat in the rays of the setting Sun, there is no disinclination in your stiff attitude towards him). The darkness has deepened with the longing of Govinda (meaning—one who attains the objectives of senses). My long entreaty resembles the long pitiable cry of the pairs of Koka (ruddy goose, separated by sitting apart on opposite banks). O' my beautiful friend! This is the proper time for rendezvous as further delay will not bear any fruit. [V-32]

The couple, unintentionally left somewhere, happened to meet each other by chance in the darkness but are pleased instantly to engage in sexual act. They embraced, kissed, nail scratchings ensued and were exerted. But through initiation of love act and expression of satisfaction they came to know each other and experienced an indescribable pleasure mixed with embarrassment. [V-33]

O' my friend with a beautiful countenance! Moved by the waves of passion while proceeding on the path in darkness, (treading softly) slowly resting under each tree, let Śrī-Kṛṣṇa, the fortunate one, receive you with awe and wonder and be pleased to achieve his object in solitude. [V-34]

Thus ends the Fifth Canto, called *Sākāṅkṣa-Puṇḍarikākṣa,* of Jayadeva's *Gītagovinda.*

Then begins the Sixth Canto: *Sotkaṇṭha-vaikuṇṭha*

[Rādhā, absorbed in the thought of Kṛṣṇa, sees him everywhere and also considers herself to be Kṛṣṇa. Rādhā, much afflicted in love, becomes very weak. It becomes difficult on her part to visit her lover Kṛṣṇa. Hence, Kṛṣṇa (the God of *vaikuṇṭha*), therefore, without hesitation (or *vikuṇṭhā*) crossing all the rules of propriety becomes eager to conduct himself (as *dhṛṣṭa*) without shame on a rendezvous in reverse to Rādhā. Thus, the canto in all fitness is named *Sotkaṇṭha-Vaikuṇṭha*]

The trusted friend on finding the devoted Rādhā in the bower, incapable of moving, spoke to Govinda, who pines for love (of Rādhā) as follows. [V-35]

'paśyati diśi diśi rahasi bhavantam' gīta (Aṣṭapadī)-XII:

She in solitude, as if in a state of drinking the sweet (intoxicating liquor-like) honey of your lips, sees you in every direction.

O' Lord Hari (who takes away the life of foes and the agony of friends)! Rādhā acutely suffers in her abode. [*pada*-1]

Attempting to go to you on rendezvous, she walks forward a few steps and falls. [*pada*-2]

She, (in order to calm down the heat generated by the fire of love) wearing a bracelet of tender leaves and lotus-stalks, lives only with expectation of your union. [*pada*-3]

She dressed like you, looks frequently at her pleasant decoration and (in absorption) finds pleasure in thinking herself to be Kṛṣṇa (the enemy of the demon 'Madhu' or the exciting atmosphere of spring). [*pada*-4]

She enquires from her friend constantly why Hari is not coming on the rendezvous? [*pada*-5]

Imagining Hari by her side, She embraces and kisses often the clouded darkness. [*pada*-6]

As you delay, her delicacy dissolves away and she, waiting to receive you in her bridal bed, moans and weeps. [*pada*-7]

May this song of Śrī-Jayadeva spread great joy in the people of literary taste. [*pada*-8]

O' Rogue! Dear Rādhā with deer-like eyes, thinking only of you and your irresistable love, is immersed in the ocean of passion. She (thinking of your love-union) gets horripilated a lot and being perplexed utters love-cries expressing internal apathy with emotional fervour. [V-36]

She (for you) puts ornaments of various kinds on her (limbs). When a leaf thrills, she in anticipation of your arrival and with a hope of getting you by her, prepares a bed and merges in your thought for long. Thus adhering to such modes of (*ākaḷpa*) ornamentation, (*vikaḷpa*) alternatives in uncertainity, (*taḷparacanā*) preparing the bed for conjugal love-play, (*saṁkaḷpalīḷā*) fancy of imagination in hundred ways; she, the beautuful lady will not be able to spend this night well without you. [V-37]

Thus ends the Sixth Canto called, *Sotkaṇṭha-Vaikuṇṭha,* of Jayadeva's *Gītagovinda.*

Then begins the Seventh Canto: *Nāgara-Nārāyaṇa*:

[Nārāyaṇa is considered to be the sole resort of all—*narāṇām ayanam.* He is very clever in preferring to live and play inside every body by making it his *nagara* or a dwelling place. Rādhā is impatient in waiting quite long for Kṛṣṇa. But Kṛṣṇa, who loves many does not restict himself to one alone. He is known as *Nāgara-Nārāyaṇa* as he derives pleasure being in play with many.]

In the meanwhile as the moon, with a black patch on his body because of the sin caused by closing down the path of unchaste women, through illumination of the intermediate space of Vṛṇdāvana (with a flood of light); looked like a mark of sandal paste on the face of the quarters (*digvadhö*) and is considered to resemble beautiful women. [V-38]

While (the disk of) the moon goes up above the horizon, Mādhava getting delayed in reaching; the lady with repentence in separation cried out loudly lamenting a lot. [V-39]

kathitasamaye' pi harirahaha n yayau vanam gīta (Aṣṭapadī)- XIII:

Ah! Hari did not turn up in the forest in time as appointed. My jubiliant youth without blemish is of no use.

I was deceived by the guilded words of my friends.Where shall I seek refuge now ? [*pada*-1]

Following whom I came even to the thicket in dark night, he now wedges my heart with one of the uneven (five) arrows of the God of Love. [*pada*-2]

My tryst is futile. There is sure sign of death for me. I have no sense left to bear the pangs of the fire of separation. [*pada*-3]

This enchanting night sweet like honey makes me depressed, while some fortunate woman enjoys Hari (the captor). [*pada*-4]

I consider the bracelets and other ornaments studded with gems to be unbearable as they carry the flames of separation from Hari (the thief, who steals). [*pada*-5]

My flower-like delicate body is so easily wounded by the arrows of the God of Love. The garland of flowers on my bosom even hurts more than his very indifferent nature. [*pada*-6]

I stay (for him) here in difficulty without caring for the forest-reeds, but Madhu-sūdana (the destroyer of all that is sweet) does not remember me at all. [*pada*-7]

This song of the poet Jayadeva, a refuge at the feet of Hari may dwell in your heart like a beautiful young woman proficient in the practice of the art of love. [*pada*-8]

Is He after some lovely lady (but how can it be, when he loves me very much) or detained by the friends in play (but how can it be, when the time for rendezvous was scheduled) or wanders in darkness of the forest nearby (but how can it be, when the place is quite well known to him) or is handsome Kṛṣṇa tired out and not able at all to come to the assignation, a beautiful arbour of *aśoka.* [V-40]

Then (Rādhā) saw her friend return without Mādhava, apprehended that Janārdana was seduced by some woman and started describing the event as if she had witnessed it. [V-41]

smarasamarocita-viracitaveśā gīta (*Aṣṭapadī*)-XIV:

Some young woman with exceptional qualities enjoys with Madhu-ripu (an enemy by not keeping up the appointment that is sweet in spring-season).

The woman is dressed appropriately to fit in, in the battle of love. Her hair is dishevelled and the flowers have fallen down. [*pada*-1]

Due to Hari's deep embrace, the abnormal condition prevails and the necklace is glittering upon her pitcher like breasts. [*pada*-2]

Beautiful is her moon-like face with the waving of curls. Kṛṣṇa is drinking from (the honey of) her lips. Her eyes are closed in ecstasy. [*pada*-3]

Her cheeks look charming with the ear-ornament (*kuṇḍaḷa*) shaking and her hips move fast while the girdle jingles (actively in erotic-enjoyment in reverse order). [*pada*-4]

As the lover stares on (with mercy), she remains bashful and smiles and makes a variety of indistinct sounds in consummation. [*pada*-5]

She is filled with ample horripilation and tremor. Her love blossoms when she in coyness sighs and closes her eyes. [*pada*-6]

She, skilled in the war of love, filled with perspiration in amorous dalliance, has thrown herself upon the chest (of my Lord). [*pada*-7]

The song of consummation by Hari as delineated by Śrī-Jayadeva may remove the evils of Kaḷi. [*pada*-8]

The moon having the appearance of pale lotus-like face of love-lorn Śrī Kṛṣṇa, the enemy of demon Mura and as a friend of the God of Love, spreads anguish in my sublime heart. [V-42]

samuditamadane ramaṇīvadane gīta (*Aṣṭapadī*)-XV:

He is thrilled while putting a 'mark of musk' comparable to the image of the deer on the moon, on the face of the lovely woman who looks delightful and is excited. She upturns her lower lip for a kiss.

Thus the victorious Murāri was found enjoying now in the forest on the bank of Yamunā. [*pada*-1]

He arranges *kuruvaka* (a red kind of *Barleria*) flowers on her hair. These flowers look as beautiful as the lightning on the dense cloud-like dark hair of the wanton face of the young woman. Moreover her dark hair resembles a forest (of dark hair) infested with deer herds (the mark as found on moon) belonging to the Love God. [*pada*-2]

Her (large and hard) compact breasts are spread out like the (large) vast sky. The mark of musk with the scratching of nails (made by Kṛṣṇa) on them appears to be the black-spot on the moon. Her fine necklace of gems resting on the breasts appears like a cluster of stars. [*pada*-3]

Her tender arms are as delicate as lotus-stalks. The palms appear like the ice-cold leaves spread out of the lotus-stalk. A bracelet of emerald appeared to be a swarm of honey-bees hovering around her arms. [*pada*-4]

The pleasure-house (*pedenda*) in between the buttocks of the nourished body is considered to be the golden seat of the God of Love. There the girdle of gems casts a welcoming archlike smile at the entrance. [*pada*-5]

He decorates her feet adorned with jewel-like nails by placing them on his chest, which is the dwelling place of Goddess Kamaḷā, for the marks of red lac-juice on his chest would avoid demeaning other women. [*pada*-6]

O' my friend! Tell me why should I live here inside this arbour for long in vain, while the mischievous Kṛṣṇa, the brother of Haḷadhara (with a plough to cultivate the field) is having sexual dallliance with some other beautiful woman? [*pada*-7]

Let not the evil characteristics of Kaḷi prevail here with the depiction of Hari's virtues in the sentiment of love by Jayadeva, the king of poets but a servant of Kṛṣṇa, the enemy of demon Madhu. [Pada-8]

O' my friend! If the merciless cheat did not come, why do you feel sorry for you are a mere messenger ? He has many paramours to dally with at his will. What is your fault, then? See! This heart longs for him and is drawn towards him by the (string of) qualities, ignoring anguish, anxiety and distress. I will cease to breathe, I am dying. [V-43]

'aniḷataraḷa-kubaḷayanayanena' Gīta (*Aṣṭapadī*)-XVI:

O' Friend! The woman, who was sexually pleased by Vanamāḷī Kṛṣṇa—

She, who is loved by Kṛṣṇa, the handsome one with eyes as good as lotus tremulous by the wind, no more feels the heat by sleeping on a bed of tender new leaves. [*pada*-1]

She, who is loved by Kṛṣṇa, the handsome one with the charming face as good as a fully blown lotus, is not afflicted by the arrow of the God of Love. [*pada*-2]

She, who is loved by Kṛṣṇa, the handsome one with the sweet words as good as nectar, is not subjected to the burn by the Maḷaya-breeze. [*Pada*-3]

She, who is loved by Kṛṣṇa, the handsome one with the lustre of hands and feet as good as a lotus on land, does not roll about in the ice-cold rays of the moon. [*pada*-4]

She, who is loved by Kṛṣṇa, the handsome one with the lustre of cluster of clouds during the rainy season, is not afflicted by the pangs of separation. [*pada*-5]

She, who is loved by Kṛṣṇa, the handsome one with the lustre of clothes as good as the lines of gold made on the touch-stone, does not snort with the mocking of the people around. [*pada*-6]

She, who is loved by Kṛṣṇa, the best of young men all over the world, does not suffer from the most pitiable pain. [*pada*-7]

Let Hari also enter into your heart through these words composed by Śrī-Jayadeva. [*pada*-8]

O' Sandal Breeze (aniḷa, derived from the root '*an*' meaning 'both give and take' with suffix '*iḷa*') pleasing the God of Love! Blowing from the south (*dakṣiṇa*) be favourable (*dakṣiṇa*) and give up your cruelty by contrary action (*vāmatā*). O' Life of the world! Putting Mādhava for a moment before me (be favourable) first and next (be cruel to) take my life away. [V-44]

O' my friend! This house appears (with my dear friends) to be an enemy, the ice-cold breeze to be burning fire, and the moon with (life-giving) nectar of rays to be (death inflicting) poison in as much as he is in my mind (but not nearby). My heart still longs for him by force. What shall I do, when the lover is verily free in ruling over the lotus-eyed woman. [V-45]

O' Maḷaya Breeze! Do not stand on my way. O' God of Love (with five arrows)'! Take my life (breathing with five vital forces) away. I shall not again go back home. O' Sister of Death (Yamunā)!

Why should you also spare me ? Ask your waves to grasp me, so that the burning fire of love in my body may at least cease. [V-46]

Thus ends the Seventh Canto, called Nāgara Nārāyana, of Jayadeva's *Gītagovinda*.

Then begins the Eighth Canto: Vilakṣa-Lakṣmīpati:

[Rādhā spends the night with unbearable agony. Then to her astonishment finds Kṛṣṇa with remarkable marks of eros to be at the threshold in the morning. Kṛṣṇa though 'Lakṣmī-pati' the noble lord of auspiciousness, is found bearing depreciable signs of a wretched paramour. Thus the canto is significantly named Vilakṣa-Lakṣmīpati.']

Somehow passing the night shattered by the arrows of the God of Love and finding her lover bent down before her and speaking words of conciliation, she spoke displeased with jealousy. [V-47]

rajanijanitagurujāgararāga *gīta* (*Aṣṭapadī*)-XVII:

O' Hari (depriver of my wealth of pleasure), O' Hari (seducer of other ladies)! You go.

O' Mādhava (the husband of Lakṣmī)! Go away. O' Keśava (*kḷiśnati* torments *iti keśa* i.e. one who torments, *va* = a lot)! Get out (of this place). Don't utter words of falsehood. O' lotus-eyed (lover)!

Follow that woman, who dispels your despondency.

Your eyes, red and indolent due to wakefulness in the last night, are distinctly indicative of indulgence in eros. [*pada*-1]

O' Kṛṣṇa! Your red lip now bears the colour of your body through the kisses of that dark-eyed woman, who adorned her eyes with mascara. [*pada*-2]

Your body that bears the marks of her hard nails during the battle of love, seems to have a record of her victory in erotic play inscribed in gold lines on an emerald piece. [*pada*-3]

Your grand chest is wet with the marks of fluid of lac flowing from her lotus-feet and puts up an outward show of new leaves on a tree of love. [*pada*-4]

The marks of teeth-bite (in passion) on your lower lip, cause pain in my mind and say:

How can this body of yours and mine be still one and the same? [*pada*-5]

O' Kṛṣṇa! Your mind must be equally dark like the rest of your body. Otherwise, how could you cheat a person who is sincerely following you and suffering from the fever caused by the uneven darts of the God of Love? [*pada*-6]

It is not a wonder that you (a ravisher) wander in the forest to devour young women, in as much as it is very well proved in the case of killing Pötanū that even then it was a nature with you as a child to be cruel towards women. [*pada*-7]

O' learned men! Listen to the lamentation of a young woman, deceived and abandoned by the lover as sung by Śrī-Jayadeva. It is as sweet as nectar (of heaven) but very difficult to have even in heaven above (the abode of God). [*pada*-8]

O' Cheat! Seeing your chest red with lac dripping from the feet of your beloved, as if spreading the passion outwardly and thus finding my full love for you to be shattered, now it causes me more shame than anguish to look at you. [V-48]

Thus ends the Eighth Canto, called *Vilakṣa-Lakṣmīpati,* of Jayadeva's *Gītagovinda.*

Then begins the Ninth Canto: *Mugdha-mukunda*

[Rādhā sent back Kṛṣṇa, but pined very much for him in separation and repented for the same.

Having come to know of this from her trusted maid, Mukunda (the giver of liberation) was both concerned and fascinated. Hence, the name *Mugdha-Mukuṇḍa.*]

Then on finding Rādhā separated from the lover on account of a quarrel, agitated by Manmatha (the agitator of mind), exasperated in sexual pleasure and remorse and then feeling sorry through the recapitulation of the conduct of Hari; the confidante spoke to her in confidence. [V-49]

Harirabhisarati vahati mṛdupavane gīta (Aṣṭapadī)-XVIII:

O' my angry friend! Do not take a pique against respectful Mādhava.

Hari is in rendezvous while the sweet wind blows. What more pleasure you can aspire at home? [*pada*-1]

Why do you not make use of your pitcher-like breasts extremely succulent and heavier than palm-fruits? [*pada*-2]

How many times it is repeated to you word for word not to leave out Hari, who is very cordial. [*pada*-3]

Why do you wail helplessly and feel yourself distressed and allow (create occasion for) the assembly of young women standing around to laugh at you? [*pada*-4]

Make your eyes worthy of seeing Hari preferring to be on the cool bed of lotus-leaves. [*pada*-5]

Why do you feel depressed at heart? Listen to my words and remember that difference between you two is not desirable at all. [*pada*-6]

Let Hari come and speak to you very sweetly. Why do you make yourself alienated? [*pada*-7]

May the deeds of Hari as elegantly sung by Śrī-Jayadeva cause happiness to people of taste. [*pada*-8]

You became rough when your lover was affectionate, you remained unbending when he was bent down before you, you were hostile when he was passionate, you turned your face away when he was looking you up. These may be proper for you to act in perversity and as such natural for you to feel sandal paste to be poison, cool-rayed moon to be burning sun, the frost to be fire and all the objects of pleasure to be torturous. [V-50]

Thus ends the Ninth Canto, called *Mugdha-Mukunda,* of Jayadeva's *Gītagovinda.*

Then begins the Tenth Canto: *Catura-Caturbhuja*:

[Rādhā's pride has come down.The bower is dark. Kṛṣṇa has arrived. At the instance of Rādhā the lady companions moved out of the bower. Kṛṣṇa, the God with four arms (accepts her anger, abuse, finding of faults and other complaints without being apprehensive, ashamed, resorting to falsehood and surrenders at her feet by applying all tactics of appeasing her) is fascinated in finding Rādhā alone. Skilfully using his charming and loving words He cunningly convinces and wins her over in such a manner that the canto goes under the name *Catura-caturbhuja.*]

Then in the evening while the fair faced woman, who in harsh anger was unable to heave high and kept bashfully looking at the face of her friend; Hari approached her and spoke gushing words with joy. [V-51]

vadasi yadi kiḍcidapi gīta (*Aṣṭapadī*)-XIX:

O' my dear one of good manners! Give up your indefinite anger towards me. Now the fire of love burns my mind. Let me drink honey from the lotus-like face of yours.

If you speak a little, the bright teeth, like moon-light, dispels the dense darkness of fear. May your moon-like face cause the *cakora*-like eyes to long for the intoxicating nectar from your lower lip. [*pada*-1]

O' lovely woman with beautiful teeth! If you are really angry with me, then (as punishment) strike me with your glances as sharp as arrows, bind me with your embrace and bite my lower lip with teeth by the kiss to derive pleasure through the same. [*pada*-2]

You are my ornament. You are my life. You are the precious gem in this ocean-like world.

To make you always compliant to me, I put a lot of effort with all my heart. [*pada*-3]

O' slender lady! Your blue lotus-like eyes now bear the appearance of red lotus. It will be proper for you to apply them as arrows of Cupid and enamour this dark man (Kṛṣṇa and God of Love both). [*pada*-4]

Let the row of gems glitter on your pitcher-like breasts and beautify the region of your heart. May the (jingling) girdle around your tight hips proclaim the command of love. [*pada*-5]

O' soft-spoken lady! Your feet that defeat the lotus on land in softness and redness, glow beautifully for their position in my heart at the time of sexual pleasure. Tell me to glisten them with shining juicy lac. [*pada*-6]

Kindly place your lovely tender foot on my head as an ornament to encounter the poison of love. Let it dispel the symptoms of burning fire of cruel Madana (who maddens one in love) in me. [*pada*-7]

Let these fine flattering words issued in respect of Rādhā by the enemy of Mura (the ego) and depicted in a very sharp effective style by the Poet Jayadeva, the husband of Padmāvatī, be victorious. [*pada*-8]

O' my dear frightened in apprehension! Put aside your doubts about me. By your firm and heavy breasts and hips you have overcome my heart. There is no place for others to enter inside, except the God of Love without a body.

Now, O' my lady-love! do whatever necessary before you embrace to begin with. [V-52]

O' attractive and infatuated (*mugdhā*) one! Administer punishment on me with the cruel biting of your teeth, fastening tight with creeper-like arms through embrace causing pain by pressing your hard close-breasts. O' angry (*caṇḍi*) one! May you alone derive pleasure (with such punishment) but let not my life quit because of cutting asunder of the arrows of the damn wicked God of Love (equipped with five arrows and thus known as *pañcabāṇa*). [V-53]

O' slender woman! Your unnecessary silence pains me. O' young lady! Please dwell upon the fifth (musical) note (as of a cuckoo) while you talk sweetly. Casting your glances cast away my suffering and do please me. O' beautiful woman! abandon your disinclination (towards me) but not me. O' beautiful and simple lady! Your most amiable beloved is present here before you by himself. [V-54]

O' *caṇḍi*! Your lower lip is (red and glistening) like *bandhuka* (*Pentapetes Phoenicia*) flower, the cheeks look pale-white like *madhuka* (*Bassia Latifolia*) flowers, the shining eyes emancipating the beauty of the blue water lily (*niḷa naḷina* i.e. *Nelumbium Speciosum*), the nose in shape occupies the position of *sesame* (*Sesamum Indicum*) flower and the teeth are white like *jasmine* (*Jasminum Multiflorum*) flower. *Puṣpāyudha* (with the five flowers as his weapon), the God of Love conquers the world by serving your face (resembling five flowers as mentioned above) [V-55]

Your eyes languid with passion are *Madālasā*, face shining like the moon is *Indulatā*, the movement fascinating people is *Manorama* and the thighs in shape surpass *Rambha*, the plantains. Full of art is your love-play.

The eyebrows are beautiful like drawn lines of a picture. O slender woman! You, endowed with heavenly beauty, are indeed on earth (in *pṛthvī*, here the metre). [V-56]

Thus ends the Tenth Canto, called *Catura-caturbhuja,* of Jayadeva's *Gītagovinda.*

Then begins the Eleventh Canto: *Sānanda-Govinda*:

[Kṛṣṇa has been able to appease Rādhā. She too, forgetting all the miseries, has beaten the drum for sexual fight. Govind (meaning, to derive sensual pleasure) in nuptial mood is also extremely happy. Hence follows the name Sānanda-govinda.]

Keśava having pleased the doe-eyed for long with supplication, when got himself dressed and went to the bed in the arbour; a maid companion told Rādhā, who was without fatigue, beautifully dressed and shining in the blinding darkness of the evening as follows. [V-57]

viracita cāṭu vacanaracanam gīta (*Aṣṭapadī*)-XX:

O' Beautiful and innocent (mugdhā) Rādhikā (meaning, Rādhā in miniature form. i.e. O' Rādhā!) You must make yourself small by giving up your pride and self-conceit in order to win over Kṛṣṇa and His divine love.)! Follow Madhu-mathana (the crusher of demon Madhu and squeezer of honey from tender flower-like ladies), the obedient one (who follows you too).

He has said beautiful flattering words and Himself fallen at your feet. Now He has gone to sleep on the nuptial bed near the *aśoka*-bower, the *kunja*. [*pada*-1]

O' lady laid with the burden of heavy breasts and buttocks! You are a little slow in your movement. Tinkling your gem-studded anklets, approach him slowly and gracefully like a *marāḷa* (swan). [*pada*-2]

Listen to the very charming (call of flute) sound of Śrī Kṛṣṇa (known as Madhuripu, not only because he kills the demon Madhu, but also because he prevails over the sweet and enchanting atmosphere of the Spring by fulfilling the desires to the fullest satisfaction and thus defeating the God of Love, enchanting for the young ladies and enjoy the emotion of love with the cuckoos which sing the glory (or announce the rule) of the God of Love with five flowers as arrows on his bow. [*pada*-3]

O' *karabhoru* (the lady whose thighs resemble the back of the fore-arm or the trunk of a young elephant)! The mass of creepers with their moving tender leaves in the wind, as if waving their hands, urging you to proceed without delay. [*pada*-4]

You (if do not believe my words) ask your pitcher-like breasts with a beautiful necklace like the stream of water (as flows on the mountain), which are throbbing with the waves of love, as if asking to be hugged by Hari. [*pada*-5]

O' lady in anger (*caṇḍi*)! All the friends know that your body is also ready for the love battle.You without bashfulness and with passion proceed to him on a rendezvous with your girdles jingling and sounding like a battle-drum. [*pada*-6]

You go to Hari playfully with the help of a friend leading by holding your hands, which with nails look beautiful like the arrows of the God of Love. With the jingling sound of your bracelets, you inform him of your approach for the battle of love. [*pada*-7]

Let this song of Śrī-Jayadeva be for good, like a woman's necklace, adorning the throats of people whose minds do rest on Hari. [*pada*-8]

O' my dear friend! She will come, look at me, talk about matters of love, get to love by hugging my entire body and then gratify by cohabitation—with these thoughts in his mind; your beloved looks for you, trembles, bristles, rejoices, sweats and faints (without getting you) in the darkness of the arbour. [V-58]

O' friend! The darkness in the arbour as if embraces every limb of the cunning passionate beautiful-eyed women in haste under a nice blue-cloak on rendezvous—putting collyrium on the eyes, a bunch of *tāpiñcha* (flowers of *tamāḷa*) on the ears, a garland of blue lotuses around the head, various designs as decoration of the breasts with musk. [V-59]

The darkness of the night gets deepened with the blackness of the *tamāḷa*-leaves. It stands as a touch-stone (black in colour) to test the gold of love of the women, as bright as the Kaśmir-women, looking still brighter because of the row of gems on them at the time of rendezvous with their lovers. [V-60]

Having seen Hari at the door of the bower, shining with the glaze of the jewels in his pearl necklace, central locket, golden girdle, anklet and bracelet; Rādhā being bashful, a companion told her: [V-61]

mañjutara-kuñjataḷa-keḷisadane gīta (*Aṣṭapadī*)-XXI:

O' Rādhā! Go into the bower and be close to Mādhava.

O' my dear! Being impetuous with smiling face, play up amorously there on the beautiful ground of the bower, a pleasure-house. [*pada*-1]

O' my dear! You are beautiful with the necklace moving to and fro on your pitcher-like robust breasts. Play upon the bed, excellently prepared with the fresh and tender leaves of *aśoka*. [*Pada*-2]

O' my dear! Your body is as tender as flowers. Go in to the fine bed-room made of flowers and play up. [*Pada*-3]

O' my dear! You are proficient in the fine art of singing amorous songs. Go into the playhouse, cool and scented with the gentle breeze and play up. [*pada*-4]

O' my dear! You are indolent with your corpulent buttocks. Go gladly into the thick bower covered with new leaves of many creepers. [*pada*-5]

O' my dear! You are emotionally passionate. Go into the bower filled with the humming of honey-bees delighted in the spring season. [*pada*-6]

O' my dear! Your teeth are beautifully set like the seeds of the pomegranate fruit. Go into the bower resonant with very sweet songs of the cuckoos. [*pada*-7]

This song composed for the happiness in the society of Padmāvatī and by Jayadeva, the king of poets, may bestow bliss on hundreds. [*pada*-8]

O' Rādhā! Kṛṣṇa keeping you ever in his mind, is very much wearied and greatly inflamed by love. He now wishes to drink your *bimba*-like lower lip facing trouble because of nectar (liked by all) in it. You adorn his lap for some time. He is sold out on the wealth of your playful knitting of the eyebrows.

Why do you then feel ashamed about one who worships your lotus-feet like a purchased slave ? [V-62]

She, with fear and joy, quickly looking towards Govinda; entered into the pleasure-house with the jingling of lovely anklets. [V-63]

rādhāvadanavilokanavikasitavividhavikāra gīta (Aṣṭapadī)- XXII:

She (Rādhā) looked upon the face of Kṛṣṇa, under the spell of great joy giving vent to amorous desires. (For her) Hari was the only flavour of love, only desired object of love and fascination.

At the sight of Rādhā's face, there were expressions of various symptoms of love in Kṛṣṇa like the ocean which rises high at the sight of the lunar disc. [*pada*-1]

He wore a long necklace of pure pearls upon his chest, which looked like the non-stop flow of Yamunā crested with masses of foam. [*pada*-2]

His dark and tender body covered with yellow thin robe looked like the blue lotus having its root encircled with yellow veils. [*pada*-3]

His pleasure in passionate love was produced by the face through its quivering sidelong glances like a pool in autumn, where a pair of wagtails play on an open lotus. [*pada*-4]

The *kuṇḍaḷa* (earrings), put to increase the lusture of his lotus-like face, dazzle themselves in beauty like the radiant Sun. His lower lip delighted with his charming smile increases the greediness for sexual-pleasure in increasing intensity. [*pada*-5]

His hair decorated with flowers looks like the clouds decorated with the moon-beams scattered on them and the sandal mark on his dark fore-head looks like a lunar circle rising in darkness. [*pada*-6]

His body becomes prickly with the thrill of joy excited for the pleasure of love-play and looks beautiful with radiating rays of the ornaments studded with gems. [*pada*-7]

The song of Śrī-Jayadeva has doubled His treasure of beauty. By placing Him in your heart for good bow to Hari who is the essence of all the virtues. [*pada*-8]

The eyes of Rādhā with fickle pupils projecting an intense desire to glance at Kṛṣṇa, went beyond their corners, elongated up to the ears and tired, fell on Him and (as the person who falls gets up immediately in shame and looks around to know, if anybody has seen them falling) then became tremulous. Rādhā was drenched with the tears of joy which looked like sweat rolling down from the eyes. This is because of the hard labour the eyes devoted to see the lord shedding a flood of tears. [V-64]

When the friends knowingly went outside the play-house with their meaningful smiles concealed by hands in the pretext of scratching their mouths; Rādhā, the doe-eyed woman, proceeding to his bed under the sway of love, when looking at him found that he was also looking for her being lovestricken; then her embarrassment went away. [V-65]

Thus ends the Eleventh Canto, called *Sānanda-govinda,* of Jayadeva's *Gītagovinda.*

Then begins the Twelfth Canto: *Suprīta-Pītāmbara*

[Kṛṣṇa, for his yellow garments known as *Pītāmbara* is 'very much pleased at the end, for his success in winning over Rādhā, the lady-love for which this canto is rightly called *Suprīta-Pītāmbara.* After long eager awaiting and suffering from pangs of love, there is final consummation of love in this canto. Kṛṣṇa treats Rādhā with utmost love and serves her every wish with delight like a handmaid.The absolute egolessness and total surrender of the Lord, the eternal lover to his beloved devotee indicates rather the strong traits of Tantricism to control or have a strong hold over one's *śakti* or the 'Goddess of love and devotion' than its influence on the so called *Sahajiyā*'s treating god as a slave of slaves, quite contrary to the conducts of *vaiṣṇava* dharma. Here, it may be recalled that *Bagaḷā*, one of the ten *mahāvidyās* in *śākta-tantra,* is very well known as *Pītāmbarā* with reins in her hand as symbol of enormous controlling power to keep the opposite overpowered and spellbound. It is also significant that recitation of the *Gītagovinda* in ecstasy is seen in the *cakra-pūjā* of *vāmācāra* practice in Tantra-worship.]

When her friends were away, Hari spoke to Rādhā who now smiles passionately with thrills on her lower lip indicating overpowering intentions of love and casting her eyes constantly upon the bed made of flowers and tender leaves. [V-66]

'kiśaḷayaśayanataḷe kuru kāmini caraṇanaḷinaviniveśam' gīta (*Aṣṭapadī*)- XXIII:

O' Rādhikā (worshipper)! Now at this opportune moment betake yourself to the beseeching Narāyaṇa (*ayanam,* the final resort of *narāṇām* all the human beings in general and of *narāṇām* ladies in particular).

O' my dear Kāmini (affectionate lady with lust)! Lay your lotus-like feet on the bed of new leaves (*pallava*, meaning having *lava*-a little grandeur of *pat*, the feet) by which the bed (envious of you and vying with you) may get a defeat from your decorated tender feet. [*pada*-1]

You have come a long way (and must be feeling very much tired). I shall serve your feet (pressing together and stroking gently) with my lotus-like hands. Please let me (be allowed to) be on your bed like your anklets (by putting them aside), which are as heroic as I in following you. [*pada*-2]

Kindly speak words of nectar trickling down from the moon-like face of yours. Let me take out the upper garment covering the breasts which stands as an obstruction and does separate us. [*pada*-3]

To extinguish the heat of love, kindly place your pitcher-like breasts on my chest as they are horripilated with passion and inaccessible but ready for the embrace of the lover. [*pada*-4]

O' conceited lady (*Bhāminī*)! Please make the nectar from your lower lip available to your slave and save him, whose mind is fixed upon you and dying with a body consumed by the fire of separation being devoid of the pleasure of love-play. [*pada*-5]

O'my dear with a face like the moon! Please let your bejewelled girdle as good as your charming voice ring (while at the reverse erotic play) into my ears and cause a relaxation to my ears vexed by the songs of cuckoos since long. [*pada*-6]

Now your eyes, embarrassed due to futile anger, cease to look at me as if closed in shame. Kindly give up your anger and sexual frustration. [*pada*-7]

The song of Śrī-Jayadeva depicting at every step the delight of the enemy of Madhu (the sweet Spring and its God of Love too) may produce an appreciation of emotion of the charming love pleasure in the minds of the persons of cultivated taste. [*pada*-8]

The horripilation at the time of close embrace, winking while playfully looking with purpose, the pleasant talk while drinking nectar from the lower lip and the attainment of excess bliss in the art of erotic warfare; though considered to be hindrances wonderfully so happened to agreeably cause the beginning of sexual union of both the lovers. [V-67]

Oh! Paradoxical indeed is the way of love, in as much as the lover having been held firmly in between the arms under control, pressed by the heavy breasts, pierced by the nails, bitten on the lower lip by the teeth, hurt by the slope of the hip and bent through dragging the hair down by the hands and captivated by the drinking of honey from her lower lip; obtained indescribable satisfaction. [V-68]

At the beginning of the battle of love-play (requiring both to be active, but the lady) to win over her lover, she courageously got upon him and undertook an adventure in haste so that the surface of her hips got numb, the creeper-like arms loosened, the breasts shaken and the eyes closed.

How can the pleasure be derived in displaying the sentiment of heroism as natural with men in the sexual intercourse, be possible in perfect manner with women in reverse (since it needs a man positively active but not only manly action of a woman reversely in love-play)? [V-69]

Her breasts were pink marked by nails, sleepy eyes were reddish, the redness from the lower lip was washed out, hair dishevelled and its garland fallen and the cord of girdle and the clothes were loosened. The mind of the lover was impaired on seeing in the morning these amazing scenes made by the arrows of the Love God. [V-70]

kuru yadunandana candanaśiśiratareṇa kareṇa payodhare gīta (*Aṣṭapadī*)- XXIV:

She told Yadunandana, the joy of her heart:

O' Yadunandana! Do decorate with your hand as cold as sandal, a design of leaves with the help of musk on my breasts resembling full pots of auspisciousness kept ready for the festival of mindborn God of Love. [*pada*-1]

O' my dear! Decorate my eyes with collyrium (through its sidelong glances as if) releasing the arrows of the God of Love, generating an impression of a swarm of black-bees because of its darkness as they have been bereft of collyrium by your kisses. [*pada*-2]

O' *śubhaveśa* (well dressed one)! Put a pair of *kuṇḍaḷa* (earrings) on both my ears, which look like snares of love and stand on the way of expansion of sidelong glances of my eyes as good as deer (in movement and innocence). (As a result, the snares then having caught the *kuṇḍaḷa* for ever, would never be able to catch my eyes). [*pada*-3]

My glossy curling hair for long appears to be a swarm of bees on my spotless lotus-like face. Kindly fasten them in a pleasing manner. [*pada*-4]

O' *kamaḷānana* (with a face like the lotus)! Now the sweating has ceased and hence put a beautiful mark with the essence of the musk like a lunar spot on my forehead which would look like the moon. [*pada*-5]

O' *mānada* (dispeller of high opinion of oneself in arrogance)! With flowers do decorate my beautful braid as luxuriant as the peacock's tail (being dishevelled in love-play, as flowers have dropped down) and a bushy tail of *camara* (*Bos Grunniens*) reckoned as a royal insignia of the Love God. [*pada*-6]

O' *śubhāśaya* (One with good intention)! Put ornaments, clothes and bejewelled girdle on my wide hips which are firm and beautiful like the dwelling cave of the elephant of love. [*pada*-7]

(O' devoted readers!) Kindly have your heart adorned with this song of Śrī-Jayadeva which will dispel the fever of the world and impurity of *Kaḷi* as it is made of nectar for remembering the feet of Hari. [*pada*-8]

Do create designs of leaves on my breasts, decorate my cheeks, put the girdle on my hips, adorn my head and hair with garland, put bracelets on my hands and anklets on my feet. And all these were carried out with pleasure by *Pitāmbara*, the yellow-robed one. [V-71]

The skill in the arts of music (*gāndharva*), the concentration of the *Vaiṣṇavas*, the discrimination of the truth of erotics which is diaplayed in the poems of all that can be easily understood by the wise people from *Śrī-Gītagovinda* of the scholar and poet Jayadeva, whose soul has Kṛṣṇa as the only object of veneration. [V-72]

As long as the words of Jayadeva bestow the essence of erotic emotion—O' Mādhvīka (locally known in Odia as *mahuli*, a sweet liquor distilled from the flowers of Madhuka-tree)! your idea of being sweet holds no good. O' *śarkarā* (a rock candy locally called *śākara* in Oḍiā)! you are hard (like a piece of pebble). O' *drākṣā* (grape)! no one will look at you. O' *amṛta* (nectar, which makes one immortal)! you are now dead(*mṛta*). O' *kṣīra* (milk)! you are liquid (tasteless) water. O' *mākaranda* (sweet mango)! you cry (*kranda*, as you are no more sweet). O' *kāntādhara* (sweet lower lip of the beloved)! you go to hell.

Thus ends the Twelfth Canto, called *Suprīta-Pītāmbara*, of Jayadeva's *Gītagovinda*.

'The singing of this sweet song is an act of piety symbolising a cow, the most loving being reared by Govinda. Where there is a cow symbolising *dharma*, there is Govinda, the God. Each song of this lyric has eight stanzas as the cow has eight hoofs or eight steps of piety, viz. *satya* (truthfulness), *śauca* (purity), *ahiṁsā* (non-violence), *anasūyā* (without malice and enviousness), *kṣamā* (forbearance), *ānṛśaṁsya* (compassion), *akārpaṇya* (without miserliness), *saṁtoṣa* (contentment). Following the above mentioned footsteps the devotees serve Him all the eight time-units of a day called *prahara* (of three hours duration each) by songs embellished with *prema, sneha, māna, praṇaya, rāga, anurāga, bhāva* and *mahābhāva* in order to get Him. The lyric sung (gīta) in praise of Govinda (with '*jaya*') by Jayadeva at the precinct of Śrī-Jagannātha, the Lord of the Universe, is called the *Gītagovinda*. It is said that Śrī-Jagannātha, in the guise of a cow, (having eight hoofs) in all eagerness followed Jayadeva to listen to his lyrical poem with twenty-four songs, each containing eight stanzas called *aṣṭapadī*. It is, therefore, sung everyday before the Lord of the Universe as service pleasing to Him. This translation true to the sense and spirit of the *Gītagovinda* began on september 26, 2004 and was casually completed on the bright night of *Kārtika* (*Rāsa*)-*pūrnimā*, November 25, 2004.]

APPENDICES

Appendix-A

A Sample Pictorial Description of the *Gītagovinda*

Dinanath Pathy

This illustrated palmleaf manuscript is in the collection of the Orissa State Museum bearing catalogue No. Ext. 166.

Poet-Jayadeva (*Sarvāṅgasundarī Tikā* by Dhananjaya Dharaṇideva)
Size-29.5 cm. x 3.7 cm.
Script-Odia
Language-Sanskrit
Date of the copy-17th century (as per museum records)
Number of folios-72 x 2 (We have followed the numbers written with the help of an ink pen on the palmleaf folio from No. 1 to No. 91)
Colophon-
Sanskrit text- *Virendrasya Mukunda Sindhunṛpate Dirneika Vandhorṇava Trinsenke pratipadithou Gurudine Kanyāgate bhāskare Tikāputtalikānvitam Vilikhitam Śrī Gītagovinda Kāvya Chāru DhananJayākṣya Dharani Devena pakṣe site*

Translation

The best of the Brāhamaṇas, Dhananjaya, has written the commentary and etched the illustrations on Thursday, the Ist day of the new moon in the month of *Kanyā* during the 30th *aṅka* of King Mukundadeva, the best of the heroes.

Four kings bearing the name Mukundadeva have ascended the throne of Odisha Kingdom.

Page 255: *Illustration from the Dharanidhara* Gītagovinda *palmleaf manuscript, Orissa State Museum.*

They are:-

1. Telangā Mukundadeva (1559 to 1568 AD)
2. Mukundadeva (1657 to 1688/89 AD)
3. The last independent king Mukundadeva (1795 to 1816 AD)
4. Mukundadeva (1876 to 1926 AD)

The time of the Telangā Mukundadeva would be too early in consideration of the style of the visuals whereas that of two other Mukundadevas (3rd and 4th) would be too late. It would be proper to ascribe the date of the manuscript to Mukundadeva (2) listed above. His 39 anka would be 32 regnal years and the date of the manuscript would be 1657 + 32 = 1689 AD, that is in the 17th century. (19th September 1689 AD). The scribe Dhananjaya has mentioned that he has done both the *tīka* (commentary) and *puttalikā* (the figures or the illustrations). All the illustrations in this manuscript are not of uniform style and are not executed by a single artist. Certain drawings are so sketchy that they appear to be made in the 20th century. These drawings have perhaps prompted a few scholars like Joanna Williams and J. P. Das to conclude that the illustrations belonged to the 19th century. In our considered view, the illustrations of this manuscript have been done over a period of time beginning from the 18th century upto the 20th century notwithstanding our calculation of the date of the manuscript based on the colophon.

Folio

1a. & 1b. No illustrations

2a On either side of the leaf two *padma maṇḍāla* are drawn within two dark squares separating the script portion with two vertical bands.

2b Nanda, the best of the cowherds commands Rādhā to escort Kṛṣṇa home as darkness descends on the forest. Dark sky has been suggested with hatching lines at the top frame of the folio. Nanda is shown bulky and bearded. The scribe has depicted Rādhā taller than Kṛṣṇa because it is Rādhā who has to escort Kṛṣṇa. The sequential composition is suggestive of a forest-scape with cows and a deer grazing. The application of red over the bodies of the cows, border of Nanda's cloth, Kṛṣṇa's girdle and Rādhā's sari border is crude and is perhaps an after thought.

3a Rādhā and Kṛṣṇa on their way back home get involved in amorous love play in a *kuñja* on the bank of the river Yamunā. A pond suggestive of the river has been shown with lilies and swans. A tiger is resting on the bank of the river (scene from the left). Kṛṣṇa

Illustration 2b. Gītagovinda *opening scene. Nanda, Kṛṣṇa, Rādhā.*

escorted by Rādhā returns home. In the first *kuñja* Kṛṣṇa is seen engaged in sexual dalliance with Rādhā. In the second sequence also the scene of sexual dalliance is continued, where Kṛṣṇa kisses Rādhā passionately. In the third *kuñja*, Kṛṣṇa kisses the breasts of Rādhā, Rādhā is very much responsive to the love play. While presenting the erotic scenes, Rādhā and Kṛṣṇa are drawn in the same height. The scribe's attitude in maintaining the differences in height of Rādhā and Kṛṣṇa in ordinary sequences and drawing them in similar heights in sequences of amorous acts is easily discernible.

3b The full portrait of a scribe resembling a Puri *Brāhmin* writing on a palmleaf is painted. This could be Dhananjaya the scribe who has written and illustrated the palmleaf manuscript. This is wrongly identified as Jayadeva by some scholars because of an inscription in Odia attached to the portrait. The portrait is flabby, unimpressive and unbecoming of a poetic character.

4a and 4b No illustrations.

5a The fish and tortoise incarnations have been shown in zoomorphic forms. In later depictions the first two incarnation figures are shown as emerging from the fish and tortoise. Of course these are late 19th century versions which were then adopted by calendar art.

5b The two incarnation figures of Nṛsiṁha and Varāha presented in a square panel are bound by two vertical borders. Nṛsiṁha is shown under a decorative arch. Both the figures have been depicted in profile, facing each other. Varāha stands amidst the sea, made dark by crisscross lines. Nṛsiṁha tears open the belly of Hiraṇākṣyapa. The demon is clad in stitched garments and sports a trimmed beard.

6a Vāmana is shown in two sequences. In the first, he resembles a priest of Puri Jagannātha temple holding a palmleaf umbrella. In the second sequence Viṣṇu is painted along with Bali depicted as a tiny figure.

Above: *Illustration 3a. Rādhā and Kṛṣṇa in a kunja.*

Illustration 6a. Vāmana and Bali.

6b Paraśurāma is drawn with a long beard, wearing stitched garments holding a bow in the left hand and an axe in the right, with a quiver, shield and sword tied to the waist. A severed head of Sahasrārjuna is placed on the right side on an altar and another head of a *kṣatriya* on the altar on the left.

Rāma stands in heroic attitude with his bow stretched, carrying a quiver full of arrows on his back. He wears an embroidered skirt and a *palāsa* flower in his matted locks. Rāvana lies dead before him. The heads of Rāvana have been depicted as if stacked one above the other vertically.

7a Balarāma is shown with a moustached face. He is portrayed holding a *musaḷa* in his raised left hand. Buddha has been conceived as a Hindu sage with flowing matted locks falling on either side of his shoulders. The sage is shown in three-quarter face with a beard and a rosary around the neck. He wears a red loincloth and sits cross-legged on a lotus. Kaḷki is shown riding a galloping horse holding a drawn up sword. He resembles a soldier in a Mughal army.

7b No illustration

8a The illustrations of Lakṣmīnārāyaṇa. Lakṣmī is painted tiny on the lap of Nārāyaṇa.

8b Sūrya Nārāyaṇa (Dinamaṇi) is seen inside the *maṇḍala* which is in the form of a wooden chariot with a single wheel. In the Kālīyadaḷana on the right side of the leaf *nāga-kanyās* with scales on their torsoes stand in water.

Above: *Illustration 6b. Rāma shooting a deadly arrow at Rāvana.*

Illustration 8b. Kālīyadaḷana.

9a In the picturisation of Girigovardhana, Kṛṣṇa lifts a bow shaped group of hills and blows a *singā* (horn). The two cowherd boys, one wearing a skirt and the other a *dhoti*, are supporting the hill with the help of their sticks.

9b Nārāyaṇa is killing Madhu in two pictorial sequences. The demon Madhu is dressed in stitched and striped garments and sports a pointed and trimmed beard. Nārāyaṇa has a long plait. In another illustration on the same leaf Rāma and

Rāvana are engaged in a duel riding their respective chariots each drawn by a single horse.

10a A vivid depiction of spring season. A forest full of tall tapering trees drawn in harmony with the standing figures. The trees are stencilled out from a brick-red background. Colours have been applied liberally to this illustration giving the impression of a miniature paper painting. A monkey in a playful mood is seen climbing up a tree. The pictorial renderings are naturalistic.

A tiger lies waiting at the foot of the trees, its body seems fixed to the trunks. The whole scene gives the impression of an *abhayāraṇya* where wild animals and human beings fearlessly roam together.

10b Mādhava in the form of Nārāyaṇa with conventional *āyudha* is seated in *padmāsana* with Rādhā under a niche. In another illustration Rādhā probably speaks her heart to a parrot.

11a Rādhā and Kṛṣṇa are inside the *kuñja.* The *kuñja* has been improvised by entwining creepers. A square black path is etched for a pond where one sees two swimming fishes, a goose and two lotuses with their stalks going deep into the water. A deer is resting on the bank. Two *sakhi* dance with Kṛṣṇa who is dressed up in a skirt made of leaves. He has a plait dangling on his back. Out of the two female dancers, one has a plait and the other a chignon. They are wearing skirts with *choḷi* and blouse. In another sequence Rādhā lowers a bough and casts a passionate glance at Kṛṣṇa. An arched *kuñja* is seen empty nearby.

11b No. illustrations.

12a The scene of an *upavana* with a large variety of flowering trees planted with a uniform symmetry. On the right of the leaf is a triarched *kuñja* resembling a temple niche. Kṛṣṇa, Rādhā and Laḷitā dressed in skirts dance together. Kṛṣṇa's skirt is made of green

Illustration 11a Kṛṣṇa dancing with Rādhā's sakhī *in a* kuñja.

leaves. A peacock, a mongoose, a deer and a wild cock enjoy the rhythm of dance in the garden.

12b No illustration.

13a Kṛṣṇa entreats Laḷitā. Laḷitā lowers a creeper and presses it under her foot probably to pluck a flower. The surface treatment of the foliages leaves a blank space in the leaf to accommodate the figures of Kṛṣṇa and Laḷitā. Little touches of light yellow and red lines have been painted on the illustrations.

13b No illustrations.

14a Kṛṣṇa in the midst of *gopī* performs *rāsakridā* in the forest of Kadamba. The *sakhī* are shown in various dance sequences on either side of Kṛṣṇa. On the left side of the leaf, Laḷitā points out to Rādhā, Kṛṣṇa's *rāsakriḍā* with the *gopī* and other maidens. She pulls Rādhā to her side and raises her accusing finger at Kṛṣṇa. Kṛṣṇa stands head above the group of dancers. Six dancers, three on either side of Kṛṣṇa form an almost symmetric dance pattern.

14b Landscape with two hillocks set in between palm and aśoka trees. A tiger sits majestically on the peak of the first hillock and a bear is seen sniffing in between the hillocks. Birds perch on the trees. A snake emerges from its hole. The hillocks have been rendered with small conical shapes and have been suggested with parallel wavy lines.

15a Rādhā and Kṛṣṇa are in close embrace. Kṛṣṇa holds a yellow flower. On the right corner of the leaf Kṛṣṇa is seated and Rādhā stands close to him with hands crossed over her breast.

15b No illustrations.

16a Rādhā with her head covered with a veil is presented before Kṛṣṇa. Perhaps Laḷitā whispers into Kṛṣṇa's ears Rādhā's desire and her intention of coming. In another sequence Rādhā and Kṛṣṇa are seen engaged in intercourse.

Illustration 14b. Landscape with tiger and other interesting flora and fauna.

16b Rādhā and Kṛṣṇa dance dressed up in skirts. Both of them have long plaits. Three companions watch them dance and enjoy the sequence.

17a *Rāsanṛtya* is enacted again. Kṛṣṇa dances with four *gopī.* He is drawn taller than the group of dancers. The dancers form a well-knit circle, a *maṇḍala,* with their hands intertwined.

17b The union of Rādhā and Kṛṣṇa. Rādhā and Kṛṣṇa are seen in five pictorial sequences twice in open rectangular spaces and thrice under arched *kuñja.* The middle niche contains the love making sequence of Rādhā and Kṛṣṇa. Rādhā reclines against a pillow. The dark, fleshy and well groomed body of Kṛṣṇa lies atop the yellow complexioned Rādhā. The treatment of costumes of Rādhā and Kṛṣṇa in these sequences show various patterns.

18a Rādhā and Laḷitā are inside the *kuñja* which has a half circled opening against a rectangular space, studded with flowers, creepers and other decorative foliages.

18b No illustrations.

19a and 19b No illustrations.

20a Rādhā is seen with her companions inside the *kuñja.* The *kuñja* look like arched *jālī* windows often found in Mughal architecture. These *jāli* also remind us of foliated tapestry.

20b No illustrations.

21a and 21b No illustrations.

22a and 22b No illustrations.

23a and 23b No illustrations.

24a Rādhā and her companion enjoy the beauty of the garden from inside the *kuñja.* The *kuñja* is set with flower creepers and the background is done with criss-cross hatched lines, to heighten the effect of the flowers. A pond with lotuses and two inverted fishes is inscribed. Steps have also been provided on both sides of the pond meant as bathing *ghāt.* The trees on the banks of the pond are smaller. Inside the garden a monkey, a deer and a bear are seen.

24b No illustrations.

25a Kṛṣṇa is in a dejected mood resting his bent head on his hands inside the *kuñja.* His plait hangs down on the back with a red flower dangling at the end. A pond with fishes is seen at the right extreme.

25b Six *gopī* are engaged in dance. They expect the arrival of Kṛṣṇa. Kṛṣṇa stands underneath a *kuñja* on the right corner of the leaf waiting for the arrival of Rādhā. The trees are set against a patch of dark clouds drawn with criss-cross lines.

26a On the right extreme corner of the leaf inside a *kuñja,* Dūti and Kṛṣṇa anxiously keep waiting for the arrival of Rādhā.

26b No illustrations.

27a Kṛṣṇa sits waiting inside a *kuñja.*

27b Illustrations with similar theme continue.

28a Single illustration of a deer beneath a tree on the right extreme corner of the leaf. There is a foliated vertical border on the right extreme.

28b No illustrations.

29a Kṛṣṇa sits on a lotus *maṇḍala* inside a *kuñja.* Laḷitā with folded hands brings some message from his beloved Rādhā. The garden is seen with long tapering trees of palms and nuts. Trees spaced symmetrically stand against a background crowded with flower droppings which look like a tapestry. River Yamunā with fishes and lotuses is visible through the trees.

29b No illustrations.

30a *Rādhā* in *viraha* inside a *maṇḍapa* pining for the love of Kṛṣṇa. Moonlit night is suggested with a round moon against a square patch of dark sky studded with stars. The artist has tried to make the moon look natural with dark patches on its surface.

Illustration 25b. Kṛṣṇa awaiting Rādhā's arrival and gopī *dancing.*

30b Two sequences of Rādhā in varying moods are illustrated on the leaf. On the left, Rādhā in *viraha* beats her breast in frustration and in the second sequence she gathers her patience and tries to spread the bed of flowers hoping for the arrival of Kṛṣṇa.

31a Rādhā in her intense longing paints the picture of Kṛṣṇa in *kasturi* visualising him as Kandarpa. The god of love holds a mango blossom and his attending crocodile (*Makara*) is painted under the pedestal. After painting Kṛṣṇa as Kandarpa, she prostrates in front of the picture.

31b No illustrations.

32a Rādhā with her companions sits inside a *maṇḍapa*. The *maṇḍapa* has been conceived like a wooden *vimāna* used in spring festival procession in Odisha. Pendants are seen hanging from the ceiling of the *vimāna*.

32b Rādhā and Kṛṣṇa are seated inside the *maṇḍapa*. She is in remorse, her hand against her cheek. Kṛṣṇa sits reclining against a round pillow.

33a Rādhā waits anxiously. Her figure is set at the left hand corner of the leaf.

33b Rādhā rests majestically against a pillow. In the next sequence Laḷitā offers a cup of honey to Rādhā.

34a Rādhā waits eagerly in a *maṇḍapa*. This sequence is repeated again in another *maṇḍapa* painted nearby. The treatment of bangles with bright touches of yellow in-between black lines suggests the glittering effect and breaks Rādhā's monotony of waiting.

34b Rādhā is in a dejected mood. In one sequence she sits with her face cast downward resting on the bed and in another sequence reclines on a pillow, face upward. These two sequences are

Illustration 30b.
Rādhā in viraha.

under two arches with pendants hanging from the ceiling. In between these two arched *kuñjas*, Laḷitā is seen standing in a pensive mood.

35a and 35b No illustrations.

36a Rādhā waits for Kṛṣṇa in a *kriḍāmaṇḍapa.* An empty bed is seen on the floor. Rādhā reclines against the bed. Her longings could be read from her face.

36b Rādhā is projected on a *maṇḍapa* on the right extreme corner of the leaf.

37a Kṛṣṇa waits for Rādhā inside the arbour shown in two sequences. In the first illustration, he sits on a bed reclining against a pillow. In the second illustration on a *padmamaṇḍala* with both hands supported against the chin gazing intently for the arrival of Rādhā.

37b There are three illustrations for the three sequences. Inside the arched arbours the sequences take place, Kṛṣṇa sits dejected and Laḷitā stands close by. By the side of the *kuñja* a pond is etched. In the middle, Rādhā stands in *viraha* probably waiting for the message from Laḷitā. In the right extreme illustration, Rādhā sits dejected and Laḷitā tries to communicate Kṛṣṇa's entreaties and convince Rādhā to surrender to his love.

38a Kṛṣṇa in *viraha* sits depressed inside a *kuñja* with coconut trees on both sides. The presence of an owl is suggestive of the night. Portions of the dark sky are seen on both sides of the *kuñja.*

38b Dominating the scene stands a wooden *maṇḍapa* with a three tiered *piḍhā* roof, and carved pillars. An empty bed is placed on the left. Kṛṣṇa in *viraha* rests his head on his knees. In another

Illustration 34b. Rādhā in frustration when Kṛṣṇa did not keep his word.

sequence, while Kṛṣṇa so sits inside a *kuñja* Rādhā sleeps on the ground dejected.

39a In the first sequence, Kṛṣṇa plays his flute beneath a *kadamba* tree. In the next sequence he waits anxiously in the *kuñja* on the bank of the river Yamunā. He spreads a bed of tender leaves.

39b The scenes of gardens on both the banks of the river Yamunā. On the right bank, Kṛṣṇa anxiously waits for the arrival of Rādhā. The illustration is divided into two sequences by a vertical plain band. On the left Rādhā's companions persuade her to proceed to the *kuñja* which is on the other side of the river.

The borders of Rādhā's sari are brightly painted with yellow. The river is shown in the fashion of a pond with fishes. An elephant with a well modelled body is shown to accentuate the feeling of a forest.

40a Rādhā and Laḷitā are engaged in conversation inside the arbour. The arbour is set with beautiful creeper motifs, running into a type of decorative panel design. Laḷita is wearing a red sari.

40b No illustrations.

41a Kṛṣṇa waits anxiously inside the *kuñja* in a dejected mood. He then spreads a bed of flowers and stands outside and watches Rādhā's arrival.

41b Rādhā and Laḷitā are conversing inside the garden. The background of the scene is treated with trees. A line bordering the figures depicts a novel way of rendering a composition.

42a Rādhā is in *abhimāna*. Dūti supplicates her in favour of Kṛṣṇa. On the right extreme corner of the folio Kṛṣṇa is painted.

42b A scene of a pavilion with a man and a woman making love in a

Illustration 39b. Sakhī *entreat Rādhā to meet Kṛṣṇa.*

garden at night. They first embrace each other and then engage in coition. The man holds the plait of the woman in the ardour of passion. This illustration presumably serves to quicken the longing of Rādhā and Kṛṣṇa. The dark background has been shown with criss-cross hatched lines. Red, lemon yellow and black colours are used by the painter.

43a Kṛṣṇa is inside a wooden *maṇḍapa*. The *maṇḍapa* is devoid of pillars and is set atop a *piḍhā* roof. Massive graphic motifs have been used in the decoration of the *maṇḍapa*. On the right, Rādhā is painted with her companions.

43b The *maṇḍapa* is with trifoil cusped arches crowned at the top with a *piḍhā* roof. The roof of the *maṇḍapa* forms a concave shape instead of straight slantings. Rādhā sits in *abhimāna*. In another sequence of the scene on the right side of the leaf Rādhā beats her breast in frustration. She then reclines on a bed. Laḷitā, her confidante, stands nearby.

44a Dark night is depicted with a dark patch. An expectant Rādhā awaits the arrival of her lover. In another sequence Rādhā, the *vāskasajjā nāyikā* has spread a bed of flowers for Kṛṣṇa and is seated on the floor inside the *maṇḍapa* waiting for the arrival of Kṛṣṇa. Kṛṣṇa did not arrive. She passed the entire night waiting for him. To suggest this unfulfilled desire, the dark background otherwise suggestive of Kṛṣṇa has been removed by the painter.

44b No illustrations.

45a and 45b No illustrations.

46a Rādhā, the *virahautkaṇṭhitā nāyikā* sits dejected inside a garden. Quite unconcerned about her mental condition, monkeys are seen playing, one pulling a branch and the other climbing a tree. The night is deepening and the moon rises on the right corner against a patch of square sky dotted with stars. A dark patch is noticed on the surface of the moon.

46b Rādhā is painted in four sequences inside flower arbours (A reading from the left is given.) She puts on an anklet on the left leg in the first sequence. In the second sequence she awaits the arrival of Kṛṣṇa. Here the tree looks prominent being set against a dark sky. In the third sequence Rādhā is spreading a bed of leaves for her lover. In the fourth sequence she spends anxious moments.

47a Rādhā is in remorse inside a *kuñja* set with thick foliage. The mood is one of remorse and depression.

47b No. illustrations.

48a Rādhā and Laḷitā in conversation beneath a tree.

48b No illustrations.

49a Rādhā and Laḷitā in the scene. Rādhā points at the moon enquiring from Lalita the time of the arrival of Kṛṣṇa. The artist always paints the round moon against a rectangular patch of dark cloud dotted with stars. Inside the moon, a motif is shown perhaps to suggest its dark patch. The moon heightens Rādhā's expectations which are riddled with ifs and buts symbolised by the dark patches. It is already time for the rendezvous, Kṛṣṇa does not turn up.

49b Finally making Rādhā elated, Kṛṣṇa has arrived. Rādhā engages with him in love play. *Viparīta rati*, lovemaking in reverse posture, is depicted. They are shown engaged in the act of lovemaking in two sequences inside the *kuñjas*.

50a After enjoying themselves Rādhā and Kṛṣṇa roam in the garden and play pranks on each other. Kṛṣṇa dresses Rādhā, puts a garland around her neck, fits a bangle on Rādhā's wrist. The branches of the trees from either side form two arches. In the first sequence Rādhā wears a green sari and changes it to a yellow one in the second sequence obviously after the love play. In the centre is a potted plant. Below is the river Yamunā, the bank shown in a straight line with fishes as if woven in a tie and dye sari border. The illustration is filled with romance.

50b Rādhā and Kṛṣṇa are on the bank of the river Yamunā in a jubilant mood. Yamunā is depicted as a black patch with swimming fish motifs. In the first sequence Kṛṣṇa paints a *tilaka* on Rādhā's forehead, in the second sequence tucks a garland of *pātali* flowers.

Illustration 50b. Kṛṣṇa adorning Rādhā after love play.

These sequences justify that the lovemaking is over and it is time for Rādhā to return back. Her dressing up is a sequel to her return.

51a Rādhā is in no mood to go home but wants to indulge in love dalliance. Kṛṣṇa invites Rādhā for another bout of enjoyment by pulling her to his side. Rādhā to show mock resistance holds on to a tree. The tree in fan-shaped foliage is painted red. Squirrels run over its trunk. Subsequently she is won over. Kṛṣṇa now massages Rādhā's feet in a mood of supplication.

51b Rādhā and Kṛṣṇa in union on the left side of the leaf. On the right, Rādhā with her companion narrates her amorous exploits with Kṛṣṇa.

52a and 52b No illustrations.

53a Rādhā reprimands Kṛṣṇa for his betrayals. Kṛṣṇa appeals to Rādhā with bended knees and folded hands. A cock is painted to indicate the end of the night. Kṛṣṇa probably could not enjoy the love of Rādhā for the entire night. At daybreak, unfortunately it is time to leave.

53b Rādhā sits near a pond, perhaps worships the Sun God and offers water. Ducks and other aquatic birds are seen frolicking in the water. One can also come across lotuses.

54a No illustrations.

54b The tension between Rādhā and Kṛṣṇa continues. Rādhā reprimands Kṛṣṇa pointing her finger at him. Kṛṣṇa wearing a green *dhoti* stands like a culprit inside an arched pavilion.

55a and 55b No. illustrations.

56a Rādhā and Dūti are standing together. Rādhā is in *abhimāna* inside the *kuñja* having a *piḍhā* roof.

56b No illustrations.

Illustration 57b. Rādhā reclining Lalitā sitting nearby.

57a Rādhā wears a green sari and reclines against a pillow on the bed and listens to Laḷitā's narration. Rādhā in a carefree mood lifts her left leg and places it on her right stretched leg crossing at the knees.

57b No illustrations.

58a Rādhā is in *abhimāna.* Kṛṣṇa appears before her, seated with folded hands. Dūti stands complacent at a distance with her right hand against her cheek. Kṛṣṇa wears a *dhoti* with parallel horizontal dark stripes. The architecture has been twisted to suit the composition. The middle pillars which should have supported the arch are missing. Kṛṣṇa has a long plait. Rādhā looks older than Kṛṣṇa.

58b No illustrations.

59a Rādhā and Kṛṣṇa are in a *kuñja.*

59b No illustrations.

60a and 60b No illustrations.

61a and 61b No. illustrations.

62a Rādhā reclines on a round pillow with her bent head resting on her hands. Her companion tries to convince her of Kṛṣṇa's genuine love, Kṛṣṇa waits anxiously inside another foliated *kuñja* on the right side of the leaf. In between the trees, a peacock is painted.

62b No. illustrations.

63a Rādhā and Laḷitā are inside a *kuñja.* Rādhā relaxes against a pillow. Her hands support her head. Her breasts are exposed with dark nipples. Laḷitā explains a point. The trees are laden with foliages and red flowers against a dark background rendered with hatched pattern.

63b No illustrations.

64a Kṛṣṇa is in *abhimāna* shown in three sequences. Scenes take place inside the *kuñja* improvised with tree motifs. All the *kuñja* are half circular. In the first *kuñja* Kṛṣṇa kneels down with anxiety, in the second sequence he stands dejected. In the third *kuñja* he reclines over a pillow with downcast face.

64b No illustrations.

65a No illustrations.

65b Kṛṣṇa waits expectantly sitting with a lotus bud in his hand to make a presentation to Rādhā. Rādhā and Laḷitā are seen outside the *kuñja.* The drawings are more sketchy and incomplete and do not seem to be the work of the same hand that has done the other illustrations. The lines are comparatively bolder and the details are not precise, though the quality of scribing of the letters in the text portion remains constant. The vague impressions of the stylus in addition to the final line suggest the work of an untrained hand. This perhaps is the work of a novice under training either of the scribe or of some person other than the illustrator.

66a and 66b No illustrations.

67a and 67b No illustrations.

68a Rādhā is in a bridal attire with a heavy veil covering her face. She is being escorted by Dūti. They both wear saris with vertical bands and similar motifs. Kṛṣṇa wearing a long plait hanging at his back sits inside the *kuñja* waiting for the arrival of Rādhā. A coconut tree is standing at the side of the *kuñja*. The flowers of the *kuñja* are painted yellow.

68b No illustrations.

69a The meeting scene of Rādhā and Kṛṣṇa in the *kuñja* having a half circled arch fashioned with the help of creepers. Three women attendants keep a watch on the *kuñja* from outside. Kṛṣṇa is wearing a *pitāmvara* with star motifs. Rādhā wears a green sari.

69b No illustrations.

70a Rādhā and Kṛṣṇa are inside the *kuñja*. The above sequence continues. The *kuñja* is a decorated half circled arch having geometric motifs.

70b No illustrations.

71a Rādhā and Kṛṣṇa are making love on a bed of flowers inside two arched *kuñjas*. In the first *kuñja* two pillars are shown and in the second, a perfume sprayer is placed by the bedside.

72a Rādhā and Kṛṣṇa engaged in coition. Four different erotic postures are depicted inside four *kuñja*. In the first *kuñja* Kṛṣṇa, his hair tied in a bun, is engaged in sexual dalliance. In the second *kuñja*, the body of Rādhā is painted yellow. In the third

kuñja, Kṛṣṇa is holding the plait of Rādhā in a flush of passion. In the fourth *kuñja* Rādhā and Kṛṣṇa are engaged in passionate lovemaking in standing postures. This *kuñja* has charming foliated arches.

72b The scenes of coition are repeated in three more sequences. In the second and third sequences *viparīta rati* is depicted, like in the preceding leaf. Rādhā is painted yellow in the second *kuñja* against a Terre Verde green Kṛṣṇa. The third sequence is almost an extended posture of the second.

73a Rādhā and Kṛṣṇa are painted inside the *kuñja.*

73b Rādhā requests Kṛṣṇa to dress her up after the sexual dalliance.

74a The illustration is on the right hand corner. Rādhā and Kṛṣṇa are seen inside the *kuñja.* Rādhā reclines on a pillow.

74b No illustrations.

75a Rādhā and Kṛṣṇa shown in romantic moods in four sequences.

(a) Rādhā sits on the lap of Kṛṣṇa. Her garments drop down from her body. Kṛṣṇa holds Rādhā firmly by her waist and fondles her cheeks.

(b) Rādhā and Kṛṣṇa are seated on a bed. Kṛṣṇa puts his hands around Rādhā's neck.

(c) Rādhā and Kṛṣṇa are seated on a cot. Kṛṣṇa puts a mark of vermilion on Rādhā's forehead.

(d) Same scene continues.

75b Same sequences continue and are shown with the help of four illustrations.

(a) Kṛṣṇa puts an ornament on Rādhā's plait.

(b) Rādhā completely naked is seated on Kṛṣṇa's lap.

(c) Kṛṣṇa unclothes Rādhā (This sequence should have preceded the former motif).

(d) Kṛṣṇa adorns Rādhā's head with ornaments. In painting, the sequence is to be read from right to left.

76a Rādhā and Kṛṣṇa are inside the *kuñja* (left side of the leaf is broken). Kṛṣṇa is massaging the foot of Rādhā.

76b No. illustrations.

77a and 77b No illustrations.

Illustration 72b. Kṛṣṇa and Rādhā in amorous pursuit.

78a Rādhā and Kṛṣṇa inside a *kuñja*. Rādhā holds a bunch of flowers. Kṛṣṇa wears a Mughal turban; on the right side is seen an erotic posture of Rādhā and Kṛṣṇa. A lamp is lighted inside the *kuñja*.

78b Rādhā reclines against a pillow inside a garden. A round moon is suggested in the sky. On the right side of the leaf Rādhā is fanning Kṛṣṇa drawn inside a *piḍhā* pavilion. He looks like a Mughal hero. These illustrations do not belong to this manuscript. No script on either side. The illustrations are sketchy and seem to be of a later date in comparison to the other drawings.

79a *Māḷava Rāga*-Scene of a dance hall (*sangitasālā*). Four women dancers, two wearing skirts and the other two saris are participating in the performance. A dancer is dancing, the second is playing on a *mṛdaṅga*. She is wearing a *choḷi* with breast medallion, the third yellow complexioned dancer is wearing a skirt and a red *choḷi*. The fourth is clapping the cymbals. On the right extreme a *nāyaka* with Terre Verde green complexion and *Nāyikā* yellow complexioned are seen in close embrace. *Nāyaka* is kissing the lips of the *Nāyikā*.

79b *Mallara Rāga*-A sage wearing a loincloth, matted locks, long beard, rosary around the neck, carries an axe on his right shoulder.

Kaśyapa Rāga-Depiction of a war scene. Kaśyapa riding a galloping horse meets the attack of spear from a footsoldier. From either side, soldiers charge at one another.

Vasanta Rāga-A young man feeds a cuckoo with a mango shoot.

Deśākhya Rāga-A wrestler practises gymnastics inside an *ākhaḍā*. A club (*mudgara*) is placed below.

Vangāla Rāga-The illustration of a bare bodied young man wearing a red *dhoti*.

80a *Gauri Rāga*-A yellow complexioned *Nāyikā* wearing a red sari feeds a parrot perched on the branch of a tree.

Kāmoda Rāga-A hermit sits cross-legged in *padmāsana* on an altar holding a rosary by the side of a pond with lotuses and fishes.

Illustration 79a. Scene of a dance hall.

80b *Dhanāsi Rāga*-A dark complexioned *Nāyikā* writing a love letter on a tablet.

Maleasika Rāga-Nāyikā with orange complexion, beating her body with a lotus.

Gaudi Rāga-Golden complexioned *Nāyikā* worshipping Kandarpa and Rati. Rati sits on the lap of Kandarpa.

81a *Kukubha Rāga*-A *Nāyikā* clad in yellow sari, in a disturbed state of mind moves here and there in response to the call of the cuckoo. Two cuckoos are seen perched on both the trees on either side.

Koḍava Rāga-The *Nāyikā* is sitting on the lap of her husband inside a wooden pavilion. The husband fondles her cheeks.

81b *Gandharva Rāga*-A *sādhu* with a beard and long matted locks flowing on either side of his shoulder is seated in *padmāsana* inside a flower *kuñja* bedecked with red flowers.

Śrī Hindola Rāga-There are three swings suspended from three pillars. In the middle, *Hindola*, swing, a dark complexioned man is sitting. The swing is being pushed by two ladies.

82a *Toḍi Rāga*-A damsel is seated on an altar wearing a red sari with star motifs. Her body is not painted, she wears her hair in a long plait and is feeding a deer with tender leaves. Two trees have been painted in the background. The background is not painted.

Varāḍi Rāga-A *Nāyaka* is seated inside a pavilion, reclining against a pillow, resting his hands on right knee, left hand crossed over the right. He has a moustache, beard and a *beṇṭi.* A yellow complexioned *Nāyikā* wearing a red sari with black stripes on the warp with a *benti* is waving a *chāmara.* Her feet are not visible.

82b *Karṇāṭa Rāga*-A king is seated on a lotus pedestal with a dagger in his right hand. Four attendants stand before him with folded hands. Two from the right corner are dressed in Mughal fashion with *kurtā*, skirt, turban and the other two are wearing *dhotis* upto the knee and *kirīṭas* on their heads.

Mālava Rāga-A yellow complexioned woman is seated in *padmāsana* inside a pavilion. Another woman is standing in front of her with a fly whisk wearing a green sari. That woman too is yellow complexioned.

83a *Paṭṭa manjari or Paḍmanjari Rāga*-A woman wearing a green sari is seated on a wooden pedestal with a downcast face. Another woman, perhaps an attendant, is seated on a low *piḍhā* (stool) waving a fan.

Velāvali Rāga-A dark complexioned woman wearing a yellow sari is planning to go on an assignation.

Gunḍakiri Rāga-A Terre Verde complexioned woman under an arched pavilion.

83b *Gurjari Rāga*-A yellow complexioned *Nāyikā* wearing a black sari is seated on a bed of flowers flanked by two trees. She is playing a *vīṇā*.

Hemaruci Rāga-The *Nāyikā* is sleeping with her face downwards. A man, yellow complexioned, is seated in *virāsana* holding a bow and arrow under an arched pavilion. The pillars of the pavilion have *Rāhu* masks as capitals.

84a *Tankuna Rāga*-The daughter of the king of *Gandharvas* is on her way to meet her husband. She is yellow complexioned and is wearing a green sari with a red border. Her husband is sitting in a majestic pose on a *divan* resting his arms on a round pillow.

Khamvāvati Rāga-She is worshipping Brahmā and waving a flywhisk.

84b *Madhukari Rāga*-The scene of *viparīta rati* is presented. The yellow complexioned woman, completely naked, is seen mounted on her husband. The man has stretched his left leg and raised his right while reclining on a round pillow inside an arched wooden *maṇḍapa.*

Nāṭya or Nāṭa Rāga-One hermit with a long beard and matted locks is playing on a *vīṇā* reclining against a pillow. A young man of Terre Verde green complexion holds a *vīṇā* underneath an arched *maṇḍapa.*

85a *Devakiri Rāga*-A yellow complexioned *Nāyikā* holds a *rangaṇi* flower in the right hand which rests around the neck of a man who is reclining against a round pillow on a bed under an arched pavilion.

Laḷitā Rāga-A woman is sitting naked on a high couch. Her sari is falling down. She is trying to cover her breasts with her left hand while in the right hand she is holding her plait. A yellow complexioned *Nāyaka* wearing a red *dhoti* with black stripes is in a dejected mood. Only the left side pillars of the pavilion

Illustration 85b. Loving Submission. Nāyaka and nāyikā.

are shown. On the right side is a tree with a cock standing close by.

85b *Himakiri Rāga*-The golden complexioned woman wearing a dark Terre Verde sari is plucking flowers. She has a long plait with red tassels. She is holding the right hand of the companion. The companion is wearing a light green sari. Two potted plants have been placed on either side of these figures.

Rāmakiri Rāga-The scene is inside an arched pavilion. The *Nāyaka* is prostrating before a *Nāyikā*. The *Nāyikā*, yellow complexioned, is wearing a black sari. The woman is sitting with folded knees, placing her hands over the knees.

86a No illustration.

Bhairavi Rāga-A woman worships the *Śivaliṅgam* in a *dipadaṇḍi* inside the pond. Water is shown dark with hatched lines. Cranes and other aquatic birds perch for fish.

Moṭakiri Rāga-A woman makes a garland of flowers sitting inside a green *kuñja*. She is wearing a green sari.

Appendix-B

Archaeological Remains at Kenduli

Dinanath Pathy and Bijaya Kumar Rath

Present Kenduli (Kendubilva of Jayadeva's time) consisting of three hamlets-Kenduli Śāsana, Kenduli Deuḷi and Upara Sāhi–is located at about 22 kms. from Bhubaneswar when one approaches through Bāliantā. This place can also be reached through Phulnakharā and Kantāpadā traversing a distance of about 40 kms from Bhubaneswar.

Kenduli, the birthplace of the great poet Jayadeva belonging to the 12th century AD, is very rich in antiquarian remains dating from pre-Jayadeva period. Several mounds in the village yield pottery of red ware, black and grey ware belonging to the 9th-10th century AD, sculptures pertaining to Jainism, Buddhism and Brahmaṇism are found here dating back to a period between the 9th century and 13th century AD. The renovated Caṇḍi temple of the 10th century AD, the later Nṛsiṁha Temple enshrining earlier sculptures and the ruins of the

Ruins of Trimāli maṭha *at Kenduli.*

A spouted terracotta vessel collected from Kenduli village, 11th century (Collection, Dinanath Pathy).

Trimāli Maṭha constitute the standing monuments of the place. A copper plate charter, the largest copper plate charter from Odisha available so far, of the Gaṅga King Nṛsiṁhadeva IV (AD 1378-1414) and a stone inscription of the 11th century have been discovered from this village.

Amongst the *Brahmaṇical* sculptures of this place one finds images of Viṣṇu, Lakṣmī-Nṛsiṁha, Lakṣmī-Nārāyaṇa, Gopīnātha, Candī (Manasā) and Bhairava which indicate a strong *Vaiṣṇava* and *Śākta* influence in the area before and after Jayadeva. This rich cultural heritage is evidently reflected in the *Gītagovinda*, the immortal creation of the poet Jayadeva.

The original Registration deed mentioning Kenduli Śāsana and other neighbouring villages and the Patta, the revenue records, mentioning Kenduli Deuḷi and Kenduli Śāsana are annexed at pp. 279-285.

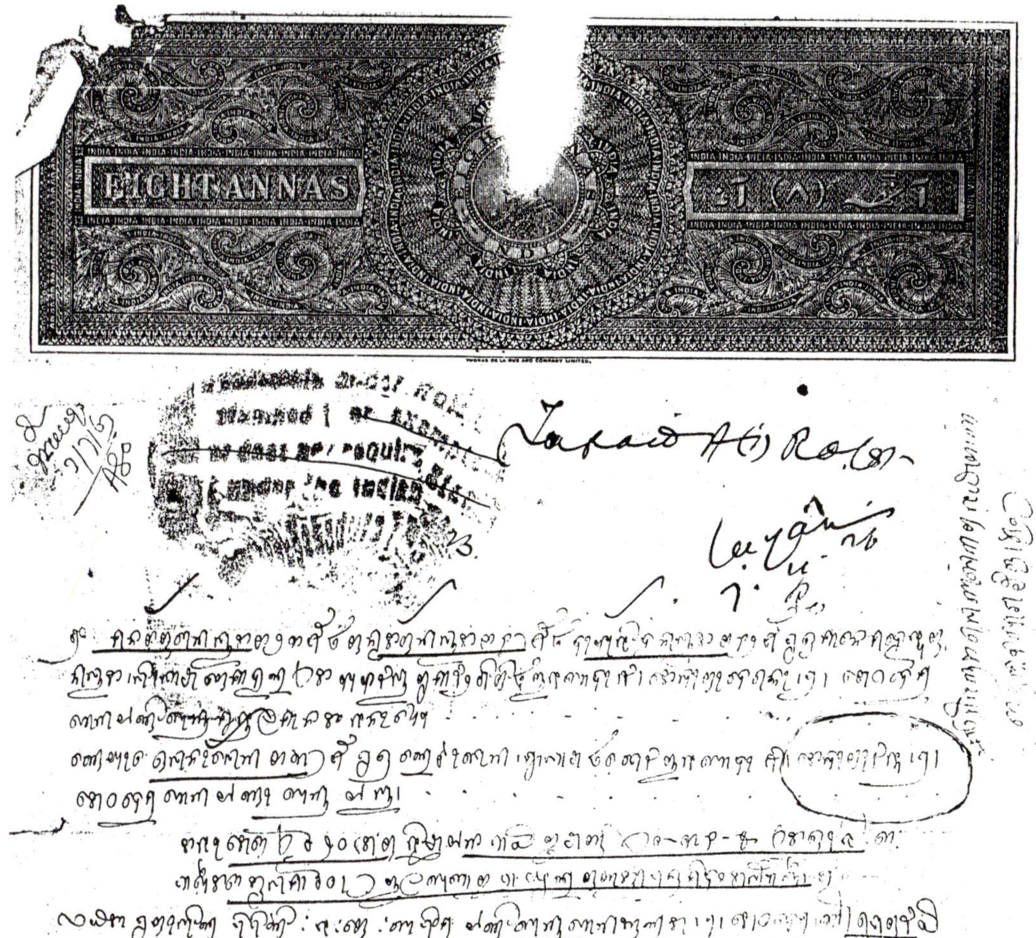

Registration Deed of 7th April 1926 mentions village Kenduli Sāsana, Pragaṇā, Kothadesa.

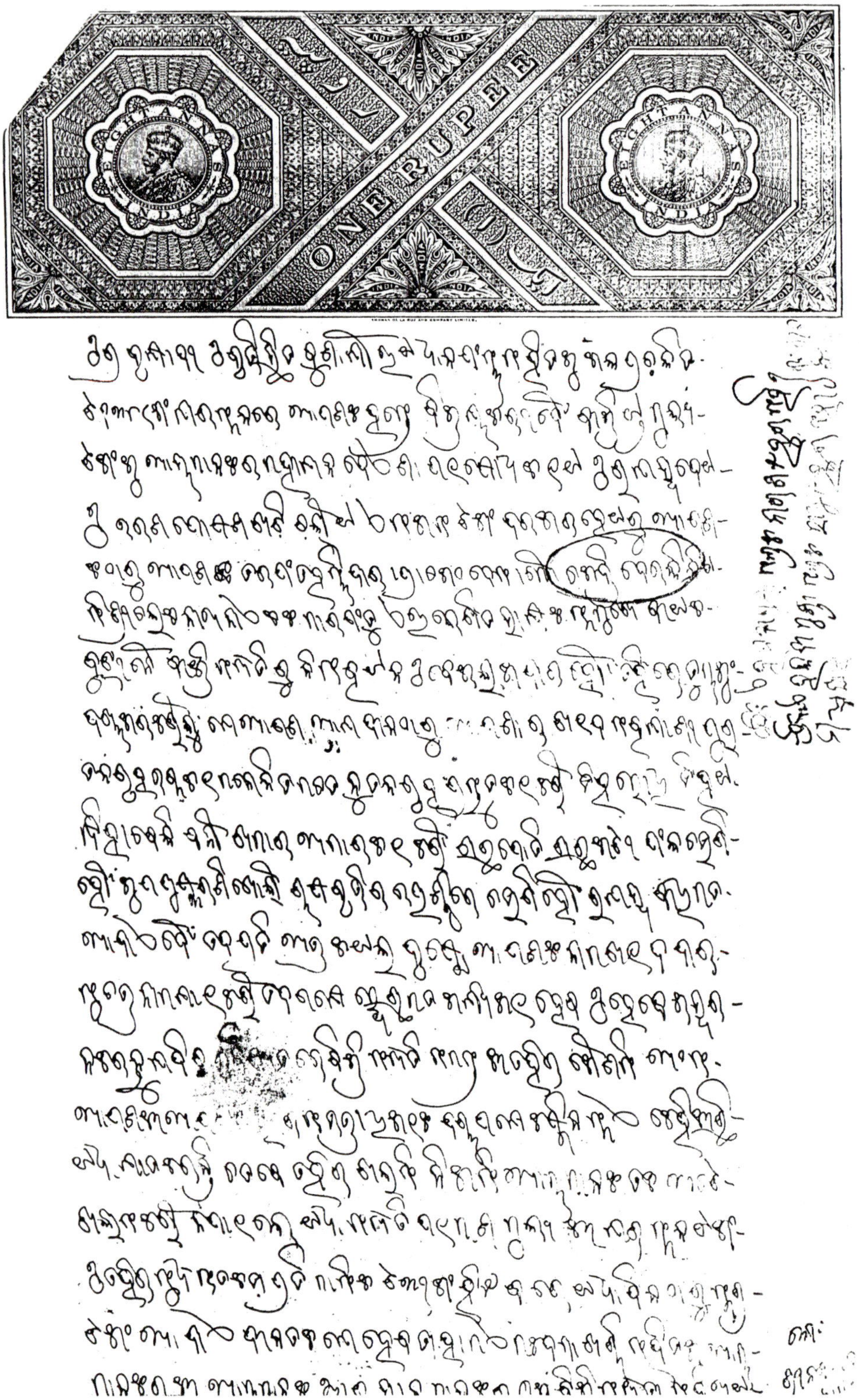

Registration Deed of 7th April 1926 mentions village Kenduli Sāsana, Pragaṇā, Kothadesa.

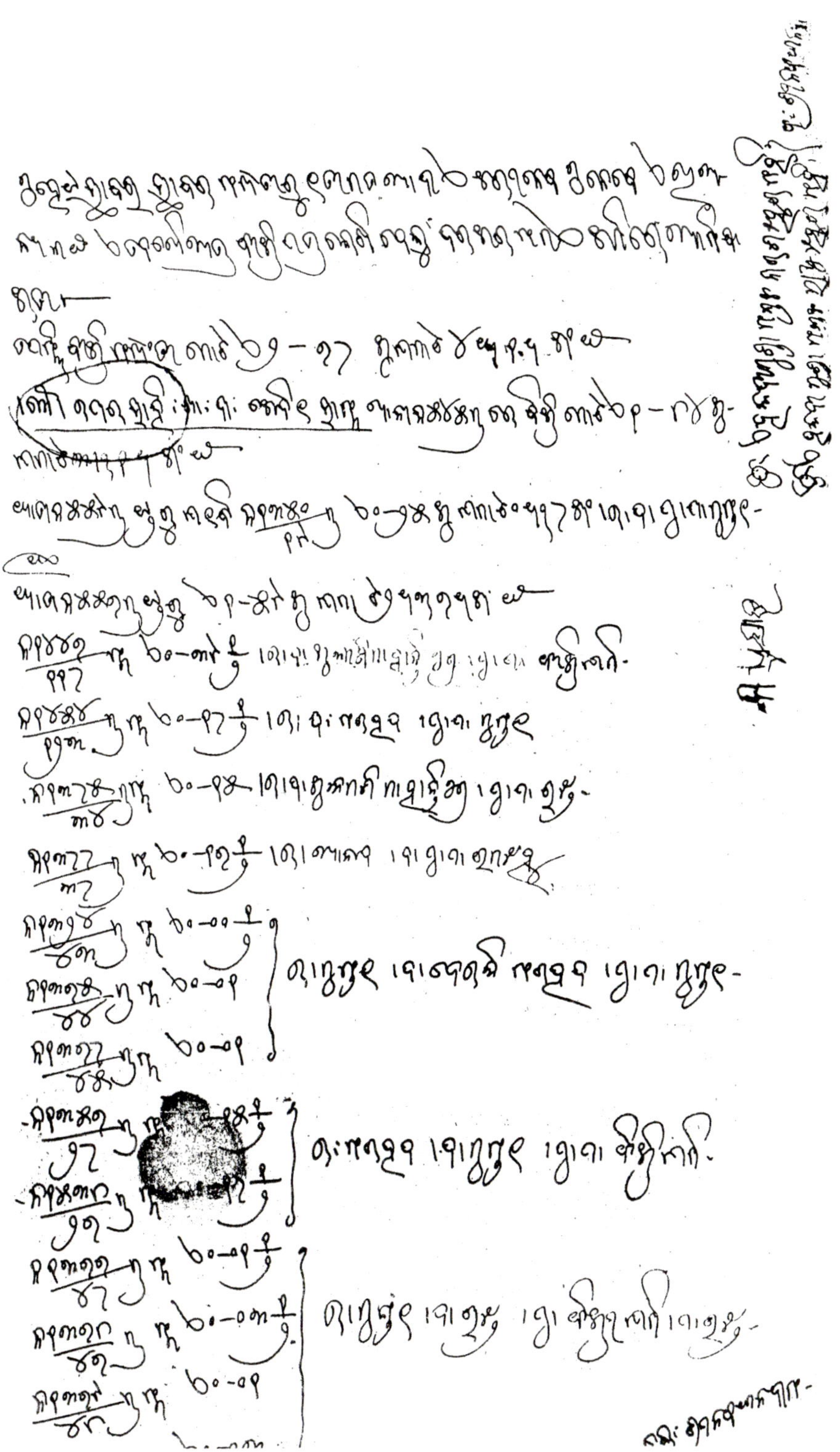

Registration Deed of (3rd page) of 30th June 1914 mentions village Uara Sāhi.

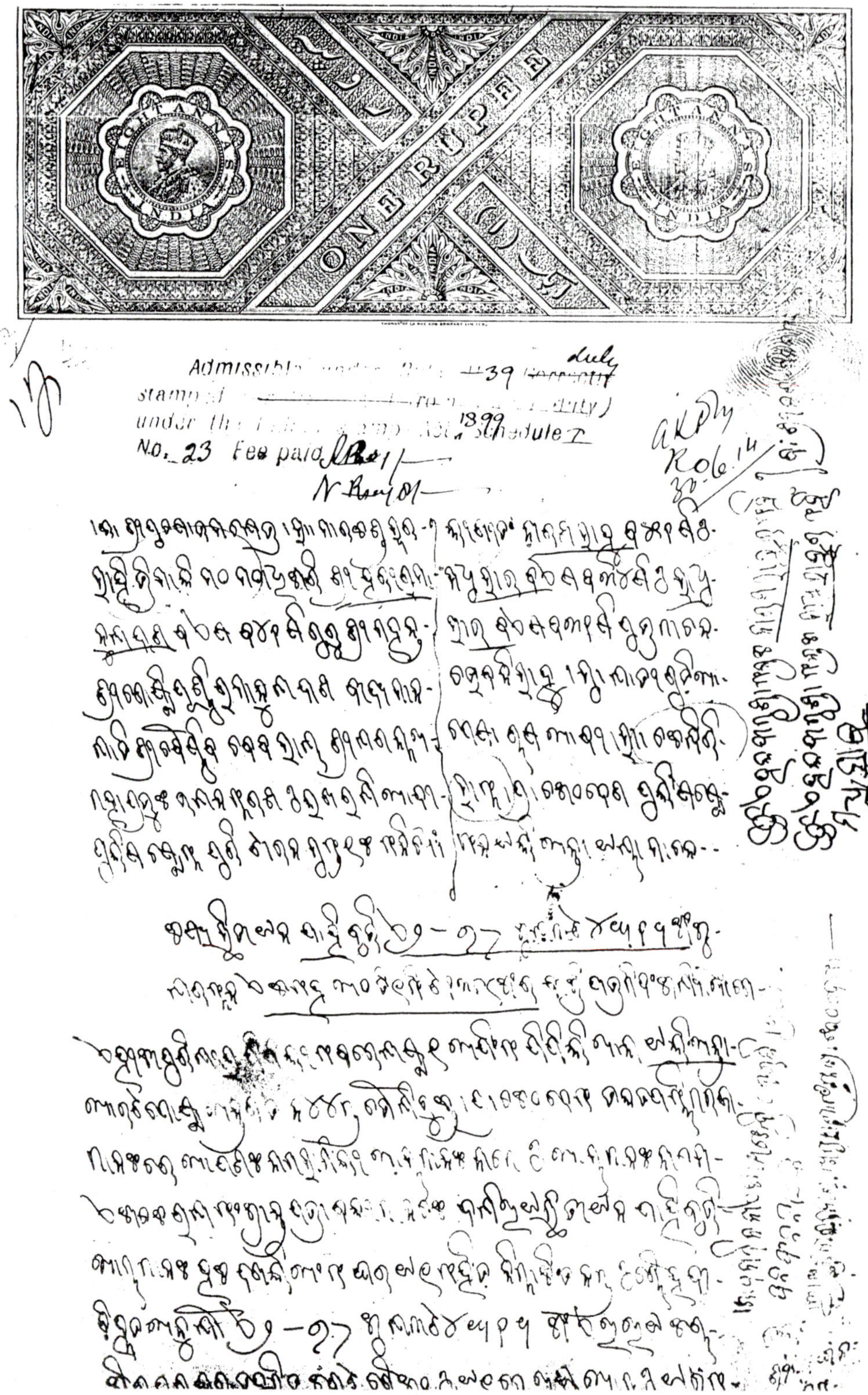

Registration Deed of (3rd page) of 30th June 1914 mentions village Upara Sāhi.

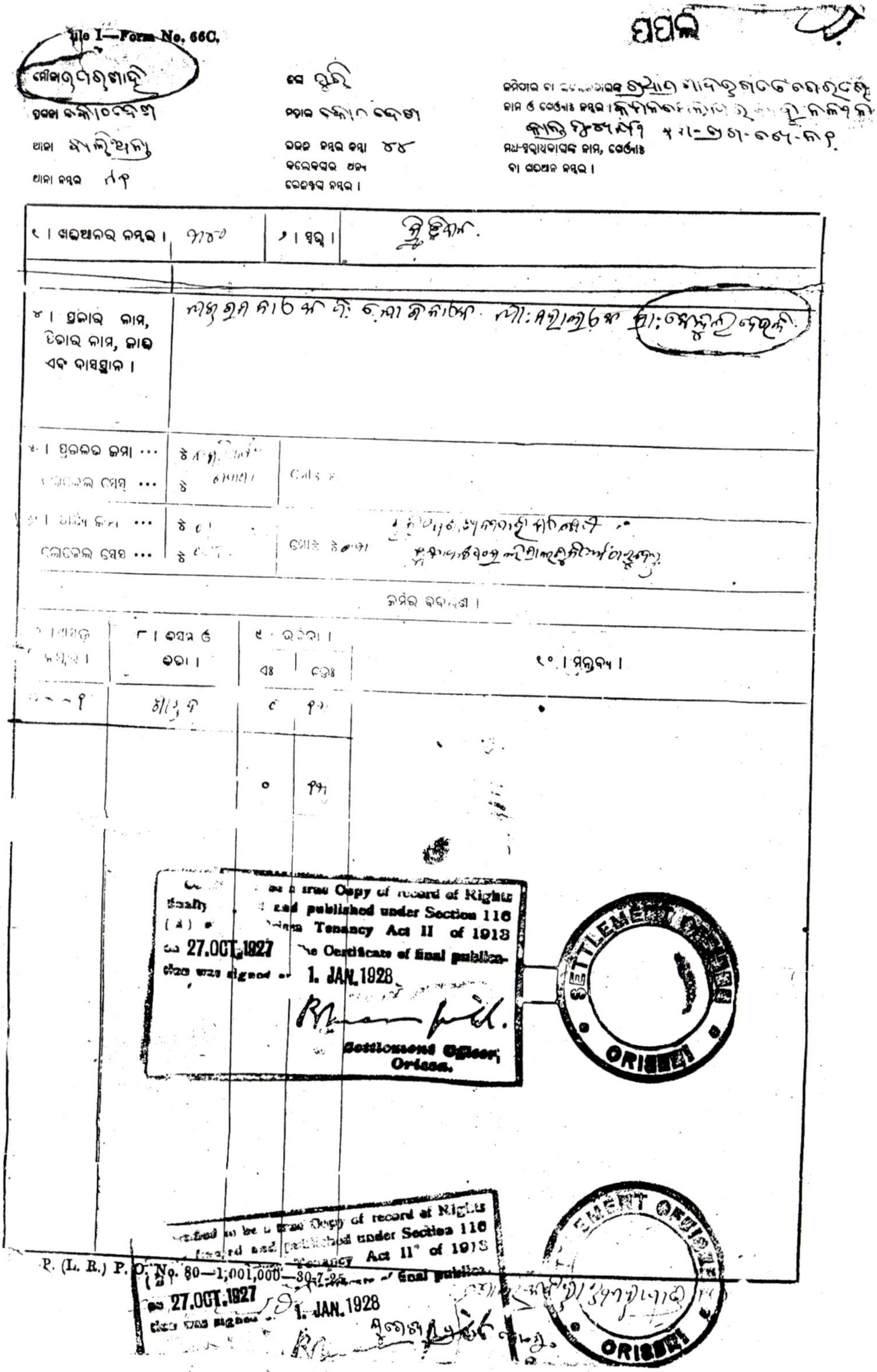
Rule I—Form No. 66C.

... a true Copy of record of Rights ... and published under Section 116 ... Tenancy Act II of 1913 ... 27.OCT.1927 ... The Certificate of final publication was signed on 1. JAN. 1928

Settlement Officer, Orissa.

SETTLEMENT OFFICER ORISSA

P. (L. R.) P. O. No. 80—1,001,000—30-7-25.

Paṭṭā (Revenue record) of 1st January 1928 mentions the village names Upara Sāhi and Kenduḷi Deuḷi.

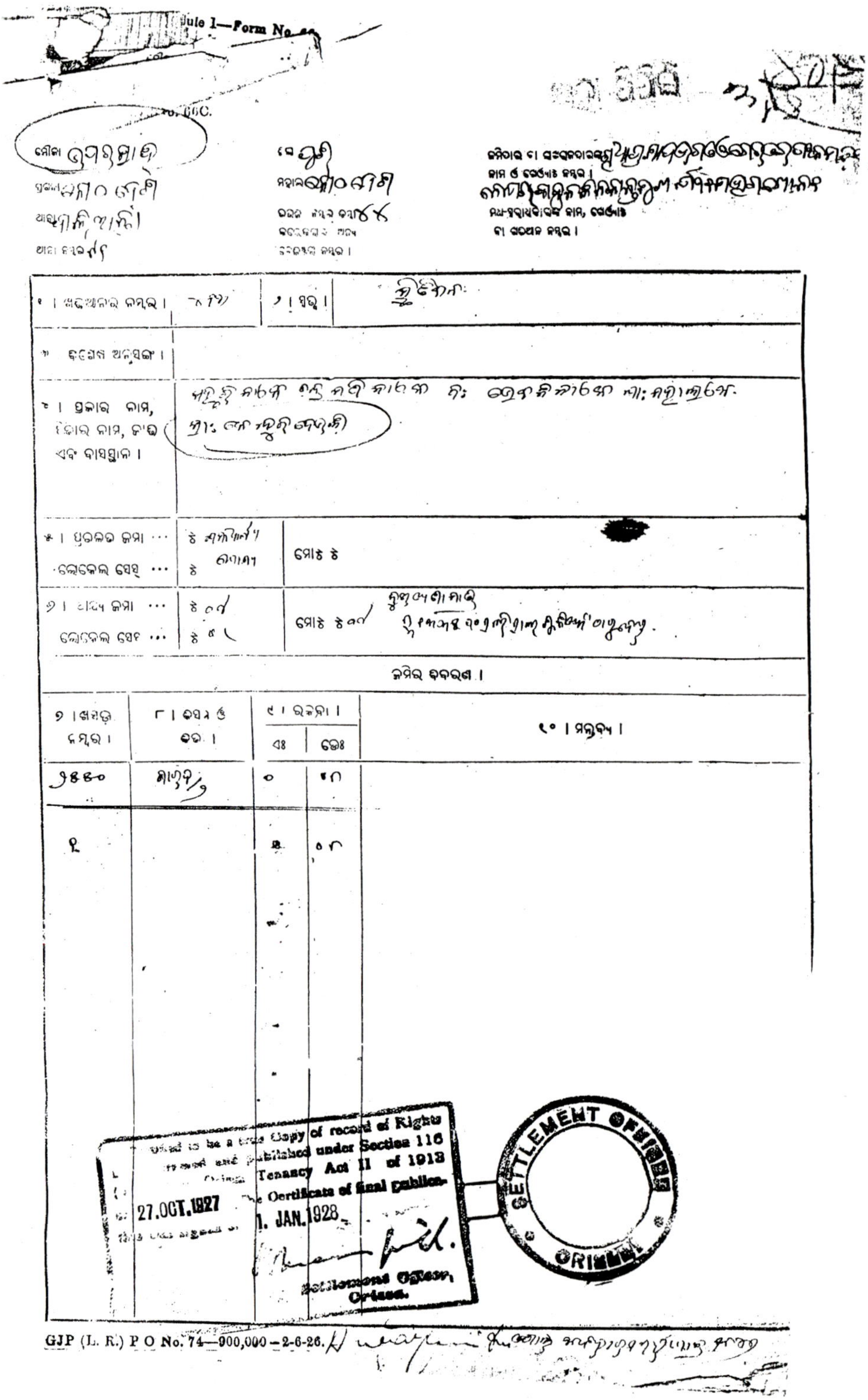

Schedule 1—Form No.

୧ । ଖତିୟାନର ନମ୍ବର ।		୨ । ସ୍ୱତ୍ୱ ।	
୩ । ବିଶେଷ ଅନୁସଙ୍ଗ ।			
୪ । ପ୍ରଜାର ନାମ, ପିତାର ନାମ, ଜାତି ଏବଂ ବାସସ୍ଥାନ ।			
୫ । ପ୍ରଚଳିତ ଜମା ··· ସେସ୍ ···		ମୋଟ ଟ	
୬ । ଧାର୍ଯ୍ୟ ଜମା ··· ସେସ୍ ···		ମୋଟ ଟ	

ଜମିର ବିବରଣ ।

୭ । ଖେସଡ଼ା ନମ୍ବର ।	୮ । ଚକର ଓ ଜାତି ।	୯ । ରକବା । ଏ:	ଡେ:	୧୦ । ମନ୍ତବ୍ୟ ।

Certified to be a true Copy of record of Rights ... published under Section 116 ... Tenancy Act II of 1913 ... Certificate of final publica...

27.OCT.1927

1. JAN.1928

Settlement Officer, Orissa.

SETTLEMENT OFFICER ORISSA

GJP (L. R.) P O No. 74—900,000—2-6-26.

Paṭṭā (Revenue record) of 20th October 1927 mentions the village names Upara Sāhi and Kenduḷi Deuḷi.

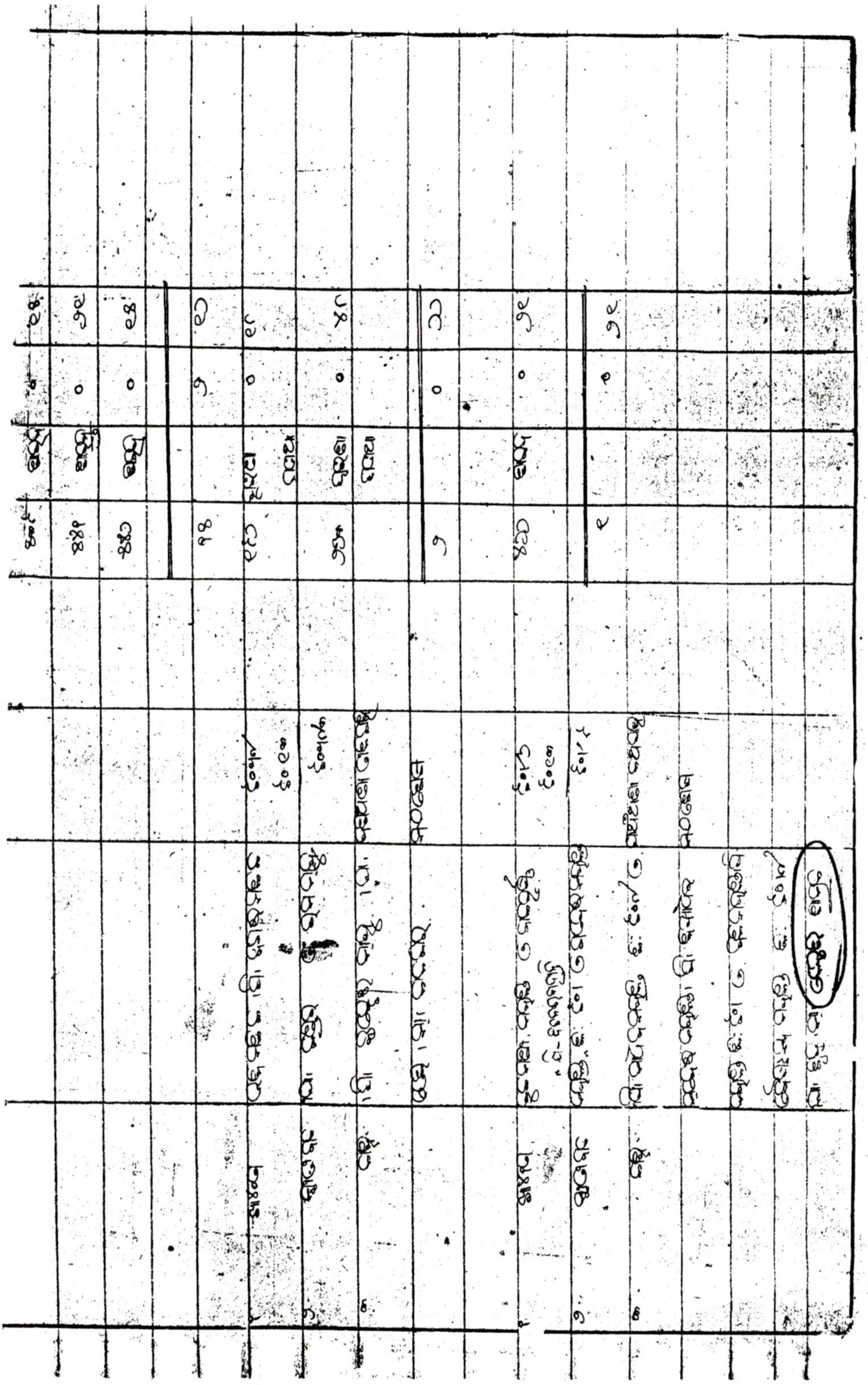

Paṭṭā (Revenue record) of 1927 mentions the village names Kenduḷi Sāsana.

Bibliography

ABBOTT, J.E. and Godbole, N.R. *Stories of Indian Saints*, English translation of Mahīpati's *Bhakta Vijaya*. Poona, 1933.

ACHARYA, P. *OHRJ*, Vol. 1, No. 4, 1953.

Aihole inscription of Pulakeśi II by Ravikīrti.

ARNOLD, Sir. *The Indian Song of Songs*. London, 1875.

AYANGAR, C.R. Srinivas. *Life and Teaching of Śrī Rāmānuja*; Madras, 1908.

BAGCHI, P.C. *History of Bengal*, Dacca University.

BANERJEE, J.N. *The Development of Hindu Iconography*, 3rd edn., New Delhi, 1974.

BANERJI, Rakhal Dās. "Eastern India School of Medieval Sculpture", *ASI*, XL VII. Delhi, 1993.

BANARJEE, R.D. *Eastern India School of Mediaeval Sculptures*.

Bāṅgāla Sāhityera Itihāsa. Vol. I-Part I, 1967 edn.

Bhāgavata.

Bharatamuni. *The Nāṭyaśāstra*.

BHATTACHARYA, S.P. "The Vṛndavana Yamaka and its author", in *V.R. Society Bulletin*, 1931.

BHATTACHARYA, S.P. (ed.). *Hari-caritam*.

BISHWAS, Sharmila. "The Maharis of Orissa" in *Attendance* 2003-4.

BUHLER, A, E. Fischer, M.L. Nabholz. "Indian Tie-dyed Fabrics", in *Historic Textiles of India*, Vol. IV.

CAITANYA, Śrī Kṛṣṇa. *A New History of Sanskrit Literature*.

Caitanya Caritamṛta, Adi, iv.

CHAKARAVARTI, M.M. *J.A.S.B. vol.LXIV*, Part I, 1895.

CHAKRAVARTI, M.M. "Uriya Inscriptions of the 15th and 16th centuries", *Journal of Asiatic Society Bengal (JASB)*, LXII,I.

CHATTERJEE, Suniti Kumar. *Jayadeva*, Sahitya Akademi, 1973.

CHATTERJI, S.K. *Jayadeva*, Sahitya Akademi. New Delhi, 1981.

DAS, A. *Catalogue of Sanskrit manuscript of Orissa*, Vol. II.

DAS, J.P. *Pata paintings of Orissa*, unpublished thesis, Sambalpur University, 1981.

DASGUPTA, A.R. *Indian Lyrics*, 1962.

DASGUPTA, R.D. *Eastern Indian Manuscript painting*.

DASGUPTA, *History of Indian Philosophy*, Vol. 3.

DASGUPTA, *History of Sanskrit Literature*, Vol.I, 1962.

DASGUPTA and De, *History of Sanskrit Literature*.

DASGUPTA and De S.K. *History of Classical Sanskrit Literature*.

DASH, G.N. (ed.). "Jagannātha and Oriya Nationalism", *in The Cult of Jagannātha and the Regional Tradition of Orissa*, A. Eschmann and Others, New Delhi, 1978.

DASH, Gaganendra Nath. "*Gītagovinda* Traditions: A Medieval Debate and Its Impact on Modern Oriya Identity', in *Text and Context in the History, Literature and Religion of Orissa*, Ed. Angelina Malinar, Johannes Beltz and Heiko Frese.

DE, S.K. *Aspects of Sanskrit Literature*, 1959.

DESAI, Kalpana. *Iconography of Viṣṇu.* New Delhi, 1973.
DEVA, Kṛṣṇa. "Northern Temples" in *Archaeological Remains, Monument and Museums, ASI*, New Delhi, 1974.
Dhoyī *Pavanadūtam J.A.S.*, 1905.
DIMOCK, Edward C. *The Palace of the Hidden Moon*, 1966.

Epigraphia Indica XIX.
Epigraphia Indica, Vol. XXXIX. *JASB* (old Series), Vol. L. XVII (1998), part I.

FISCHER Eberhard, Mahapatra Sitakant and Pathy Dinanath. *Orissa Kunst und Kultur in Nordost Indien, Zurich*, 1980.

GARGAVATU, Ratnākara. *Kapila Samhitā* published.
Gītagovinda, Canto-I, Verse-1.
Gītagovinda, Canto-I, Verse-2-4, *Prabandha.* 1-2.
Gītagovinda, Canto-III Verse - 1-6.
Gītagovinda, Canto, VII, Verses 1-9.
Gītagovinda, 3rd canto: *Varṇitam Jayadevakena hareridam pravaṇena Kinduvilva samudra sambhava rohiṇi ramaṇena*".

HIRACHAND, H. (ed.). *Gītagovinda*, Bombay, 1865.
History of Bengal Dacca University, Vol.I.

KANE, P.V. *History of Dharmaśāstra Literature*, Vol. I.
Kane, P.V. *History of Sanskrit Poetics.*
Kāvyādarśa, I.
Kāvyamīmāmsā, Kāvyanuṣāsana, VIII.
Kāvyaprakāśa ed. *Jhallkikar, Sūtra* 49 and *Vṛtti* thereon.
KEITH, A.B. *A History of Sanskrit Literature, London*, 1966.
KEITH, A.B. *The Sanskrit Drama.*
KINSLEY, D. *The Sword and the Flute*, 1977.
KOTHARI, Sunil. *Odissi: Indian Classical Dance Art.*
KṚṢṆADĀSA Kavirāja, *Caitanya Caritāmṛta.*
KṚṢṆAMACHARIYA, M. *History of Classical Sanskrit Literature*, 1974.
Kṣemarāja, Śrī Kṛṣṇa Dāsa's *Bhaktamāḷā*, Venkatesvara Press, Bombay.
Kṣemendra Laghukāvya Saṁgraha, published by the Osmania University.
KULKE, Hermann. "Jagannātha - Kult and Gajapati Koenigtum" *Suedasien Institute der Universtaet Heidelberg.* Vol. 23, 1979.
KULKE, Hermann. "*King Anangabhima III, the Veritable Founder of the Gajapati Kingship and of the Jagannātha Trinity at Purī*".
KULKE, Hermann. "Some Remarks about the Jagannātha Trinity" *Indologen-Tagung*, 1971. (Wiesbaden, 1973).

LAYDEN, R.N. von. "Ganjifa, the playing cards of India" in *Marg*, Vol. III, No. 4, 1979.

Macdonell's *History of Sanskrit Literature.*
MAHANTY, A.B. (ed.). *Mādaḷāpāñji.* Cuttack, 1940.
MAHAPATRA, Chakradhara. *Utkala Itihasara Eka Ajnata Adhyaya*, Cuttack, 1959.
MAHAPATRA, Kedarnath. "New Light on Poet Jayadeva, the Author of the *Gītagovinda*", *OHRJ*, VII, No. 3/4, 1958-59.
MAHAPATRA, Kedarnath. "Govardhana Ācārya and Udayana Ācārya", *OHRJ*, VII, No. 1, 1958.
MAHAPATRA, Kedarnath. "Studies in the *Naiśadhīya Caritam* of Śrī Harsa", *OHRJ*, VIII, No. 1, 1959.
MAHAPATRA, Kedarnath. "Jagannātha Puri as a Centre of Culture through the Ages", *OHRJ*, VI, No. 4, 1958.
MAHAPATRA, Kedarnath. "Śrī Jayadeva was not a poet of the Court of Lakṣmaṇa Sena", *OHRJ*, XXII, No. 2, 1976.
MAHAPATRA, Kedaranath. *Descriptive Catalogue of Sanskrit Manuscript of Orissa*, Orissa Sahitya Academy, 1960.

MAHAPATRA, K.N. *Souvenir on Jayadeva.*
MAHAPATRA, K.N. "New light on Poet Jayadeva", *OHRJ* Spl.Vol.
MAHAPATRA, K.N. *Jayadeva was not a Poet of the Court of Lakṣmaṇa Sena.*
MAHAPATRA, K.N. "Govardhana Acharya and Udayana Acharya" *Orissa Historical Research Journal,* (*OHRJ*), Spl. Vol.82.
MAHAPATRA, K.N. "*Abhinava-Gītagovinda* by Gajapati Puruṣottamadeva (1466-1497 AD)", in *Orissa Historical Research Journal* (*OHRJ*), 1961.
MAHAPATRA, K.N. *A Descriptive Catalogue of Sanskrit Manuscript of Orissa, Bhubaneswar,* Vol.II, 1960.
MAHAPATRA, Kedarnath. *Śrī Jayadeva O Śrī Gītagovinda* (Oriya), Bhubaneswar, 1973.
MAHAPATRA, Kedarnath. *Govardhana Ācārya and Udayana Ācārya.*
MAJUMDAR, M.R. "The Gujarati School of Painting and Some Newly Discovered Vaiṣṇva Miniatures", *JISOA*, X, p. 15, 1942.
MANSINGH, Maydhar. *History of Oriya Literature,* (*Odia version*).
MILLER, Barbara Stoller. *The Gītagovinda of Jayadeva,* Delhi, 1977.
MISHRA, B. *Purāṇu Maṭha Samskriti* (Oriya), Puri, 1988.
MISHRA, K.C. *The Cult of Jagannātha.* Calcutta, 1971.
MISRA, Binayaka, *Orissa under the Bhumakara kings.*
MISRA, Keśava. *Alamkāraśekhara, Kāvyamālā,* 1926.
MISRA, Premalata (ed.). *Sangītarāja.* Varanasi, 1963.
MITRA, Debala. *Konark,* pl. XXIV.
MITRA, R.L. *Antiquities of Orissa,* Vol.II, 1880.
MOHANTY, Bansidhar. *Jhankār.* April, 1969.
MOHANTY BC and Krishna Kalyan. *Ikat Fabrics of Orissa and Andhra Pradesh,* Ahmedabad, and Plates 19 and 19a, 1974.
MUKHERJI, P. *Gajapati kings of Orissa.* Calcutta, 1953.
MUKHERJEE, Prabhat. *History of Medieval Vaiṣṇavism in Orissa.* Calcutta, 1940.
MUKHERJEE, P. *History of Medieval Vaiṣṇavism in Orissa.*
MUKHERJEE P. (ed.). *Prapannāmṛta, History of Medieval Vaisnavism in Calcutta,* Orissa, 1940.
MUKHOPADHYAY H.K. *Vīrabhum Vivaraṇa,* 1323 Sal.
MUKHOPADHYAY, Harekṛṣṇa. *Kavi Jayadeva O' Gītagovinda* (Bengali), 1983.

Nāṭyśāstra, SVI.

PANDA, B. (ed.). *Gītagovinda,* Directorate of Culture, Orissa.
PANDITA, Bhupati, *Prema Pancāmṛta.*
PANIGRAHI. *Archaeological Remains at Bhubaneswar.*
PANIGRAHI, K.C. *History of Orissa* (*Hindu Period*), Cuttack, 1981.
PANIGRAHI, K.C. *Chronology of the Bhauma-Karas and the Somavamsis.*
PANIGRAHI K.C. *Jhankāra* Vol. XXI., No. 10, Jan. 1970.
PATHY Dinanath. "Sakhīnāṭa: Angarag's Passionate Project" in *Angarag,* Spring. 2008.
PATHY, Dinanath. *Rethinking Odissi.*
PATHY, Dinanath. *History of Orissan Painting.*
PATTANAYAK, N. "Administration of Jagannatha Temple in the 18th century." in *Man in India,* 43,3, 1963.
PATTANAYAK, Sudhakara (ed.). *Cakadāpothi O cakada basana ba cayini cakada.* Cuttack, 1959.
Prācī Māhātmaya
PRADHAN N.N., *Oriya Sāhityare Jayadeva.*
Prastavana, *Gītagovinda,* Nirnaya Sagar Press. Bombay, 1949.

RAJAGURU, S. N. *Inscriptions of Orissa, Vol. III, Part II.* Bhubaneswar, 1975.
RAJAGURU, S.N. *Inscriptions of Orissa,* Vol. III, Part (i). Bhubaneshwar, 1960.
RAJAGURU, S.N. *Inscriptions of Orissa, Vol. I Part (ii),* 1958.
RAJAGURU, S.N. *OHRJ,* Vol. I, No.3 (1952).
Rājaśekhara, Bālarāmāyaṇa.
Rāmadāsa, *Mādalāpānji.*

Rāmadāsa, *Darḍhyatā Bhakti.*
RAO Subba, *The History of Kaliṅga.*
Rasikaprīyā published with the *Rasamanjarī*, a commentary on the *Gītagovinda* in the *Kāvyamālā* series.
RATH, Banamali. "Orissa, the Land of Jayadeva" *OHRJ*, XXII, Nos. 3/4 (1977).
RATH, Banamali. "Contribution of Orissa to Indian Lyrics" in the *Proceedings of the International Sanskrit Conference*, Vol. I, Part I, 1975.
RATH, Banamali. "A family of poet-cum-rhetoricians in Orissa" in *Jhankar*, (Oriya) Feb. Vol. IX, No. 12, 1958.
RATH, Banamali. *A Study on the Srikṛṣṇalīlāmṛtam.*
RATH, B.K. *Cultural History of Orissa*, (AD 1885-1110).
RATH, Bijay Kumar. "Nātamaṇḍapa in Odishan Temple Architecture; A Pavilion for Dance Performance" in *Angarāg*, No. 7, Spring 2009.
RATH, P.C. "Saintalā" *JOHRS*, Vol. II, No. 2; *Bolangir District Gazetter*, ed. N. Senapati, *OHRJ*, Vol. X No. 4, 1947
Raverty, *Tabaqat-i-Nasiri* Translation.
RAY, P.K. *Praci Valley : Archaeological Survey Report* (1974-75).
RAY, P.K. "A Unique image of Viṣṇu-Kṛṣṇa in the Orissa State Museum" *OHRJ*, IX, No. 4, 1963.
RAY, P.K. (ed.). *Prachi Valley Survey Report*, Orissa State Archaeology. Bhubaneswar, 1975.
RAY, P.K. (ed.). *Archaeological Survey Report, Praci Valley*, Bhubaneswar, 1975.
RAY, Nihar Ranjan. *Bāṅglāra Itihāsa; History of Bengal*, Dacca University.
"Record of Rights", Part II, *Orissa Gazette*, Cuttack; Calico Museum of Textiles. Ahmedabad, 1956.

SAHOO, Itishree. *Odisi Music.*
SAHU, N.K. (ed.).*Souvenir on Jayadeva*, Jayadeva Sānskṛtika Pariṣad.
SAHU, N.K. (ed.). *Souvenir on Jayadeva.* Bhubaneswar.
SAHU, N.K., Kar K. (ed.). in Souvenir on Jayadeva *Pīyūṣalaharī.*
Śankarācārya Granthāvali, Published by Dharmajṇāna Pracāra Mandir.
SASTRI, S.N. *The Laws and Practice of Sanskrit Drama.*
SASTRI, H. Krishna "Two statues of Pallava kings and Five Pallava Inscriptions in a rock-cut temple at Mahabalipuram", in *Memoirs of the Archaeological Survey of India*, No.26.
SHASTRI, Haraprasad. "Notes on Vishnupur Circular Cards" in *Asiatic Society of Bengal*, Vol. LXIV, Calcutta, 1895.
SHASTRI, D.N. *Critique of Indian Realism*, Agra, 1964.
SEN, S. *Banglā Sāhityera Itihāsa.*
SEN, Sukumar (ed.). *Sekh Subhodaya.* Introduction, Asiatic Society, Calcutta.
SEN Sukumar and SEN Sunanda(ed.). *Purusottama Das by Kanci Kaveri.* Calcutta, 1957.
SEN Sukumar and Sen Sunanda. (ed.). *Kānci Kāveri*, 'Genealogy of the King of Oḍradeśa' Local Records, Vol.60, Calcutta. Telugu Manuscript, Oriental Manuscript Library, Madras, 1957.
SIEGEL, Lee. *Sacred and Profane Dimensions of Love in Indian Traditions as Exemplified in the Gītagovinda of Jayadeva*, London, 1979.
SINGH, Jagabandhu. *Prācina Utkala*, Puri, 1929.
SIRCAR, D.C. *Indian Epigraphical Glossary*, 1966.
Sridharadāsa, *Saduktikarṇāmṛtam*, Firma KLM, 1965.
"Śrikṣetra" *Bengali.*
Śrī Gopālasahasranāmastotram, Gita Press Gorakhpur.
Śrī Kṛṣṇa Caitanya, A New History of Sanskrit Literature.
Srikṛṣṇalīlāmṛtam. (the manuscript of the *Śrikṛṣṇalīlāmṛtam* is preserved in the Manuscript Library of the Orissa State Museum, Bhubaneswar).
Śrimad-bhāgavata.

TRIPATHY, K.B. *Evolution of Oriya Language and Script*, Bhubaneswar, 1962.
TRUMPP, Ernst. "Die aeltesten Jindui-Gedichte", *Sitzungs berichte der philosophischen-philologischen and historischen class der K.B. Akademie der wissenschaften zu*, Munchen, Vol. I, Munich, 1879.

Uttarabhārat ki Santha Paramparā.

VASU, Nagendranatha (ed.). *Bānglā Viśvakoṣa.*

VATSYAYAN, Kapila. "*Gītagovinda* and its Influences on Indian Art," in *Chavi, Rai Krishnadāsa Felicitation Volume.*

VATSYAYAN, Kapila. "The Illustrated Manuscripts of the Gita Govinda from Orissa", *Madhu,* ed. by. M.S. Nagaraja Rao, p.275. Delhi, 1981.]

VIŚVANĀTHA, Kavirāja. *Sāhitya Darpaṇa.*

WATT, George. *Indian Art at Delhi,* 1903.

WILSON, H. *Viṣṇu Purana.*

WINTERNITZ, M. *Geschichte der Indischen Literatur,* Vol. III, 1920.

Yugavani (A Bengali Weekly), 7th June, 1969.

Index